Animated 'Worlds'

Animated 'Worlds'

Edited by
Suzanne Buchan

Associate Editors
David Surman
Paul Ward

British Library Cataloguing in Publication Data

Animated 'Worlds'

A catalogue entry for this book is available from the British Library

ISBN: 0 86196 661 9 (Paperback)

Published by
John Libbey Publishing, Box 276, Eastleigh SO50 5YS, UK
e-mail: libbeyj@asianet.co.th; web site: www.johnlibbey.com

Orders: **Book Representation & Distribution Ltd**. info@bookreps.com

Distributed in North America by **Indiana University Press**, 601 North Morton St, Bloomington,
IN 47404, USA. www.iupress.indiana.edu

Distributed in Australasia by **Elsevier Australia**, 30–52 Smidmore Street, Marrickville NSW 2204, Australia. www.elsevier.com.au

Distributed in Japan by **United Publishers Services Ltd**, 1-32-5 Higashi-shinagawa, Shinagawa-ku, Tokyo 140-0002, Japan. info@ups.co.jp

Printed in Malaysia by Vivar Printing Sdn. Bhd., 48000 Rawang, Selangor Darul Ehsan.

Contents

Introduction

What do we mean by the term 'animation' when we are discussing film? Is it a technique? – A style? – A way of seeing or experiencing a 'world' that has little relation to our own lived experience, or to other cinematic experience, for that matter? What effect have digital technologies had on our understanding and perception of animation film? What are the methods, terminologies and languages we use to describe what we view on screen? To answer these questions, animation studies needs a language that can be specifically used in critical and theoretical writings on animation film. Critics and scholars are developing and defining filmologist Etienne Souriau's prerequisite of a 'well-made language', essential to any scientific discipline.[1] The fine-arts base of pre-digital animation are as varied as fine art production itself: sculpture, painting, drawing, graphics, illustration, collage and many other artistic media flow into animation filmmaking, and the filmmakers' skill is evident not only in artistic creativity, but also in the transformation of static images and objects into time-based visual narrative. These narratives are the 'worlds' the spectator is confronted with.

Texts in this anthology originated at the Animated 'Worlds' conference held at Farnham Castle, England in 2003. The call for papers addressed these and other questions and encouraged contributors to consider how we can better define specific queries around animation that are essential before we can begin to articulate answers to them. The contributions in this book reflect especially on the generous and encompassing concept of animated 'worlds' – a term I use to describe realms of cinematic experience that are accessible to the spectator only through the techniques available in animation filmmaking. The astonishingly rich diversity of media used in animation encourages interdisciplinary approaches and excursions into other fields, and a prerequisite for this is a solid understanding of what animation is – first and foremost, it is a time-based visual medium. Yet it is a complex film medium, one that makes use of many artistic forms of creativity, and one that in most cases is not photorepresentational, as live action (pre-digital) cinema is. For this reason, animation remains a difficult art form to describe and isolate from other media. It is helpful to consider Gilles Deleuze's formulations about the meeting of disciplines. In an interview called 'The Brain is the Screen', he suggests 'The encounter between two disciplines doesn't take place when one begins to reflect on another, but when one discipline realises that it has to resolve, for itself and by its own means, a problem similar to one confronted by the other'.[2] The conference aimed to encourage speculation on what the 'problem' of animation is and initiate discussion about what a filmological language of animation scholarship could be. Many of the approaches in the essays align to the relatively recent 'turn' in film studies, a shift away from 'Grand Theory' that should apply to all films, and increasingly towards 'piecemeal' approaches that concentrate on individual films. Some address current debates in film studies around cognitive theory, emotion and phenomenology that are freeing the spectator from the passive role that earlier theory posits. The conference especially hoped to encourage contributors to present microanalyses of films that illuminate our understanding of individual films, rather than hypotheses based on broad and idiosyncratic corpi, and I am pleased that most authors did indeed take this on board. These microanalyses can provide methodologies that, in turn, may initiate future exploration into other works.

The essays in the *Animated 'Worlds'* anthology are wide-ranging in their different approaches to animation film and are organised in thematically arranged clusters. Despite the diversity, there are passages in some that seem to speak to other texts in the anthology, which may be evidence in part of the intense exchange and lively discussions that took place at the conference during presentation of the original papers. The majority of them take pre-digital animation as their subject, although the differences between traditional techniques and digital animation are permeable in some texts. Rachel Kearney's contribution, 'The Joyous Reception: Animated Worlds and the Romantic Imagination', excavates Romantic concepts of mind and elides these with 20th century visual media aesthetics. By focusing on the metamorphic contour of Disney, and digital media's ability to blend indexical and software-based data, a concurrence is suggested between the formal qualities of these images and the Romantic process of mind. Approached through the theories of Eisenstein, Schelling and Coleridge, Kearney proposes that the imagination's dialectical synthesis, a reunion of subject and object, is symbolically revealed in the animated form. She develops a fascinating argument for the relationship between animated image and spectator as one that encourages a sense of joy. The theme of spectatorship is continued in my essay 'Animated "Worlds'" and Animation Spectatorship' that reviews and critiques a number of approaches to animation spectatorship. Its basic premise is that the phenomenal and the noumenal 'worlds' animation confronts us have an uneasy relationship with notions of 'reality' and representation. I posit some suggestions towards under-standing the phenomena spectators experience when watching animation film, and how this understanding of animated 'worlds' relates to our lived experience of reality. The essay explores ways of understanding a variety of animated 'worlds' and exemplified by the Quay Brothers' *Street of Crocodiles* (1986), it speculates on the hybrid nature of puppet animation, in contrast to 2D animation, and its material relation to the tangible world outside the film.

The Quay Brothers' films are also the focus of the next two essays. Richard Weihe's brief yet extremely apposite philosophical musings on this film in 'The Strings of the Marionette' are underpinned by concepts of Heinrich von Kleist's 'On the Marionette Theatre', the automaton and spectator involvement. The essay focuses on *Street of Crocodiles* as a prime example of puppet animation film set within live action. The viewer is presented with a marionette that is liberated seeing its strings cut loose – thereby embody-ing the principle of animation – alongside various forms of automata, most poignantly demonstrated by a ballet of screws that screw and unscrew themselves without the help of a screwdriver. By relating their film to literary examples of the automaton (E.T.A. Hoffmann) and the marionette (von Kleist), Weihe considers the question of how these diverse art forms present automotion as a principle of 'life'. What is the aesthetic status of marionette 'strings'? How is it that the puppet's decapitation in the Quays' film is perceived as an act of cruelty, evoking our compassion though we are viewing a realm of dead matter? How is the puppet's motion trans-formed into spectator emotion? In his analysis, Weihe reveals the intrinsic relationship between animator and puppet and expands this to consider the implications of the process of animation film for these concepts. The Quay Brothers' work in with dancers in film is central in Heather Crow's essay 'Gesturing towards Olympia' that explores the dancing female body through concepts of subjectivity, hysteria and the uncanny to shed light on the relationships between gesture, the human body and the animate. Crow examines the dynamics of bodily movement in two of the Quays' films: *The Comb (From the Museums of Sleep)*, and *The Sandman*. She shows how these films bring to light (or rather, to life) the uncanniness of gesture and of the gesturing body by invoking two overdetermined figures, the hysteric and the automaton. Exploring the uncanny choreography of embodied subjec-tivity through gesturing puppets and mechanised female bodies, Crow suggests *The Comb* and *The Sandman* question the familiarity, stability, and animateness of the living body.

The second cluster of essays takes interdisciplinary approaches to a variety of films and their origins and inspirations in other artistic creativity and literature. In 'Literary Len: *Trade Tattoo* and Len Lye's Link with the Literary

Avant-Garde' Miriam Harris unravels the intricate synergies behind Len Lye's film, which was created in 1937 from rejected documentary takes from the General Post Office Film Unit in Great Britain, and merged with stencil patterns, direct animation and Cuban dance music. It evolved from Lye's multidisciplinary activities and interests in avant-garde literature and visual culture of the 1920s and 1930s, as outlined by modernist poetry theorist Charles Altieri, and Harris examines the influence of writers upon Len Lye's writing. Having established the unique characteristics of Lye's aesthetic and symbolic literary innovations, Harris closely examines the film in terms of Lye's aesthetic and symbolic innovations. Moving from literary inspiration to adaptation, Paul Wells' 'Literary Theory, Animation and the "Subjective Correlative": Defining the Narrative World in Brit-lit Animation' lays forth various theoretical relationships between written word and image, exploring the pertinence of modernist literary theory in the critical evaluation of animated literary adaptations. Wells begins with an address of the relationship between word and image in the practice of contemporary artists embracing mnemonic idioms, and the role of the illustrated Victorian novel. The discussion draws together theoretical perspectives on modernist literature; and the terms and conditions of the animation *langue*, to create the critical concept of the 'subjective correlative' which is then used as a tool for the analysis of literary adaptations.

Contemporary filmmaking through character and narrative are addressed in the next two essays. In 'Animated Fathers: Representations of Masculinity In *The Simpsons* and *King of the Hill*' Suzanne Williams-Rautiola raises a number of pertinent queries about these popular American television series, revealing how the different narrative 'worlds' promote either a hegemonic, culturally enforced masculinity or one that is less prescriptive. Williams-Rautiola suggests Homer Simpson and Hank Hill offer two very different and complex animated worlds of masculinity. *The Simpsons* is an example of Roland Barthes' 'writerly text' with a drawing style and open narrative that provide a 'discursive reserve', allowing Homer to recreate himself with each challenge to explore a variety of both positive and negative masculinities. In the 'readerly' text of *King of the Hill* the drawing style and cultural references tie the text to where the hegemonic masculine values of Hank Hill. The animated text takes the contrasts and dilemmas to their extremes, challenging and interrogating the simplistic answers offered by Hank's hegemonic definition of masculinity. In his essay on animated documentary, 'Animated Interactions: Animation Aesthetics and the World of the "Interactive" Documentary', Paul Ward explores the relationship between two animated films – *Snack and Drink* and *Going Equipped* – and the real 'pro-filmic' interviews they re-present. He suggests in animated films there may be a tension or contradiction between an attempt to represent a pre-existing reality and the aesthetic and technological 'intervention' that animation techniques produce. Ward proposes the construction of *a* world via animation techniques in order to re-present a real person from *the* world of actuality is the contradiction at the centre of these two films. Unpacking animation's aesthetic and technological interventions Ward ably demonstrates that animated documentaries are perfectly capable of re-presenting and 'embodying' knowledge about the real world, arguing for an innate relationship to the indexical and convincingly eliding the assumed divorce between these two worlds.

The final four essays are loosely connected by a focus on the creation, experience and aesthetics of digital worlds. By exploring how digital media can create different kinds of material orientations for viewers, Thomas Lamarre's 'New Media Worlds' undertakes an aesthetic investigation to reveal how digital media can create different kinds of media worlds for the spectator to experience. In particular Lamarre looks at the construction of media worlds in two animated films, both targeted for mass audiences: the photoreal or hyperreal world of *Final Fantasy: The Spirits Within* (Sakaguchi Hironobu, 2001) and the multilayered world of *Metropolis* (Rintarô, 2001). Lamarre reveals that these films tell us far more about how new media orientate viewers, especially in relation to worlds of cinema and to cel animation. The active and interactive spectator is central in David Surman's essay, 'Style, Consistency and Plausibility in the *Fable* Gameworld'. He explores how stylistic devices used in computer games worlds can incite or frustrate player's belief in these worlds. Surman sees gameworlds as the expression of a complex cultural and textual interaction, in which the foundational structures of the videogame solicit investment and belief from the player. Style arbitrates this solicitation, causing all aspects of the gameworld to conform to a common aesthetic line. Surman queries the efficiency of this process, and reveals how contemporary videogames such as *Fable* demonstrate the messiness of this ideological contract between the ambiguous roles of producers and consumers of videogames.

Through her questioning of the aspirations of digital filmmakers towards photorealism, Vivian Sobchack's essay 'Final Fantasies: Computer Graphic Animation and the (Dis)Illusion of Life' on synthespians and a digital world opens up a wealth of avenues for animation studies to explore. What is the underlying urge in the history of animation, particularly computergraphic animation toward photorealism? Using *Final Fantasy: The Spirits Within* (2001) as a paradigmatic text, in her essay Sobchack asks not only what we want from animation but also what animation wants from us, and she explores both the rhetorical lure and semiotic disappointment at the irresolvable paradox of this impossible desire for complete computergraphic simulation of human beings. The mutability of the digital image is central to the final essay, 'An Unrecognised Treasure Chest: The Internet as an Animation Archive', in which Karin Wehn effectively argues for the urgent need to archive web animation's plethora of Flash, brickfilms, machinima and other web-based films that exist only in digital formats. Considering to what extent is the Internet an archive for animation, Wehn starts off with some general observations on the challenges for digital archives, and argues for the Internet having the potential to be an archive for animation in a double sense. She puts forth that on the one hand, the Internet is a repository for traditional animation; on the other, as a new medium it has brought about its own art forms that need to be preserved. Wehn concludes with some reflections on what human and computerised equivalents of gatekeepers, curators, archivists exist and what may be the best solution to preserve these ephemeral works and the programs that generate them for future generations.

The anthology aims to provide a focused collection of insights into and hypotheses about the extremely rich and complex 'worlds' of animation – whether digital or celluloid based – and hopes to provide its audiences with new ways of seeing the films, techniques and technologies implicit in the form. The interdisciplinary nature of a number of the essays may open up ways of thinking about animation and related disciplines, revealing both the similarities and the differences between these and the animated form, and perhaps make some progress towards solving the 'problem' animation faces as a discipline with complex relationships to so many others. The emphasis on spectatorship and the participating spectator in many of the essays engages with an area of scholarship that is central to contemporary discourses around the moving image. The anthology hopes to make a contribution to the ever-growing field of animation studies, one that had long been relegated to an relatively marginal position within cinema studies and is increasingly establishing itself as a viable field of its own within visual moving image culture.

This publication would not have been possible without the support of a number of individuals and institutions. I would like to thank my Associate Editors, David Surman and Paul Ward, for their editorial engagement and support. I am grateful to the University College for the Creative Arts for significant financial support for the conference and for printing costs, and to my publisher, John Libbey, for his wise professional guidance and ongoing interest in ensuring animation studies reaches its readership. Heartfelt gratitude is due to my assistant Kerry Drumm and her team of students, who were instrumental in organising the Animated 'Worlds' conference, the impetus for the essays that appear here. Most of all, I would like to thank the authors, who have been a joy to work with, for their enthusiasm, collaboration and patience during the long process of preparing this book.

Suzanne Buchan

Notes

1. Etienne Souriau, 'Die Struktur des filmischen Universums und das Vokabular der Filmologie' [transl. Frank Kessler], in: *Montage/av*, 6/2, 1997, [Original title 'La structure de l'univers filmique et le vocabulaire de la filmologie', in: *Reveue internationale de Filmologie* 2, 7–8, 1951]: 141. Translation by the author.

2. Gregory Flaxman (ed.). *The Brain is the Screen. Deleuze and the Philosophy of Cinema.* (Minnesota: University of Minnesota Press, 2000): 367

Chapter 1

The Joyous Reception: Animated Worlds and the Romantic Imagination

Rachel Kearney

The 'world' I wish to suggest for animation is one of the imagination, specifically one that corresponds with 19th century Romantic notions of the creative mind.[1] Although it may appear historically incongruous to place such an interpretation on an art form associated primarily with Modernist or Postmodernist ideologies, what I wish to promote in this essay is the idea that the Romantic Imagination, its function and product, can transcend apparently opposing cultural contexts and operate within different technologies.

The Romantic aesthetic conveys a sense of unity, a symbolic loss of division between the mind and the ontological, within the formal qualities of the image.[2] Its appeal is not based merely upon a lack of the quotidian in content, or the special effect, but on a formal construction that enables a deep communication between the image and viewer; a revelation of unconscious thought activity. Richard Coyne has stated that 'the twentieth century is every bit a Romantic age represented through … the entertainment and leisure industries that pervade mass media'.[3] It is within animation produced for mainstream distribution and culture that I intend to search

Abstract: This essay contends that Romantic notions are relevant to animation associated with twentieth century aesthetics. By focusing on the metamorphic contour of Disney, and digital media's ability to blend indexical and software-based data, a concurrence is suggested between the formal qualities of these images and the Romantic process of mind. Approached through the theories of Eisenstein, Schelling and Coleridge, it is proposed that the imagination's dialectical synthesis, a reunion of subject and object, is symbolically revealed in the animated form. This ultimately allows an active communication between viewer and image, one that reflects the Romantic experience of joy.

1

for this aesthetic, firstly through an examination of the cel animation of Disney, and secondly by extending these notions into films that digitally integrate live action and software-based animation.

Cel animation is sometimes considered to be a subversive medium. Due to its graphic freedom from the rational and indexical, it has sometimes been connoted as an anarchic comment upon modernist society and culture, a 'world upside down'.[4] In the case of Disney I will argue that subversion is present but unconsciously produced: it is identifiable in its retreat from society rather than an engagement with it, the signification of a Romantic unity rather than the fragmentation of Modernism. These elements are also present, I believe, in the theoretical approach taken by Sergei Eisenstein in his work on Disney.[5] I will therefore employ Eisenstein's notions of the 'plasmatic' and the 'ecstatic'.[6] These will be read into an aesthetic that is comparable to the early 19th century German Romanticism.[7] The Romantic notions I will focus upon here are ideas surrounding the artist as genius, notions of the dialectic as the essence of evolution and freedom, and the reunion of man and nature in the face of mechanistic alienation.

Eisenstein himself had undergone a theoretical shift in the 1930s, moving away from mechanism in his theoretical and filmic approach towards organic modes.[8] During the 1920s, Eisenstein's work had reflected the dominant ideology of Leninist dialectics and a Pavlovian physiology, treating the mind as a materialist function, a reflex manipulated by his concept of montage. In 1931 however, following the 1925 publication in the Soviet Union of Engels' *Dialectics of Nature*, and a shift towards Hegelian idealism at the Soviet Writers' Congress, Nicolai Bukharin warned against the mechanisation of 'spiritual life'.[9] This ideological shift, in conjunction with implementation of Socialist Realism's 'revolutionary romanticism' (which, as Margaret Rose has pointed out, is never wholly differentiated from the original),[10] and Eisenstein's own reading of James Joyce, led Eisenstein to reformulate his approach towards one of organic unity. This theoretical combination of biology, mind, and art however suggests to me an earlier philosophical approach, that of the late 18th and early 19th century Romantic aesthetics and German 'Naturphilosophie'.

Eisenstein identifies his organic aesthetic in a range of artistic styles and epochs, from Mayan architecture to the paintings of Goya,[11] however in his essays on Disney he not only locates this universal aesthetic but also defined a cultural cause for it. As Thomas Elsaesser has noted in his work on German Expressionist film, this style reified Romanticism as 'the expression of a frustrated desire for change'.[12] German Romanticism in general has been interpreted as a retreat of the mind from social immobility and technological alienation, and Disney's content reflects this. His use of European folklore and rural settings suggest the Romantic immersion in nature.[13] In relation to the work of Disney Eisenstein was to express a similar point; that this animation and its animism was a flight from the mechanised constrictions of American life. He argues that the *Silly Symphonies* shorts (Walt Disney, USA, 1929–1939) are a response to 'the age of American mechanization' and are 'a glimpse of freedom within a capitalist state'. He goes on to compare 'America and the formal logic of standardization'[14] with 18th century Europe's 'restrictive and artificial life', caused by the rationalist division of man and nature. Here, 'man was confined to his soul, and the whole soul was allotted to reason ... separated from matter'.[15]

The freedom that Eisenstein confers on the animation of Disney can then perhaps be compared to the reading of Romanticism as a reaction to the restriction and division of the 18th century. For the German Romantics of this period, mind and nature were conceived of as being fundamental elements of a greater whole, Johann Gottfried von Herder arguing that they should be viewed as a dissoluble unity, 'one interpenetrating, all animating soul'.[16] The aim of the Romantic movement was to achieve a reunion of these elements through art, an aim shared by Johann Wolfgang von Goethe, who observed that a work of art must be 'spiritually organic'.[17] However, in my attempt to show the work of Disney as Romantic, I intend to employ the concepts of a philosopher who incorporated the ideals of Herder and Goethe, namely Friedrich Schelling.[18]

Schelling's early idealist work on 'Naturphilosophie', *Ideas Towards a Philosophy of Nature*, contends that mind and nature are one, the original product of an absolute whose essence is a striving for freedom within matter. This striving takes the form of a dialectical progression, engendering evolution and, ultimately, man, who has achieved ultimate freedom through self-reflection or self-consciousness. The resulting division of self-conscious purposeful intelligence and unconscious objective nature is not, however, absolute. Nature remains lodged within the unconscious of man, an aspect that is spontaneous and free, the internal representative of the unconscious development of matter in evolution and objective reality. Schelling's belief is that 'Nature should be Mind made visible, Mind the invisible Nature'.[19]

In his aesthetics Schelling identifies this unconscious element as being crucial to artistic production. Art is the product of a yearning for dialectical synthesis between conscious purpose and unconscious development, achieved within the faculty of the imagination. Schelling writes that 'unconscious force must be linked with conscious activity'[20] to produce the highest art, and that this process will be symbolically manifested in the product or artwork. For this reason art and aesthetic acts are uniquely championed in the philosophy of Schelling and in the Romantic movement as a whole. Art is philosophy visualised, and as such it can communicate the process of thought and universal unity to the spectator, with an immediacy and appeal that Schelling knew could not be achieved in his writing. Interestingly, Eisenstein takes an inverse approach, claiming that his aesthetic can be used for philosophical purpose, a visual revelation of 'this dialectic principle'.[21] Although ostensibly working within a materialist framework, his use of Engels' organic dialectic and the notion of a universal structure appear to reflect the ideas of Schelling and Romantic aesthetics. In his essay 'On the Structure of Things', Eisenstein claims that a work of art can only fully communicate when its construction corresponds to 'the laws of the structure of organic phenomena of nature'.[22] He relates this construction to an unconscious element of mind or 'inner speech' that combines with the logic of consciousness to produce the artwork. Like Schelling, Eisenstein believes that art is created by a 'dual process: an impetuous rise along the lines of the highest conceptual steps of consciousness and a simultaneous penetration by means of the structure of the form into the layers of the profoundest sensuous thinking'.[23]

For Schelling, the unifying process of the imagination is inherent in all humans, but it is only the artist of genius who can project this unconscious process symbolically within the form of art. He states that 'the artist ought indeed to emulate this spirit of nature, which is at work at the core of things and which speaks forth in shape and form only'.[24] Eisenstein appears to concur on this point, claiming that Disney is 'the great artist and master' who creates on the level of unconscious nature: 'the realm of the very purest and most primal depths ... on the conceptual level of man not yet shackled by logic, reason or experience'.[25] For Eisenstein this is the same law that dictates 'how butterflies fly ... how flowers grow'.[26]

Eisenstein calls this unconscious and universal dialectic, which dictates both nature and art, the 'plasmatic',[27] an essence defined by the freedom of form. A transformational quality, it can evolve seamlessly from shape to shape, or into any recognisable organic form. For Schelling this evolutionary essence reveals itself in progressive developments and the 'ultimate fusion of manifold forms',[28] apparently reflecting Eisestein's belief that the attraction of the plasmatic is revealed symbolically, through 'infinite changeability' and 'continuous coming into being'.[29] He defines it in Disney as the metamorphic quality of the line, a 'varying contour-expanding or ... variations of species'.[30] Its presence can communicate a revelation of freedom held within the unconscious of the spectator, an ecstatic experience, or as Schelling notes, an 'infinite harmony'.[31]

In his essays on Disney, Eisenstein focuses on the *Silly Symphonies* to exemplify his aesthetic. If we apply these notions in their Romantic context to Disney's later feature length work *Dumbo* (Ben Sharpsteen, USA 1941)

4

specifically the 'Pink Elephants on Parade' sequence, this notion of unconscious freedom, reflected through form, is highly evident. There is, I believe, a reflexive quality to the content of the film and to this segment in particular: its setting is within the circus, an arena of the visual mass entertainment where, like the cinema, the 'suspension of disbelief' is habitual. The hallucination scene itself, 'Pink Elephants on Parade', I intend to read as an expression not only of the Romantic aesthetic through its metamorphic qualities, but also as a depiction of this form of artwork's creation and reception.

Dumbo's intoxication allows him to behave in the manner of the creative artist and he can be read reflexively as representing Disney the artist, as genius creating animation. Drawing up the alcohol infused water in his trunk, Dumbo expels and creates bubbles that exemplify the aesthetic of growth and coming into being through their contour. The line metamorphosises and expands in a paradigmatic example of the plasmatic freedom of form. As a bubble transforms itself into the contour of an elephant, this then seamlessly replicates itself, dividing into a multitude of pachyderms. Limbs stretch and scale is distorted as they march, step over one another, and remerge into one vast creature. Species begin to mutate: an elephant with a snake for a trunk wanders across the screen, leaving human footprints, a cobra transforms into a belly dancer and another elephant transmutes into a car. Dumbo is now positioned as the spectator of his own images. The plasmatic appeal of the freedom of form causes his own hypnotism or ecstasis; it allows him to employ his own unconscious to gain the freedom of flight, to defy gravity.

This communication of unconscious nature, of growth and development, through the animated line of Disney demonstrates Schelling's belief that 'the basic character of the work of art is that of an unconscious infinity'.[32] Eisenstein believes that these animated films or cartoons achieve this aesthetic comedically in a way live action cannot, the stretching and transformational qualities literally revealing the plasmatic.[33] He also cites Disney's literal animism and anthropomorphism as an element that brings the spectator back to an originary oneness with nature, the 'world soul' of Schelling, a period prior to the division of man and matter.

For Eisenstein, Disney's animation is the apotheosis or teleological consummation of the illustrations of John Tenniel, best known for his caricatures in *Punch* and for illustrating Lewis Caroll's 'Alice' books, and the German satirical cartoonist Wilhelm Busch. The stretching and transformation of form depicted statically is now allowed the movement it represents in the graphic animation of Disney. Similarly, Schelling believes that this aesthetic is universal, that it will progress dialectically and re-emerge in different forms. It will be represented by a period's specific art. He claims:

'to be sure, an art the same in all respects as that of past centuries will never come again; for nature never repeats itself ... but there will be another who has attained to the highest level of art in the original manner'.[34] This art will be relative to its culture, yet a Romantic essence of freedom will survive within it.

In relation to Disney's animation as mass entertainment, I have noted that Schelling believed that art should be exposed to as wide an audience as possible. The role of the artist is primarily to communicate, to be relevant to society and to produce work that can convey the fundamental unity of mind and matter. Schelling is of the opinion that 'without some relation to a creative public opinion the artist is condemned to isolation and eccentricity'.[35] As an animator operating within the capitalist structure of Hollywood production and distribution, Disney was wholly reliant on public opinion and society to maintain his studio and output. Despite the working structures imposed by industrialisation, he does therefore reflect Schelling's individual notion of the artist.

We can now take this aesthetic forward, applying it not to the cel animation of Disney, but to the Hollywood film of the late 20th, and early 21st century, assessing whether it has any relevance to post-industrial digital technology or the culture of Postmodernism that informs it. Films such as *Spider-Man* and *Spider-Man 2* (Sam Raimi, USA 2002 and 2004) and *Hulk* (Ang Lee, USA 2003), similar to what Eisenstein noted on the illustrations of Busch in relation to Disney, have overcome their strip cartoon's status. The evocation of animism (*Spider-Man*), and union with natural elements (*Hulk*), allow an escape from the quotidian through the omnipotent freedom which nature bestows. Here, however, this union of conscious and unconscious essence is achieved not by the artist of genius but abiotically, by a technological function. I now wish to suggest that the digital combination of live action and software-based animation in the film image can also signify in a manner synonymous with the Romantic Imagination.

Post-industrial technology and Romantic theories of mind may appear incongruous, but to foreground my claims, I will employ an observation made by Rosen and Zerner. They write that Romantic theory 'is calculated for growth ... planned to allow the appropriation of anything human or even non-human'.[36] It is within the non-human, in technology and in a culture often cited as threatening the freedom of the imagination, that I shall attempt to discover this element of Romanticism. Mind and technology are enthusiastically and sometimes optimistically linked, and I do not intend to make such far-reaching assertions in this essay. My suggestion is simply for a similarity of working practice. Malcolm Le Grice offers some illuminating insights that support this. In his concept of the intelligent machine, Le Grice points out that although all machinery employed in communication reflects the investment of intellect and the culture that informs it, digital technology is its most sophisticated embodiment. He contends that

> all machines embody the application of the intellect to the fulfilment of a need or desire, the greater the complexity of the intelligent machine, the more difficult it is to differentiate the intellect of the machine from its user ... or the centre of authorship for any product.[37]

Authorship of the product, he believes, is submerged in the interaction with the intelligent machine. The product, or in this case the film image, is imprinted with the intelligence of the technology itself. He states 'that the language of the technology is inseparable from the other constituents of symbolic language of the discourse'.[38] As I have already claimed, the Romantic Imagination can exist within cultures and technologies apparently hostile to its aesthetic. In the case of digital technology, with its sophisticated embodiment of intellect, I suggest it is capable of acting in a way analogous to the process of Romantic notions of mind. This is primarily due to its ability to be programmed to combine its own animation with indexical footage. This integrating quality, which I call a 'synthetic imagination', corresponds to its Romantic counterpart in its mediating process between thought and objectivity.

To expand upon this idea of the synthetic imagination I will employ Coleridge's critical theory, attempting to discover any correlations between his notions of the imagination and the computer.[39] Coleridge's theory of the imagination was extensively informed by Schelling's aesthetics,[40] which Coleridge formulated into his own theory of artistic creation. Championing the imagination as the basis of all creativity, Coleridge divided it into the primary and secondary. The primary imagination is 'the agent of all perceptions', the site where the objective world and subjectivity coincide.[41] The secondary imagination is a faculty only available to the artist, one in which the actions of the primary, the coming together of conscious thought and unconscious nature can be revealed symbolically in the artwork. It is the manner in which the secondary accomplishes this that I will focus upon in relation to the synthetic imagination of the computer. Coleridge states that the secondary imagination

> coexists with the conscious will ... differing only in degree and in the mode of its operation. It dissolves, dissipates in order to recreate, or when this process is rendered impossible, yet still at all events it struggles to idealize and unify. It is essentially vital, even as all objects (as objects) are fixed.[42]

This merging of opposites into new wholes defies the 'formal logic of non-contradiction' that governs the duality of subject and object. It is not mimetic and is not governed by association or transposition. Coleridge calls this activity 'esemplasticity', a 'synthetic and magical power'.[43] It is an activity that I feel also accords with Eisenstein's notion of the plasmatic, a metamorphic quality.

The synthetic imagination accords with Coleridge's theory of the creative process on two major points: the union of ontological and subjective information which overcomes the rational division of mind and matter, and the break from mimetic transposition involved in achieving this dialectical synthesis. If we compare the former to ideas put forward by Lev Manovich, we can find correspondences. In his book *The Language of New Media*, [44] Manovich argues that through digitisation film attains the plasticity of form only previously thought possible in cel animation. This is achieved, he believes, because the computer does not distinguish between live action footage and images simulated in the computer; all material is reduced to an abstract numerical code, visualised in pixels to be easily altered and substituted for one another. He declares that filmmakers adopting this technique work with 'elastic reality'.[45] Lucia Santa Braga similarly highlights this function, observing that 'the digital code transforms each fragment into an entirely discontinuous and quantified element ... the result is that the numerical image is under perpetual metamorphosis'.[46]

The ability of digital media to overcome the process of associative transcription is dealt with by Timothy Binkley. In his essay 'Refiguring Culture', Binkley points out that the integration of live action and animation attains a 'synthesis that has until now been the exclusive province of sentient beings',[47] and discusses the conversion qualities of digital media. Conversion, Binkley argues, is unique to the computer. Unlike traditional analog media that transcribes images and is therefore mimetic, conversion bestows malleability on the information it receives, breaking the cycle of repetition. As a result, the database is 'essentially mediated not by physical processes but rather by conceptual constructs'.[48]

It is this process of integration and conversion, exclusive to the computer that I propose allows for comparison to the Romantic Imagination. As Le Grice argues, it is difficult to differentiate intellect and authorship from the user and machine, and I hope to have made a case for the idea of the computer working in a manner similar to that of the imagination, producing images comparable to that of the Romantic artwork.

What I would now like to address is the imprint digital technology places upon these images, how they are defined, and how the symbolic qualities they possess enable them to communicate with the spectator's imagination. Unlike films such as *Who Framed Roger Rabbit* (Robert Zemeckis, USA 1988) that retain the visual differentiation of the cartoon placed in indexical representations, James Cameron, the director of *Terminator 2: Judgment Day* (James Cameron, USA 1991) has observed that almost 'organic results' can be produced by the integration of live action and computer generated images in the special effect.[49]

If we return to my earlier idea of Eisenstein and his concurrence with Schelling's aesthetics, I suggested that both see the indwelling aspect of nature as revealed by metamorphosis, or a freedom over form. Coleridge confirms this theory within his concept of the secondary imagination, but he also adds the concept of the impossible image, an overcoming of the logic of duality to produce an illogical form. However, unlike more traditional modes of animation, this is achieved with an apparently indexical photorealist perfection, allowing this aesthetic to be experienced on a more intense and immediate level. It is these two qualities – a highly realistic fluidity and the impossible – that I will focus upon here as products of the synthetic imagination, examining how they are produced and integrated into the film text. My choice for this investigation is a single film, *The Matrix* (Larry and Andy Wachowski, USA 1999), the first of a trilogy.

The Matrix is of special relevance because it can be considered a paradigmatic representation of Postmodern ideology in film. The film's references to the Postmodernist theory of Jean Baudrillard are explicit: in an early scene we see Neo use Baudrillard's *Simulacra and Simulation* as a hiding place for the programmes he sells. Baudrillard's philosophical contention – that Postmodern culture has witnessed the implosion of the real and its representation, causing the disappearance of the imagination – is also employed in the film's narrative. In his reading of the science fiction genre, of which *The Matrix* is an example, Baudrillard writes that the text will focus on 'models of simulation … and contrive to give them the feeling of the real, of the banal, of lived experience, to reinvent the real as fiction precisely because it has disappeared from our life'.[50]

Baudrillard's theory is apparently fulfilled by *The Matrix's* presentation of the real as a deception formulated by an artificial intelligence. Playing upon the notion of a confusion of reality and representation, the film uses live action to depict the simulation of the computer program and, paradoxically, it uses digital animation to portray the real world. Like the simulacra in Baudrillard's thesis, the matrix is a 'copy without original' of an earth that no longer exists.[51] By destabilising the real, technology has also confounded the separation of subject and object. People exist in the matrix program as simulations within a simulacrum.

Despite the overt reference to the Postmodern theory I have noted in the film, I believe that a Romantic theme is concealed within it. The central character of Neo has been read as an analogy of Christ, chosen to lead humanity to self-awareness. I would like to contend that this figure can also be read as an interpretation of the Romantic artist, who has the power of utilising his imagination to transform reality (or in this case the filmic representation of it), consequently communicating this unconscious power to the spectator through the image.

This comparison unfolds when it is revealed to Neo that his perceived reality, the conscious objective world that he interacts with, is merely a computer program. This simulacrum in which he projects his simulated self through thought can be perceived as the primary imagination of Coleridge, 'the prime agent of all human perceptions'.[52] With the attainment of this awareness he chooses to experience the world he has been unconscious of, the unconscious freedom of nature defined by the secondary imagination. Neo's character is reborn; literally passing through the looking-glass, breaking the umbilical cord that attaches him to the program, escaping from his womb-like pod and being flushed into reality.

Released from the matrix he can now return to it with powers analogous to the artist. Armed with the knowledge that his presence within the program is only a simulation, he can now reshape it with the power of his imagination. In preparation his intelligence is endowed with phenomenal skills, giving him the ability to act physically through his mind when placed into the matrix. As with the Romantic artist, Neo's artwork is his own body. His physical self becomes the created symbolic object, the site where the secondary imagination can reveal his own creation of self in the program. It can be perceived in the impossible physical skills he acquires and the metamorphic transformations he undergoes.

The computer enables the rendering of these skills and transformations in a highly photorealist representation. Theories surrounding digital images often place them within a Postmodern framework. For example, Andrew Darley claims that they present a depthlessness that denies the imagination; he also suggests that these impossible yet perfect images are a spectacle detached from the film text, communicating merely their artifice and a foregrounding of the technology that produced them.[53]

My approach advocates an alternative interpretation. Here, digital technology produces not merely an excessive artifice, but a site where the synthetic imagination can function within a visual narrative, offering a symbolic union of mind and matter through the amalgamation of live action and animation. Michele Pierson argues that 'as the 1990s draw to a close ... computer-generated images have ceased to be objects for contemplation'.[54] Citing films such as *The Lost World: Jurassic Park* (Stephen Spielberg, USA 1997), she assigns to these images an 'assimulationist' aesthetic that fully integrates them into the film text.[55] In the case of *The Matrix*, the impossible images of physical virtuosity, created by the seamless blending of digital animation and live action, allow two examples of the synthetic imagination to be perceived symbolically in filmic form: morphing and bullet-time photography. Of these two techniques, the first I will consider (although not original to this film) is that of 'morphing'.

On the morph, used extensively in *Terminator 2: Judgement Day* (James Cameron, USA, 1991), Yvonne Spielmann contends it is the site where the analog and digital coincide, where 'two different moments hit each other in a single image unit'.[56] This technique is employed in the scene where Neo merges with the liquefied glass of the mirror, overcoming his division from ontological matter. It exemplifies the fluidity and metamorphic qualities of form, the symbolic revelation of the unifying power of the imagination in the image. It recalls not only the esemplastic of Coleridge, the merging of opposites that 'defies the formal logic of non-contradiction', but also the essence of Schelling's aesthetic – a dialectical synthesis realised on a scale of photorealist perfection through the process of the synthetic imagination.

The second technique, 'bullet-time photography', was introduced into Hollywood cinema for the first time in *The Matrix* and could be considered a digital reworking of stop frame animation. The dislocation of the camera from its subject matter enables it to glide around the static yet floating figures. This defiance of gravity recalls Eisenstein's notion that 'there is yet another plasmatic factor: the figures hover in space',[57] a recollection of the primal plasma, the originary freedom granted by a oneness with nature. The digital interpolation of still images into the live action is not visible; thus an impossible image with highly realist qualities is created.

It is my view that these techniques reveal the freedom that the imagination has placed within the body of Neo, a fusion of mind and nature in the artwork, here formulated by the synthetic imagination of the computer. As the characters in *The Matrix* are empowered directly by the input of technology into their minds, the film is imbued with these elements by the digital images infused into the live action, the animation of reality.

What, however, do these images present to the spectator? What kind of reception can they offer? As I earlier observed, Postmodern theory interprets these images as depthless, contending that despite their impossibility and fluidity, the imagination is denied to the spectator. As I have suggested in my own approach, the computer can communicate differently through the synthetic imagination. Binkley observes that digital images can readily accommodate two-way interactions, because they are formulated by machines configured for the input and output of information. This capacity for interaction allows for the possibility of an alternative reception, in which the spectator can recognise the process of the synthetic imagination of the computer through its images. By perceiving such qualities as a freedom of form and the non-logical, in the combination of live action and animation, it is possible for the viewer to regain awareness of his own indwelling nature, or the primal unity of mind and matter, rather than a mere fore-grounding of technology.

For Eisentsein, this revelation is one of 'ecstasy', or it is an 'infinite harmony' in Schelling's thesis. For the Romantics the experience is one of 'joy'. For Coleridge, joy is apprehended when the intermittent moments of unity between man and nature are experienced. Firstly for the artist or poet, who achieves this in his secondary imagination, conveying it symbolically in his work, and secondly for the spectator who perceives it. Joy is an emotion felt in undividedness, in the recognition that the organisation of mind and matter are not inseparable. It is felt by perceiving the creation of all as a unified whole.

Romantic thought revelled in the tension created by uniting opposites, and for that movement it was the imagination that could attain that goal. What I hope to have suggested in this essay is a continuing relevance for these Romantic notions, an indication that within the field of animation, this world of freedom and wholeness can survive despite cultural and techno-logical change. This is firstly achieved through the metamorphic quality of line perceived by Eisenstein in the *Silly Symphonies*, and consequently within the blending qualities of the computer's synthetic imagination, symbolically revealed in films such as *The Matrix*. Ultimately, my view is that the technology which has enabled these two forms of animation, and which has often been hailed as precipitating the death of Romantic ideals is perhaps, finally, that which sustains it: a retrieval of a lost freedom and unity, a universal and timeless aesthetic.

This essay is the outcome of a paper given at the Animated Worlds Conference organised by Suzanne Buchan, to whom I am grateful for her positive response to my work. I would like to thank my supervisor Michael O'Pray for his suggestions and support in the writing of this essay.

Notes

1. For a general introduction to Romantic notions of mind and the imagination see C.M. Bowra, *The Romantic Imagination* (London: Oxford University Press, 1950), Richard Kearney, *The Wake of Imagination,* (London: Routledge, 2001): 155–188 and Mary Warnock, *Imagination* (London: Faber and Faber, 1976): 43–69.

2. Romantic aesthetics are admirably dealt with in the following texts: Freidrich von Schiller, *On the Aesthetic Education of Man,* (first published in 1795) trans. E. Wilkins and L. Wiloughby (Oxford: Clarendon Press, 1967). M.H. Abrams, *The Mirror and the Lamp: Romantic Theory and the Critical Tradition* (Oxford: Oxford University Press, 1953), and Monroe. Beardsley,*Aesthetics: From Classical Greece To The Present* (Tuscaloosa: The University of Alabama Press, 1966): 244–282.

3. Richard Coyne, *Technoromanticism: Digital Narrative, Holism, and the Romance of the Real* (London: MIT Press, 1999): 31.

4. See the chapter of the same name in Norman Klein, *Seven Minutes: The Life and Death of The American Cartoon* (London: Verso, 1993): 68–74.

5. Eisenstein's essays are collected in *Eisenstein on Disney*, ed. Jay Leda (London: Meuthen, 1988).

6. These notions are also discussed at length in Sergei Eisenstein, *Nonindifferent Nature: Film and the Structure of Things* trans. Herbert Marshall (Cambridge: Cambridge University Press, 1987). They are further dealt with in relation to Disney by Michael O'Pray, 'Eisenstein and Stokes on Disney', *A Reader in Animation Studies*, ed. Jane Pilling (London: John Libbey, 1996): 195–202.

7. For an overview of German Romanticism and its key figures see Roger Cardinal, *German Romantics in Context* (London: Macmillan, 1975), and Marshall Brown, *The Shape of German Romanticism* (New York: Cornell University Press, 1979).

8. Eisenstein's move towards organicism is examined by David Bordwell in his essay, 'Eisenstein's Epistemological Shift', *Screen* (Winter, 1974/1975): 32–46. See also Oksana Bulgakowa, 'The Evolving Eisenstein: Three Theoretical Constructs of Sergei Eisenstein' in *Eisenstein at 100: A Reconsideration* (London: Rutgers University Press, 2001): 38–51.

9. Nicolai Bukharin, 'Poetry, Poetics and the Problems of Poetry in the USSR' in *The Soviet Writers' Congress 1934: The Debate on Socialist Realism and Modernism* (London: Lawrence and Wishart, 1977): 191.

10. Margaret Rose, *Marx's Lost Aesthetic: Karl Marx and the Visual Arts* (Cambridge: Cambridge University Press, 1984): 147.

11. See Eisenstein, 1987, op. cit.

12. Thomas Elsaesser, 'Social Mobility and the Fantastic: German Silent Cinema' in *Fantasy and the Cinema*, ed. James Donald, (London: British Film Institute, 1989): 24.

13. For an in-depth study of Disney's European influences see Robin Allen, *Walt Disney and Europe* (London: John Libbey, 1999).

14. Leyda, 1988, op. cit: 42.

15. Ibid: 34.

16. Johann Herder, 'Deutscher Art und Kunst' quoted in *The Mirror and the Lamp: Romantic Theory and the Critical Tradition* , op. cit: 205.

17. Johann Goethe, 'Uber Wahrheit und Wahrscheinlichkeit der Kunstwerke' quoted in *The Mirror and the Lamp: Romantic Theory and the Critical Tradition* , op. cit: 206.

18. For translations of Schelling's major works see *Ideas for a Philosophy of Nature* (first published in 1797) trans. Erroll Harris and Peter Heath (Cambridge: Cambridge University Press, 1988) and *System of Transcendental Idealism (1800)*, trans. Peter Heath (Charlottesville: University Press of Virginia, 1978). For an overview of Schelling's philosophy and its contemporary relevance see Andrew Bowie, *Schelling and Modern European Philosophy: An Introduction* (London: Routlege, 1993).

19. Schelling, 1797/1988, op. cit: 42.

20. Friedrich Schelling, 'Concerning the Relation of the Plastic Arts to Nature: An oration on the name day of the King, 1807' in *German Aesthetic and Literary Criticism: Kant, Fitche, Schelling, Schopenhaur, Hegel*, ed. David Simpson (Cambridge: Cambridge University Press, 1984): 149–158.

21. Sergei Eisenstein, 'A Dialectic Approach To Film Form' in *Film Form: Essays in Film Theory*, ed. Jay Leda (London: Harcourt Brace, 1977): 46.

22. Eisenstein, 1987, op. cit: 11.

23. Eisenstein, 1977, op. cit: 144.

24. Schelling, in Simpson (ed.), op. cit: 151.

25. Leyda, 1988, op. cit: 2.

26. Ibid: 2.

27. Ibid: 21.

28. Schelling, in Simpson (ed.), op. cit: 155.

29. Leyda, 1988, op. cit: 45.

30. Ibid: 64.

31. Schelling, 1800/1978, op. cit: 223.

32. Ibid: 255.

33. Leyda, 1988, op. cit: 39.

34. Schelling in Simpson (ed.) op. cit: 157.

35. Ibid: 157.

36. Charles Rosen and Henri Zerner, *Romanticism and Realism: the Mythology of Nineteenth Century Art* (London: Faber and Faber, 1984): 22.

37. Malcolm Le Grice, *Experimental Cinema in the Digital Age* (London: British Film Institute, 2001): 240.

38. Ibid: 280.

39. For Coleridge's critical approach and his theory of the imagination, see *Biographia Literaria* (London: Dent, 1967), and *The Notebooks of Samuel Taylor Coleridge* ed. K. Coburn (London: Routledge 1990).

40. Warnock, op. cit: 91.

41. Coleridge, 1967, op. cit: 167.

42. Ibid: 167.

43. Ibid: 174.

44. Lev Manovich, *The Language of New Media* (London: MIT Press, 2001).

45. Ibid: 300–301.

46. Lucia Santa Braga, 'The prephotographic, the photographic and the postphotographic', ed. W. North, *Semiotics of the Media* (Berlin: Mouton de Guyter, 1997): 125.

47. Timothy Binkley, 'Refiguring Culture' in *Future Visions: New Technologies of the Screen* ed. P. Hayward and T. Wollen (London: British Film Institute, 1993): 116.

48. Ibid: 92.

49. R. Baker, 'Computer Technology and Special Effects in Contemporary Cinema' in Hayward and Wollen, op. cit: 40.

50. Jean Baudrillard, *Simulacra and Simulation* (Michigan: The University of Michigan Press, 1994): 124.

51. See Jim Rovira, 'Baudrillard and Hollywood: Subverting the Mechanism of Control and The Matrix' http://www.uta.edu/english/apt/collab/texts/hollywood.html

52. Coleridge, 1967, op. cit: 167.

53. See Andrew Darley, *Visual Digital Culture: Surface Play and Spectacle in New Media Genres* (London: Routledge, 2000).

54. Michele Pierson, 'CGI efects in Hollywood science-fiction cinema 1989–95: the wonder years', *Screen* (40: 2 Summer, 1999): 175.

55. Ibid: 159.

56. Yvonne Spielmann, 'Expanding film into digital media', *Screen* (40:2 Summer, 1999): 144.

57. Leyda, 1988, op. cit: 70.

Rachel Kearney is a lecturer at the University of East London. Her current research explores concurrences between animation and Romantic notions of the imagination. By employing theories of a dialectical synthesis of mind and matter, and by applying these to the formal qualities of the animated image, she wishes to suggest a correspondence or communication, between the viewer and the viewed.

Chapter 2

The Animated Spectator: Watching the Quay Brothers' 'Worlds'

Suzanne Buchan

To say the poetic image is independent of causality is to make a rather serious statement. But the causes cited by psychologists and psychoanalysts can never really explain the wholly unexpected nature of the new image, any more than they can explain the attraction it holds for a mind that is foreign to the process of its creation.
Gaston Bachelard, *The Poetics of Space, 1958*

Silent, sombre blackness fades up to an abstract composition of rough vertical and horizontal rectangular forms that frame thick and mottled glass panes. The camera pans up, to the left, back to the right and down again. The rhythmic sound of a tram passing in the distance suggests an open, off-screen space. Slightly visible in the lower left a movement commences: slowly, ponderously, a rotating form rises like a behemoth from its fixings, a thick, oily screw which doggedly emerges from its invisible existence below the visible surface. Eerie, restrained and cyclical music accompanies this unfamiliar and compelling vision; a squeaking violin implores the screw to strain higher, higher, revealing the spiralled ridges of its cylindrical form. Then, in the foreground, two smaller screws begin to twirl upwards to complete an industrial *pas de trois*, a visual fugue,

Abstract: Using a framework of phenomenological concepts that reviews other authors' approaches to animation spectatorship, the essay explores the viewer's experience of the 'worlds' of animation film in screening, particularly investigating the relationship between the images on screen and their tangible, extant counterparts in the real world outside the diegesis. With a focus on puppet animation exemplified by the Quay Brothers' *Street of Crocodiles*, the essay posits a number of propositions as to how animation as a form addresses and engages its audience. If aims to articulate the difference between *a* world, created with the animation technique, and *the* world, the phenomenal world we negotiate in our daily lives.

the smaller screws more urgent, in a hurry to free themselves from their wooden prison. They spiral upwards faster than the rotating column in the background, jerkily, as a new sound weaves itself into the background violin, high-pitched, nervous, yet endearing. Hesitating at the last moment before disengaging themselves, they fall on their sides and roll off-screen, one trailing a curled wisp of old twine, the other gathering sticky dust, as they venture off to – where?

This brief description is of a scene from the Quay Brothers' *Street of Crocodiles* (1986). There may be a few incidental films in each of our personal cinema experiences in which the essence of poetic cinema seems to coalesce in a particular instant, a scene or a secondary gesture. They are fleeting yet remarkable instants of film which transcend lived experience and enter interior realms of the metaphysical. There is a discrepancy between the phenomenal world and the noumenal, or supersensible, 'documentation' of what is intimately trapped in our own imaginations. This essay explores the experience of such cinematic moments that transpose similar visions on screen.[1]

During work on a recently completed formal and aesthetic analysis of the films of the Quays, my thoughts became increasingly entangled in philosophical and phenomenological debates on cinema. Most of the approaches I used were not reliant on established, a priori or prescriptive theories of cinema. They were much more related to the *experience* of watching the Quays' films, if you like, through a phenomenological filter. This has meant taking a cue from Jean-Paul Sartre's understanding of phenomenology as 'allowing one to delineate carefully one's own affective, emotional, and imaginative life, not in a set of static objective studies such as one finds in psychology, but understood in the manner in which it is meaningfully lived'.[2] The cinema is a place we recurrently slip into, to allow ourselves that most pleasurable experience of being moved, intellectually, affectively and emotionally, by what unfolds on screen.

Animated 'Worlds'

The aesthetic representation of 'worlds', imaginary or otherwise, through cinematography is thematised in philosophical, cognitive and psychoanalytic discourses with impact on almost all areas of the humanities. The concept of 'worlds' was the glue that brought some of my musings together:

> What exists beyond the [film] text and what kind of description can be adequate to it? Here we encounter the exciting and dangerous term 'world'. A film elaborates a world which it is the critic's job to flesh out or respond to. But what is this cinematic world?[3]

What Dudley Andrew considers 'exiting and dangerous' is exactly what attracts and is daunting at the same time: to describe an experience of the 'world' of *Street of Crocodiles* and of other Quay films through a framework that takes into account the 'lived' experience of the films. I hope to posit some suggestions towards understanding the phenomena we experience when watching their films, and how this understanding relates to our lived experience of reality. The experience of scale, for instance, or of how we understand the 'worlds' we see in animation – the intrinsic differences between the often exaggerated 'worlds' of 2D films and the puppet anima-tion 'world' that the Quays' films invoke. By formulating a few indicative questions and approaches for these and other works, the essay explores a concept of animated 'worlds' that may open new avenues of enquiry specific to spectatorship for the 'worlds' other techniques and technologies evoke, such as 2D and computer animation.

In an added section of the enlarged edition of his philosophical enquiry into the ontology of film, *The World Viewed* (1979), Stanley Cavell responds to Alexander Sesonske's criticism (included in this response) brought against his text which is worth quoting here at length:

> Cavell: [T]here is one whole region of film which seems to satisfy my concerns with understanding the special powers of film but which explicitly has nothing to do with projections of the real world – the region of animated cartoons. If this region of film counters my insistence upon the projection of reality as essential to the medium of the movies, then it counters it completely. Here is what Sesonske says about cartoons (he is thinking specifically of Disney's work, which is fair enough: if any cartoons are obviously to be thought of as movies, even to the point of containing stars, these are the first candidates):

> [Sesonske:] [N]either these lively creatures nor their actions ever existed until they were projected on screen. Their projected world exists only *now*, at the moment of projection – and when we ask if there is any feature in which it differs from reality, the answer is, 'Yes, every feature'. Neither space nor time nor the laws of nature are the same. There is *a* world we experience here, but not *the* world – a world I know and see but to which I am nevertheless not present, yet not a world past. For there is no past time at which these events either did occur or purport to have occurred. Surely not the time the drawings were made, or the frames photographed; for the world I know and see had not yet sprung into existence then. It exists only now, when I see it; yet I cannot go to where its creatures are, for there is no access to its space from ours except through vision.[4]

> [Cavell:] Each of these remarks is the negation or parody of something I claim for the experience of movies. But of course they do not prove my claims are false except on the assumption that cartoons are movies, and that, therefore, what I said about movies, if it is true, ought to apply to cartoons in the way it applies to movie. But on my assumption (which I should no doubt have made explicit) that cartoons are not movies, these remarks about their conditions of existence constitute some explanation about *why* they are not.[5]

Sesonske's rebuttal on how animation differs from reality is especially interesting. He is of course referring to drawn animation, as Cavell notes above. Disney's works have often been described as fictional hyperrealism and as exhibiting a style of animation which comes closest to a depiction of reality (shadows, anthropomorphism, scale and perspective). Sesonske continues, however, by saying that '[t]here is *a* world we experience here, but not *the* world'. Cavell describes cartoons as a 'region' of film that completely counters his insistence on the projection of reality as essential to the medium of movies. In other words, Cavell seems to consider cartoons (no mention of object animation) as not belonging to the domain of his conception of cinema, and he puts forth that maybe we can't consider them as films at all.

But Cavell's concern is with 'reality'. His explanation of the 'region' of cartoons and his reasoning as to why they do not belong to film is closely bound to his own philosophical conceptions of reality. If we think of the profilmic materials of cartoons, drawings that *represent* ideas, objects and characters through graphic composition, colour, tone and style, then the 'reality' of these drawings is their material base – paper, cel or otherwise. What Cavell fails to point out is that the cinematic apparatus enables movement and the experience of these drawings as a 'reality' particular to the 'region' of animation. Taking a cue from Sesonske, I would like to address what the 'special powers of film' could be in puppet animation. If animation has nothing to do with projections of the real world, then what is it projecting, and how do we understand it? There are, as well, different realities that have to be taken into account. Cavell's perception of reality is different from mine and from any other spectator in the cinema. There is consensus within philosophical schools on different definitions of reality, but, in our discussion, we will seek a more precise definition of what Cavell means by 'a region', and what Sesonske means by 'a world'. We will consider how the Quays' puppet films present 'real' spaces (sets) and figures in the cinematic illusion, not drawn ones. The idea of an animated 'realm' created by the technique demands a different approach towards understanding the spectator's experience of their cinematic worlds.

I am not expecting to solve the complex 'problem' that animation presents as a unique form of cinematic illusion. Rather, the point is to reflect upon why these films are meaningful and have enriched my life and informed my own imagination of other 'worlds' and as they have, in different ways, for many others. Maurice Merleau-Ponty's phenomenology is also concerned with how the manner of experiences of our own bodies is different from our experience of inanimate physical objects. He describes a situation that can be understood as analogous to cinema. A man is in a room looking at a reflection of part of the room in a mirror canted at a 45-degree angle:

Fig. 1: Street of Crocodiles, *Quay Brothers, 1986. [Image courtesy of the Quay Brothers.]*

After a few minutes, provided he does not strengthen his initial anchorage by glancing away from the mirror, the reflected room miraculously calls up a subject capable of living in it. This virtual body ousts the real one to such an extent that the subject no longer has the feeling of being in the world where he actually is, and that instead of his real legs and arms, he feels he has the legs and arms he would need to walk and act in the reflected room he inhabits the spectacle. ... It is, then, a certain possession of the world by my body, a certain gearing of my body to the world.[6]

There are intuitions and experiences at play when we inhabit the Quays' 'world' instead of a mirror. A cinematic world allows us to experience spaces and to haptically possess material objects that, in our physical world, are inanimate, but through the 'special powers' of animation, are endowed with a semblance of life. The 'universe', 'realm' or 'world' particular to the Quays' films is determined by their formal techniques and style applied to objects that occupy 3D space (Fig. 1). If we recall how Cavell seemed 'stumped' (but curious) by animation, we need approaches that can help us get a better grasp of the images in the Quays' and other films in terms of how they relate to our own experiences of realities, including overlaps between the phenomenal world and the 'world' the film presents.

In drawn animation, the moving figures and sense of space they 'inhabit' can only be experienced in projection – the artwork itself is planar. (Fig. 2)

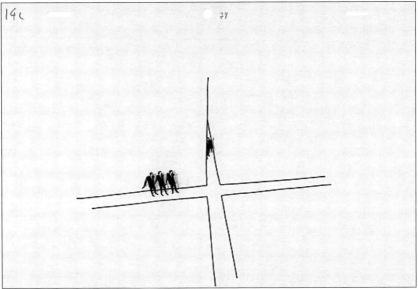

Fig. 2: Drawing from The Crossing, *1991, Raimund Krumme. [Courtesy of Raimund Krumme.]*

Although they offer ample spatial cues that can mimic our lived experience of space, and techniques like the Multiplane camera and planar focus shifts can actually introduce 3D space and perspective to graphic animation, the worlds that conventional 2D animation represents do not have a corollary

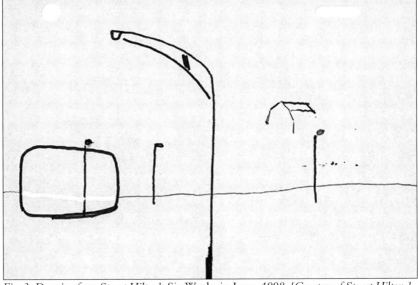

Fig. 3: Drawing from Stuart Hilton's Six Weeks in June, *1998. [Courtesy of Stuart Hilton.]*

in our lived experience. We do understand them through spatial and cultural clues and can imagine what the referents represent through the suggestions made by the images. This of course does not necessarily hold for abstract film or for some kinds of non-narrative film, which are not concerned with a coherent representation or interpretation of reality. For instance, cel, drawn or rotoscoped animation tend to use principles of composition, scale and perspective which at least suggest an analogy with the world we live in. Even if architecture and spaces are reduced to minimalist lines like in *The Crossing* (Raimund Krumme, 1991) or, as in *Six Weeks in June* (Stuart Hilton, 1998), that uses isolated graphic elements to suggest the distorted vision experienced by the ennui of a long road trip to a point of abstraction that challenges our perception, enough is there for us, after some conceptual and visual acrobatics, to reconstruct the referent (Figs. 2 and 3).

Of course, one could say the same about a live action film: the moment of shooting is unique. Yet the actors, settings and the physical world in which they carry out actions are extant, tangible and constitute a part of the real world. Let us return to the screws described at the outset. Puppet animation elicits a different set of questions as it is a complex hybrid form in this respect. The sets and puppets exist, and although they may appear to have anthropomorphic proportions on screen, they are constructed on a smaller scale. Yet although the events we see on screen *did not* occur, the objects *do* exist. Puppet animation thus represents a different 'world' for the spectator, something between '*a* world', created with the animation technique, and '*the* world', in its use of real objects and not representational drawings. Vivian Sobchack mentions Yuri Lotman in this context: 'For Lotman, the development of cinematic technology is the active intentional realization of perceptive and expressive choice-making within the context of a world'.[7] '*A* world' as different from '*the* world' is a distinction of ultimate relevance in a phenomenological investigation of the visual experience of object animation, what it represents and how we perceive this world.

Spectatorship(s)

Robert Stam et al. mention three types of cinema spectator: one based on the empirical, sociological model; the consciously aware viewer provided by the [Neo-]Formalist approaches; and the psychoanalytic model.[8] Contemporary discourses in spectatorship are homing in on the 'consciously aware' viewer, and this is the one that especially interests me. Without the contextual knowledge of what informs the Quays' films the viewer is usually puzzled or baffled.[9] This is not to say that only an informed audience can enjoy the films, or that these other models cannot apply. It does mean

21

that there is an additional level of pleasure available to spectators who can engage imaginatively with the films' aesthetic and stylistic complexities.

In *Cinema and Spectatorship*, Judith Mayne reflects on the changing status of spectatorship within cinematic theory. She notes a shift from innocent consumption to what she terms 'critical spectatorship'.[10] Mayne's study is of mainstream narrative, yet a number of issues she raises are pertinent to queries about animation spectatorship as well. In her opinion, spectatorship is at once the most valuable area of film studies and the one that has been most misunderstood largely because of the obsessive preoccupation with dualistic categories of critique versus celebration, or 'critical' versus 'complacent' spectatorship.[11] Over the ten years since Mayne's book was published, the spectator has become central in new theories of cognition, emotion and empathy. The spectator's emotional response to film initiated a major discourse in cinema studies that began in the late eighties, encouraged notably by Murray Smith, David Bordwell, Edward Branigan, Torben Grodal, Carl Plantinga, Gregory Currie, Christine Noll Brinckmann and Noël Carroll. There has been a shift away from SLAB theories invoking a passive spectator towards approaches that posit one who is actively involved in film reception.[12] Many of these theories are premised on a cultural understanding of what we see (Bordwell, Grodal, Carroll, Thompson). It also ties in with the 'piecemeal' (Carroll) and Neoformalist methods that the Wisconsin school initiated. It is generally agreed that '[t]hese theories are designed to overcome the conceptual problem raised by the "paradox of fiction", namely the paradox of the spectator responding emotionally to what he knows does not exist'.[13]

Animation is sometimes included in the heterogeneous corpus of indexed film titles serving as examples in cinema theory texts. Often the reference is to a particular technique in a discussion of non-animation film. For instance, throughout his 1984 study, Edward Branigan refers to a few animation films and their characters. Edwin S. Porter's *Dream of a Rarebit Fiend* (1906) is invoked in the context of dream states expressed using matte shots. Discussing the subjective tracking shot, he makes no distinction between the point of view of a 2D Pinocchio and the figure of Shaft from the eponymous 1971 film.[14] Point of view is itself a fascinating issue in animation film, and one could easily expand on Branigan's example of Pinocchio's subjectivity. He continues with a discussion of another Disney film:

> In *Bambi* (Walt Disney, 1942), Bambi twists his head to look at some opossums hanging from their tails upside down on a branch. The next animated drawing is rotated 180 degrees so that we see the animals from Bambi's inverted viewpoint, hanging 'straight up' and so apparently defying gravity.[15]

This quotation raises pertinent issues on the nature of animation spectatorship. It is interesting, for instance, that Branigan discusses inverted point-of-view by stating that the next drawing has been rotated. This is a profilmic event and technically speaking, out of economy, it is possible (and likely) that instead of re-drawing the opossums hanging on the branch the anima-tors simply rotated the initial drawings and shot them upside down for this scene. That they are 'apparently defying gravity' refers to the fact that these are drawings of opossums, yet despite this illusory effect Branigan's refer-ence remains the reality of what a real opossum cannot do, namely, defy gravity. Branigan's remarks are also indicative of the emphasis on technique that many texts on animation engage with.

That Bambi 'exists', twists his head and looks, is the result of the cinematic animation of a series of developmental drawings. Puppets have a different materiality and occupy real space, yet our query here concerns the evident acceptance of an animated figure's movement and ability to look. Bambi talks and moves, ergo Bambi 'is' – what is the significance? We can develop this further by considering the implications of Branigan's idea for object animation. If we recall the screws mentioned at the beginning of this essay, they also apparently defy gravity, by unscrewing themselves upwards from the floorboard and 'rolling' themselves off-camera. They are not an artist's rendering, they 'exist' as tangible objects in the physical world. Taking Branigan's cue, would we then talk about these screws as having points-of-view? And since they don't have eyes, in terms of the consciously aware viewer, what does this imply about how we take their 'cues' and attribute them with attitude and intention?

I would suggest there is a permanent doubling of point of view in *Street of Crocodiles* and other puppet animation films. That of the camera (character, omniscient author, etc.) is always also that of the director – but in a directly active sense, since, in the Quays' films that are mostly made by the two of them, the person animating determines not only formal parameters but also controls the profilmic inter-frame adjustments that result in the illusion of movement, character and 'acting'. Regardless of how much control a director will try to have over his or her actors' movements, actors are much more the 'possessors' of a point-of-view – but puppets' actions and gaze structures are entirely created and determined by the animator. This means that when a puppet looks off-screen or there is a match cut to what it is looking at, it calls attention to a much greater degree to the *intention* of the person animating the figure, as well as the actual action of *moving* the puppet. Their personality and intentions are what the conscious viewer tries to understand as expressed through the puppet. In other words, this kind of point-of-view is much more mediated than in live action, because whether we have an omniscient or subjective point-of-view we are con-stantly aware of the animator's creation of the 'world' we see.

Grodal investigates what he calls 'a systematic relation between the embodied mental processes and configurations activated in a given type of visual fiction and the emotional 'tone' and 'modal qualities' of the experienced affects, emotions and feelings in the viewer'.[16] This recalls what Stam et al. call a 'consciously aware viewer' and is a direct link to phenomenological concepts of experience. Grodal:

> Imagination, consisting of hypothetical simulations of possible relations and processes, is a central aspect of everyday life; the difference between art and everyday imagination is not one of kind but one of degree, of direct 'interestedness' and of 'art understood as superior know-how'.[17]

Appreciation of the Quays' films requires the 'superior know-how' Grodal mentions. This chimes with the expanded knowledge that Kristin Thompson and Noel Burch attribute to spectators in some of their studies.[18] Because we can experience the film's 'world' in the cinema, and the affects and associations that the film elicits carry over and are incorporated into our daily experience.

Over the years I have had many engaging discussions about animation and audience with students and established scholars from multiple disciplines. Summarised, one of the reasons why animation tends to be misunderstood or ignored by the academic community is that viewers are overtaxed by the sheer amount of visual information on screen, and that they perhaps tend to focus on the less demanding aspects of humour or narrative. Grodal supports this, assuming that 'laughter, like other types of automatic response, is a reaction to overload, an "escape-button alternative" to voluntary reactions'.[19] He also suggests that peripetia, sudden change or reversal, cause comic reaction. 2D animation's graphic potential to visualise sudden changes that would be impossible in live-action film is rampant, for instance, in the chase and slapstick films of the 1920s and 1930s exemplified by Felix the Cat shorts or the Fleischer Brothers' surreal grotesques. Thus another relevant example Grodal invokes is the parodic grotesque, that 'underlines the patterned and thereby the mechanical elements of the features they exaggerate and deform, for instance by upscaling certain features or by simplifying certain schemata of thoughts and actions'.[20] This is a feature of many Hollywood cartoons of the 1940s and 1950s, a zenith perhaps being Tex Avery's surreal and absurd distortion of body parts and his character's actions.

But discussions with other colleagues led to me amending this conclusion with a suggestion that 2D animation can also present a simplicity of form that is far less demanding than a live-action film. Puppet animation, on the other hand, can offer the excess of information that live-action cinema provides, and it can provoke the spectator to engage with the imaginative cinematic realms it creates that include material, three-dimensional elements from the lived world. The Quays' films draw on a plethora of references combined in what is often described as alchemy into a 'world' that we can experience, respond to emotionally and interpret. In a film like *Street of Crocodiles*, its 'world' bears relation to our own through spatial cues, anthropomorphism and an array of aesthetic references to fine art, literature, architecture and music. The spectator must not only find the cues that relate to his or her own experience of the world and of the experienced worlds of live-action cinema. He or she must also actively engage in developing new hypotheses that relate all of this to developing comprehension of and engagement with the animated 'world'. Neoformalism and new areas of spectatorship studies are useful here to posit the spectator as actively involved in developing hypotheses and understanding cues within a film 'world'.

Animation spectatorship

What, then, is going on inside the mature viewer when s/he watches animation? Is the experience the same as for other forms – say, when watching fiction film or documentary? Is the system of the cinematic apparatus unchanging for all forms of cinema experience? I do not think so. The animation film is utterly unique in its representation of graphic and plastic universes and impossible spaces and in its 'ability' to transcend physical laws which govern our experience. It is therefore crucial to our understanding of animation spectatorship to develop and describe our understanding of this particular set of conditions, which in turn can assist an approach to individual films. Although the 'worlds' that animation depicts contain cultural referents, they can be represented in contexts that do not mirror our understanding or experience of the world we live in. Animation spectatorship therefore presents a set of intricate complexities that need to be formulated in order to scrutinise what is happening in the viewer when they watch an animation film.

In the final chapter of *Understanding Animation*, Paul Wells contemplates the animation audience and states the need for further research in this field of enquiry:

> The points raised as matters of definition and interpretation are essentially couched in the assumption of the audience as a specific kind of *subject*, which differs from the assumed subject of the live-action film because of the unique conditions created by animation. Equally, the discussion has largely been predicated on particular approaches to animation as a text, and as such does not engage with other types of address which may look, for example, at the cognitive effects of the animated film, and the specific role of the individual.[21]

Although he raises a crucial point about other types of address, Wells does not pursue this in detail, concentrating instead on an analysis of Disney films in terms of a broad audience. He does state that the specificity of the effect of animation needs further research, reminiscent of Cavell's 'special powers of film'. A number of queries arise. Just what is this 'specificity'? How can we define the spectator's experience of watching animation? How does he or she understand the various levels of abstraction and the unreal images on screen? What can we say about point-of-view in animated cinema, about identification, emotion, or empathy? In a theory of animation spectatorship I am currently refining, experiential factors that diverge from accepted norms of 'reality' play an important role in determining perceptual and psychological phenomena of watching animation – I suggest this is the 'specificity' Wells means. These, in turn, assist us in structuring an approach to understanding the viewing experience of the Quays' films that are unique in animated cinema.

I'd like to take a step back in time and posit some ideas about relationships between Early Cinema spectatorship and develop the unique conditions of animation Wells mentions. Tom Gunning describes the 'cinema of attractions' as a cinema based on the quality of its ability to *show* something:

> From comedians smirking at the camera, to the constant bowing and gesturing of the conjurors in magic films, this is a cinema that displays its visibility, willing to rupture a self-enclosed fictional world for a chance to solicit the attention of the spectator.[22]

Animation film, in its visual presentation of imaginary worlds, retains a quality that locates it in a permanent condition of being a kind of 'ahistorical' cinema of attractions. Methods and techniques used to create animation permanently rupture the 'world' it creates because the impossibility of what we see draws attention to the fact that it is an illusion:

> To summarise, the cinema of attractions directly solicits spectator attention, inciting visual curiosity, and supplying pleasure through an exciting spectacle – a unique event, whether fictional or documentary, that is of interest in itself. The attraction to be displayed may also be of a cinematic nature, such as the early close-ups just described, or trick films in which a cinematic manipulation (slow motion, reverse motion, substitution, multiple exposure) provides the film's novelty. ... The cinema of attractions displays little energy creating characters with psychological motivations or individual personality ... its energy moves outward towards an acknowledged spectator rather than inward towards the character-based situations essential to classical narrative.[23]

In many ways animation film has not lost its 'attractiveness', and the spectator's response to the use of new technologies has striking similarities to those of early cinema.[24]

Inquiry into animation spectatorship is itself a relatively new area. Of the few authors that do engage in spectatorship, predominantly sociological and psychoanalytic methods are used to explain the experience of watching animation. The form is rarely addressed using critical approaches around emotion or phenomenology. Reasons for this can be attributed to theories that regard cinematic experience as primary, without making considerations for different techniques or genres. These include semiotics, psychoanalysis, structuralism and socio-cultural approaches. Another reason might be because animation creates its own visual culture and obeys a different set of rules than non-animated cinema. This ranges from subversion of natural physical laws that govern representations of live-action film to the appropriation of cultural codes and imagery that partially informs the 'worlds' and figures it can allow us to experience. Exceptions are Joanna Bouldin, Vivian Sobchack's recent work, or Laura Marks' fascinating essay on the Quay Brother's *Institute Benjamenta*.[25] It is also telling that Sobchack and Marks include the Quays' work in their phenomenologically oriented writing.

The dominant approach to animation spectatorship has been from a socio-cultural standpoint. North American studies on audience dominate and prefer to investigate ideologies and the influence and effect of animation viewing on broadly defined groups of children, teenagers or simply as 'audience'. This has been fruitful in determining, for instance, the effect of violence in animation on school-age viewers, or the relationship between consumer habits and television animation series created for children (especially by the numerous private channels in the USA). The Quays' films are *auteur* animation films (as are those of many other animators) and attain a complexity in narrative structure, visual abstraction and aesthetic and stylistic wealth that need appropriate approaches that diverge from socio-historical ones and that posit the viewer in a different sort of way than do these types of studies.

In addressing Disney's hegemonic domination of audience, ideology within the context of animation spectatorship has received considerable attention. Wells comments upon the state of spectatorship studies:

> Critical reaction to the Disney canon has always been mixed, and largely constitutes *the* discourse about animation itself (see Peary and Peary, 1980: 49–58, 90–92; Smoodin, 1994), but scant address has been given to the *actual* agendas of the viewing public who attend Disney films. One might presume that this is part of the overall neglect of animation, but also add that such work might suggest certain disparities between particular responses and the eagerness to promote a specific highly idealised model of innocent, ideologically sound, relentlessly optimistic, family entertainment, somehow safe from the vagaries and difficulties of the world. It has probably always been the case that the particular experience of watching Disney films has been much more complex, testing a range of psychological and emotional issues in spectators.[26]

Disney's films are pointedly and naïvely ideological and promote (and sometimes strangely undermine) conservative values of American society. Carl Plantinga notes that '[s]pectator emotions have a powerful rhetorical force because they involve thinking, belief, and evaluation'.[27] The emotional response to films that convey a particular ideology are triggered by conflict and resolution:

> The Disney film is self-evidently operating on terms which the broad spectrum of audiences recognise *as* animation, i.e. cel-animation characterised by human/animal figures who play out plausible, if highly fanciful fictions. Other kinds of animation are, indeed, now reaching a wider audience, and further research will reveal how the reaction to what we have defined as orthodox animation differs from the response to developmental or experimental animation.[28]

Wells then interprets the results of his study by constructing a paradigm of dominant themes: empathy and identification; fear and concern; treats and occasions, and codes of contentment.[29] What we can divine from this set of themes is that the responses are to conventional narrative fictions that adhere to genre conventions and highlight the pleasure aspect of viewing animation.

The question then arises: what kind of emotions does a film like *Street of Crocodiles* elicit? The film is oriented towards a mature audience with complex anticipations of pleasure and aesthetic experience. It strongly triggers intellectual, emotional and sensual engagement with its visual surface and poetic structures, much more so than the kind of conflict and resolution that more conventional narratives present. Because of the film's puzzling narrative, here is indeed a hiatus in processes of belief and evaluation, and the spectator can give him- or herself over to the pleasure invoked by the loosely structured, haptic images choreographed to music and underlaid by unusual sound.

Unconventional films that do not align with themes related to the anthropomorphic qualities of the orthodox style and choice of narrative are fertile objects of study. A film like the Quays' *Rehearsals For Extinct Anatomies* (1987), with its elliptical, almost anti-narrative structure, alienated animated automata and sombre, highly aestheticised mood, offers little in the way of, say, contentment, and any pleasure it affords has more to do with the aesthetic and haptic surface of the film than with identification or narrative resolution. There is however, a pleasurable sense of alienation that the film's macro lens-filmed vignettes of strangely sealed-off and repetitive movements and events affect. We may be drawn much more into the experience and strangeness of the film's 'world' than into the paradigm Wells sets out. Disney's films (or Nick Park's, for that matter) do not want to draw attention to the 'otherness' of the world they create, though there are a number of notable exceptions to this such as Hayao Miyazaki, George Dunning or Mamoru Oshii. Conventional narrative animation wants to engage the audience in familiar rituals and conventions of human behaviour that live-action film also deploys. Disney's films are attractive to audiences because what they see acted out is familiar from their own everyday 'worlds', but the characters acting out these events are mainly anthropomorphised, idealised animals and objects. This brings us to an interesting concept of omnipotence.

Wells quotes an article from Michael O'Pray that reviews concepts of the experience of omnipotence while watching Disney films. O'Pray's commendable text interweaves Freud's definition of the omnipotence of thought, Eisenstein's cryptic unfinished concept of plasmaticness and English aesthete Adrian Stokes' synthesis of Melanie Klein's psychoanalytic theories and the synchronised ballet-like movement of Disney's *Silly Symphonies*. Although these concepts diverge from that of the consciously aware viewer, in order to illuminate the concerns of these authors, the full version of O'Pray's quote is worth repeating:

> The central concern here seems to be the idea of a certain pleasure achieved by animation (not all of course) wherein we identify with its virtuosity. Stokes and Eisenstein speaks respectively of a 'patness' and an 'absolute perfection' (one, we should remember, that frightened Eisenstein). They stress the force of this virtuosity. It is not simply a characteristic of the animation but somehow is an integral part of how it affects us. In this virtuosity where form and content reach a perfection, there is the deepest pleasure because we are confronted with a control and importantly, the very fantasy of that control in the animated figures. In other words, in the plasmatic element – the sheer virtuosity of the lines, say, in Disney, or for that matter, in the animation films of Robert Breer or Len Lye – we have an objectification of our own desire for omnipotence. Our desire to will something without in fact acting upon it is acted out in animation itself through the virtuoso use of forms.[30]

Studies of object animation need different approaches than those of 2D 'orthodox' animation, because it presents physical space and materials that occupy this space instead of a mimetic, drawn rendering of the same. Objects and the materials from which they are constructed are tangible and have an intrinsic set of references to our lived experience which is not the case in the fully graphic fantasy of 2D animation. In *Street of Crocodiles* 'form and content' achieve virtuosity through the choreography of objects, and the use of materials that lend themselves to the musically driven trajectory of the objects and figures in the film.

The concept of omnipotence is what links the pleasure of 2D animation with that of puppet animation, particularly in terms of space and the uncanny, as I have described in more detail elsewhere.[31] As Grodal puts it: 'According to psychoanalytic theory, man is torn between id and superego, between principles of pleasure and principles of reality'.[32] In these terms, the pleasure in watching 2D animation that has a graphic representational relation to reality, and is not reality itself, thus relating it more to a pleasure principle than to a reality principle. Object animation enables both the pleasure principle (an element of the omnipotence O'Pray mentions) and the reality principle, because the images are photographic representations of physically extant objects and spaces.

Omnipotence is twofold – not simply an affect of the spectator, but also, because they are so artificial, an awareness that the animator created these images. An often-used simile suggests the animator is like God – completely responsible for all the images the spectator sees and more importantly, responsible for the impossible 'bringing to life' of inanimate forms. This confirms a desire for control, grandeur, a God-like ability to be able to ultimately control life. This may be an unconscious release from disavowal of the spectator's own helplessness. But identification is both with the objects and figures and with the animator who has made the film.

Understanding the object

There is no 'object' in drawn animation – the image is an artistic rendering, an interpretation of something that exists in the lived world or in the artist's imagination. But in puppet animation, the representation does have a direct relation to objects. Yet these objects are artificially constructed, thus the representation of a puppet, although identical with the object represented, has a different quality than objects that are not manipulated or constructed. A human being is essentially the same – an actor's appearance can be altered by make-up, costume, lighting and framing. The puppets in the Quays' *The Cabinet of Jan Svankmajer* (1984) have anthropomorphic appearances, yet the head of the child puppet is a *bricolage* of a porcelain doll's head out of which sheaves of a book protrude like hair. Although it may appear 'alive', it is not, and although its gestures and actions may represent those of a human being, the puppet itself is inanimate and a construction of the artist's making. Grodal makes a succinct point about this:

> When watching a visual representation of phenomena without any centring anthropomorphic actants, we often 'lose interest' owing to lack of emotional motivation or the cognitive analysis of the perceived, a fact which many makers of experimental films have discovered when presenting their films to a mass audience.[33]

Thus, one issue that is of central importance to understanding the experience of viewing animation is clarification of the *status* of the animated object and how we relate to it. We see a moving image, but we know that the objects we see appear 'alive' through pure artifice. Jean Mitry concedes that '[o]ne might say that any object presented in moving images gains a meaning (a collection of significations) it does not have 'in reality', that is, as a real presence.[34] We also know that in contrast to live-action figures they do not 'exist' except as inanimate objects beyond their animation on screen.

Fig. 4: Street of Crocodiles, *Quay Brothers, 1986. [Image courtesy of the Quay Brothers.]*

Is the spectator constantly aware of this fact, or is there a process of denial, wish fulfilment or sublimation that allows us to perceive animated objects as living? Do we invest them with a living state outside our experience of them in the cinema? For instance in *Street of Crocodiles* the main protagonist moves through and explores a labyrinthine architectural space. (Fig. 4) The film's experimental narrative is partially based on point-of-view structures of the puppet and relies to some degree on the Kuleshov effect, which I would suggest is heavily relied upon in puppet animation.[35]

The anthropomorphic figures in *Street of Crocodiles* (or almost any other puppet animation film) are invested by the animator with human-like qualities. Grodal investigates how we understand what he calls 'human-ness', a term that sometimes appears in quotation marks and sometimes not, a concept perhaps as riddled with meaning as that of 'worlds'. He does remark that divining the essence of humanness is deeply philosophical. Grodal suggests that '[m]assive viewer-interest indicates that the phenome-non of 'humanness' has very strong cognitive and affective appeal'.[36] This phenomenon is a distinguishing feature of puppet animation and explains the immense popularity of animation film with audiences. Grodal also provides some pertinent insights into the mental workings of animation audiences:

Important for the mode of perception is an evaluation of whether the seen or heard has its source in, or represents, an exterior hypothetical or real world or and interior mental world (or belongs to intermediary positions), or whether the source is ambiguous. If the perceived is constructed as belonging to an exterior world it cues the mental stimulation of an enactive world; *whereas, if the perceived is constructed as belonging to a mental world, it cues a purely perceptual-cognitive, proximal experience* [italics mine]. Equally important is the relation to agents of fiction. The viewer may perceive the agents with the same emotional distance that typifies his relation to inanimate objects, but he may also make a cognitive and empathic identification with them.[37]

Grodal's distinctions between types of worlds are suggestive of the different origins of the profilmic materials for 2D (e.g. hypothetical) and puppet (e.g. real) animation posited earlier. While viewing animation, the spectator executes shifts between hypothetical, real and interior mental worlds.

In his discussion on representation, Andrew reflects on different theories of image processing, how the spectator reads the images on screen and in what kinds of relationships he or she enters into with them during viewing:

If every film is a presence of an absence, we are still obliged to differentiate the types of imaginary experience possible within various ratios of this relationship. A filmed image may be considered the presence of a referent which is absent in space (live TV coverage) or in time (home movies). It may also be taken to be an image which is non-existent or whose existence is not in question one way or the other.[38]

In Andrew's definition a 2D graphic animated image is a filmed image that would fall into the category of 'non-existent' or 'not in question'. This ties in to Cavell's 'region' and is one of the 'special powers of film'. Andrew does not differentiate between a sequence and an image. This differentiation is crucial to animation film and recalls Sesonske's comments about not having access to these worlds, since the illusion of animation is non-existent without movement of the film through the projector. The drawing or painting does exist (as profilmic cel or drawing), but the movement of the images on screen is illusory, in other words, non-existent. Marketing strategies that create commercial products such as stuffed toys and figurines can introduce substantially real versions of 2D characters to our lived experience, but they are inanimate.

The puppet's 'world'

Watching any of the Quays' animation films means entering a dream world of visual and aural poetry. Whether the early collage-based artist's documentaries, the public-funded puppet animation masterpieces, the elusive *Stille Nacht* shorts or the Art Brut-inspired *In Absentia* (2001) the ambiguous, anachronistic 'world' of their puppets has attracted a fiercely loyal follow-

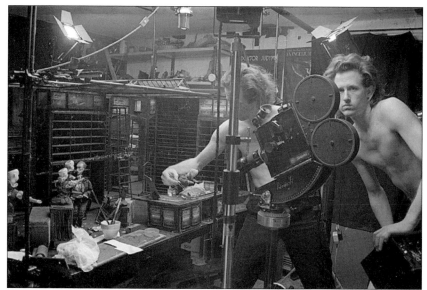

Fig. 5: Stephen and Timothy Quay in the studio filming Street of Crocodiles.
[Image courtesy of the Quay Brothers.]

ing.[39] What can we say about the referent when it is a puppet? What is its 'world'? And how does the spectator understand this world when it is not one in which he or she can make direct experience? What is its 'history'? How is the character defined? Andrew gives us some starting points:

> Every fictional film likewise relies on some substratum of spectator understanding of the type of world that becomes the subject of the film. We bring our own sense of boxing to *Rocky* and of the strictures of bourgeois life to any Douglas Sirk film. But the fictional film, at least in most of its genres, quickly transfers our interest to the world of the image, calling on, but not playing to, our knowledge of the referent.[40]

Again, Andrew is not concerned with what the images are representing, and he makes no detailed description of whether a scene must contain an actor, a particular set of spatial orientations or action of some sort. Significant is what he says about how the film relies on the spectator's understanding of a *type* of world.

Puppet animation does represent an image of spatial and object relations that are possible to experience in two contexts. The object can be both haptically experienced in cinema and physically accessed in the 'real' world. Although the movements of the puppet are limited to the screening experience, the spaces and sets that the puppets are filmed in, and are not animated, do retain a direct relation to our own lived experience. We can understand that this space exists outside the cinematic experience, albeit in miniature. (Fig. 5) A cinematic image of living beings that are represented and understood by the spectator as participants in the tangible world we experience in our daily lives is perceived by using sets of codes and previous experience. A still or single-frame image can still be contextualised as a moment isolated from a continuum of living and moving through the world, whether cinematic or 'real'. There is a direct relation between the still image and its living and moving counterpart. This is not the case for the puppet.

I asked the Quays whether they found that the alienating effect afforded by using familiar inanimate objects and materials helped audiences understand the 'world' of the puppets:

> It's a greater leap, potentially. If you create the density of the world that you're out to create, the audience will make that leap and be won by the fiction. It's like the difference between if it senses that the puppet is just a little ragamuffin and thinks 'Aha, you use little bits of mop for the hair', then you've lost. It's as if, right away, the fiction – the orders of power – abduct so powerfully, into beyond. And even then, if I go in close up, I think you wouldn't know if you looked at one of our puppets – you really believe that it's come from some other realm, that it hasn't been made.[41]

The heavy saturation of visual and aural reference to fine arts, literature, poetry, dance, architecture, graphics and sculpture throughout their films also means that an objective evaluation, say, of spatial composition is difficult to describe in simple terms. The referents in the world of their puppet animation – the 'world' of the inanimate object made animate – are also found in the world of the fairy tale. Fairy tales are integrated into Robert Walser's writings, a literary source for a number of the Quays' films, and Bruno Schulz's story 'The Street of Crocodiles' has a fairy tale-like grotesqueness. Walter Benjamin has considered the relationship between fairy tales and the matter children use to create their own 'worlds' that evokes the 'worlds' of the Quays' films:

> Children are fond of haunting any site where things are being visibly worked on. They are irresistibly drawn by the detritus generated by building, gardening, housework, carpentry, tailoring or whatever, In these waste products they recognize the face that the world of things turns directly and solely to them. In using these things they do not so much imitate the works of adults as bring together materials of widely differing kinds in a new volatile relationship. Children thus produce their own small world of things within the larger one. The fairy-tale is such a waste product – perhaps the most powerful to be found in the spiritual life of humanity: a waste product that emerges from the growth and decay of the saga. With the stuff of fairy-tales the child may be as sovereign and uninhibited as with rags and building blocks. Out of fairy-tale motifs the child constructs its world, or at least it forms a bond with these elements.[42]

The way the Quays visualise fairy tale elements in their films is in a sense

Fig. 6: Puppet from Street of Crocodiles, *Quay Brothers, 1986.*
[Image courtesy of the Quay Brothers.]

a collecting of the 'detritus' of which Benjamin speaks and rearranging it in a way that they produce their own 'world' out of the materials they find. (Fig. 6) Bringing 'materials of widely differing kinds' is a feature of their set and puppet constructions, and we will see that the 'volatile relationship' they create with these new constructions is part of the appeal their films have for spectators.

We could try to allocate *Street of Crocodiles* to a particular genre: but the anachronistic, eclectic iconography of its 'world' and its labyrinthine narrative structure, hermetic locations and lack of a genre-supporting ideology hinders an easy or exclusive classification. If anything it belongs to a hybrid category of poetic-experimental film and is postmodernist in that it exhibits reflexivity, fragmented narrative structures and thematises the dehumanised subject, especially in its use of automata. As auteurs in a cinematic form that itself is ultimately perhaps the most auteurist of all, the Quays continue to create films that express their own particular vision of 'a world'. Over the years, this 'world', its construction, design, has continued to develop but remains as unmistakable as Stephen or Timothy Quay's own ornate, embellished and stylised calligraphy. It is the world of their imaginations that, by giving a chiaroscuro cinematic life to a unique assemblage of fragments of cloth and metal, drawing on literary tropes, a word, a gesture, is transformed on the cinema screen into one we can understand but are often at a loss to describe – this is the 'world' of the Quays' films.

Postscript: 'A well-made language'

I have suggested elsewhere that one of the 'problems' the study of animation is faced with and needs to resolve is one of language – to move beyond the inarticulate 'mmm ... .' that is often the response to what we see on screen.[43] First and foremost, we need to determine what the questions are that need to be asked – in this instance, I have tried to formulate some oblique queries around animation spectatorship. 'Since filmology is a science, it must be and must want to be one. And if a science is not, in the famous words of Condillac, simply a "well-made language", then it clearly requires one as its precondition'.[44] Etienne Souriau wrote this in 1951. More than half a century later, animation critics and scholars are beginning to develop and define a 'well-made language' that can be specifically used in critical and theoretical writings on animation film. Before, the recourse was often to adumbrate filmological definitions for live-action film with subjective neologisms and skirted the real challenge – to develop a set of queries and approaches that are clearly set out in a language that is specific to the animated form. Choosing animation film as an academic and critical endeavour means developing approaches that pose essential queries specific to the form that can, in some cases, rework theory that has been successfully developed for live action cinema. But it also means responding to Souriau's call to develop a language for animation studies that clarifies ongoing and increasingly detailed discourse around the form.

If we are going to continue developing the 'well-made language', there are a number of questions we need to ask persistently when thinking about, for instance, animation spectatorship. Besides the stylistic elegance, what do these images affect in our perception that is different from when we watch films that show the actions and dialogues of living, sentient beings? How can a piece of metal be endowed with a gesture that moves us emotionally? In what kind of world can a screw 'be'? Or for that matter, what entails the experiential difference between a screw animated on screen and one that we twirl in our fingers? If we get the questions right, the definitions, terminology and 'answers' to these questions should follow.

Notes

1. This essay is a revised version of "Animation Spectatorship: The Quay Brothers' Animated 'Worlds'" that appeared in the online journal *Entertext*, Vol. 4, No. 1, Winter 2004/05. http://people.brunel.ac.uk/~acsrrrm/entertext/4_1/buchan.pdf

2. Dermot Moran, *Introduction to Phenomenology* (London: Routledge, 2000): 5.

The Animated Spectator: Watching the Quay Brothers' 'Worlds'

3. Dudley Andrew, 'The Neglected Tradition of Phenomenology in Film Theory', in: *Wide Angle* 2, No. 2, 1978, pp. 44–49): 47.

4. Alexander Sesonske, cited in: Stanley Cavell, *The World Viewed: Reflections on the Ontology of Film*. Enlarged edition (Cambridge, Massachusetts: Harvard University Press, 1979): 167–168.

5. Ibid.: 167–168.

6. Maurice Merleau-Ponty, *The Phenomenology of Perception (Phénomènologie de la perception*. Paris: Gallimard, ©1945). Translation ©1958, Routledge & Kegan Paul (London and New York: Routledge Classics, 2002): 291.

7. Vivian Sobchack, *The Address of the Eye. A Phenomenology of Film Experience* (Princeton: Princeton University Press, 1992): 249.

8. Robert Stam, Robert Burgoyne and Sandy Flitterman-Lewis, *New Vocabularies in Film Semiotics. Structuralism, Post-structuralism and Beyond* (London: Routledge, 1992): 146–147.

9. For an expansive description of Neoformalism, see Kristin Thompson, *Breaking the Glass Armor: Neoformalist Film Analysis* (Princeton, New Jersey: Princeton University Press, 1988).

10. Judith Mayne, *Cinema and Spectatorship (Sightlines)* (London: Routledge, 1993): 3–4.

11. Ibid.: 4.

12. A much-debated term coined by Bordwell that refers to Saussure's semiotics, Lacanian psychoanalysis, Althusseriam Marxism, and Barthes' textual theory.

13. Malcolm Turvey, 'Seeing Theory: On Perception and Emotional Response in Current Film Theory', in: Allan Richard and Murray Smith (eds), *Film Theory and Philosophy* (Oxford: Oxford University Press, 1997): 431.

14. Edward Branigan, *Point of View in the Cinema. A Theory of Narration and Subjectivity in Classical Film*. Approaches to Semiotics 66. (Berlin: Mouton Publishers, 1984): 80.

15. Ibid.: 106–107.

16. Torben Grodal, *Moving Pictures. A New Theory of Film Genres, Feelings, and Cognition* (Oxford: Clarendon Press, 1997 (pbk 1999): 3.

17. Ibid.: 11.

18. Noël Burch, *Theory of Film Practice* (1969), (New Jersey: Princeton University Press, 1981); Kristin Thompson, 1988.

19. Grodal: 188.

20. Ibid.: 202.

21. Paul Wells, *Understanding Animation* (London: Routledge, 1998): 223.

22. Tom Gunning, 'The Cinema of Attractions: Early Film, Its Spectator and the Avant-Garde', in: Thomas Elsaesser and Tom Barker (eds), *Early Cinema. Space– Frame – Narrative* (London: BFI Publishing 1990): 57.

23. Ibid.: 58–59.

24. See Elsaesser 1990 and Andrew Darley, *Visual Digital Culture. Surface Play and Spectacle in New Media Genres* (London: Routledge, 2000).

25. Joanna Bouldin, 'Bodacious Bodies and the Voluptuous Gaze: A Phenomenology of Animation Spectatorship', in: *Animation Journal*, Vol. 8, No. 2, Spring 2000: 56–67; Vivian Sobchack, 'Nostalgia for a Digital Object. Regrets on the Quickening of QuickTime' in: *Millennium Film Journal* No. 34, Fall 1999; Laura Marks, 'The Quays' Institute Benjamenta: An Olfactory View'. In: *Afterimage*, September/October 1997: 11–13.

26. Wells: 224.

27. Carl Plantinga, 'Notes on Spectator Emotion and Ideological Film Criticism', in: Allan and Smith: 389.

28. Wells: 225.

29. Ibid.: 233.2

51

ANIMATED 'WORLDS'

30. Michael O'Pray, 'Eisenstein and Stokes on Disney', in: Jayne Pilling (ed.), *A Reader in Animation Studies* (London: John Libbey, 1997): 200.

31. Suzanne Buchan, 'Uncanny Space, Narrative Place: The Architectural Imagination of Animation', in: *What is Architecture?/ Text Anthology (Co To Jest Architektura? / Antologia tekstow)*, Adam Budak (ed.), (Krakow: Bunkier Sztuki Contemporary Art Gallery, RAM, Goethe Institut, 2002): 373 ff.

32. Grodal: 5.

33. Ibid.: 89.

34. Jean Mitry, *The Aesthetics and Psychology of the Cinema* (Transl: Christopher King) (Bloomington and Indianapolis: Indiana University Press, 1997): 45.

35. Grodal points out that this is a means to manipulate by montage and argues there are finer nuances in facial expressions that inform our understanding of a subject actant: 89 ff.

36. Grodal: 106.

37. Ibid.: 158.

38. Andrew: 44.

39. An ongoing series of short animation films, *Stille Nacht I, II, IV* and *V* were commissioned by music groups as pop promos. *Stille Nacht III*. *'Tales From the Vienna Woods [Ich bin im Tod erblüht)* was made used to pitch the first feature film project to potential funders. See http://www.zeitgeistfilms.com/directors/tbrothers/filmography.htm for a complete filmography

40. Andrew: 44.

41. Interview with the Quay Brothers, 1992.

42. Walter Benjamin, 'Old Forgotten Children's Books', in: *Selected Writings* [translation of '*Alte vergessene Kinderbücher*' GS III] (Harvard: Harvard University Press, 1999): 16–17.

43. Closing lecture, Animated 'Worlds' Conference, Farnham, England, 2003.

44. Etienne Souriau, 'Die Struktur des filmischen Universums und das Vokabular der Filmologie' [transl. Frank Kessler], in: *Montage/av*, 6/2, 1997, [Original title 'La structure de l'univers filmique et le vocabulaire de la filmologie', in: *Reveue internationale de Filmologie* 2, 7–8, 1951]: 141. Translation by the author.

Suzanne Buchan is Reader in Animation Studies and Director of the Animation Research Centre at the University College for the Creative Arts, Farnham College, England. She taught film studies at the University of Zurich 1995–2000 and was a founding member and 1995–2003 Co-Director of the Fantoche Animation Festival in Switzerland. She curates programmes for and advises festivals and has taught at universities and art colleges around the world. Her research explores interdisciplinary approaches to animation film, theory and aesthetics, She is founding Editor of *animation: an interdisciplinary journal* (Sage Journals). Activities and publications include *Trickraum: Spacetricks* (Christoph Merian Verlag, 2005) that accompanied the eponymous museum exhibition co-curated with Andres Janser at the Zurich Museum of Design and *Metaphysical Playrooms: The Films of the Brothers Quay* (University of Minnesota Press, forthcoming 2006). She is currently writing on a book on animation spectatorship and developing an animated short film project inspired by James Joyce's texts.

Chapter 3

The Strings of the Marionette

Richard Weihe

P uppet and object animation are categories of 3D animation that define themselves in the manipulation of objects in spatial settings, relying on representational imagery rather than self-generated digital images. The following remarks are limited to the aesthetics of puppet animation, drawing on the example of *Street of Crocodiles* by the Brothers Quay. In a comparison between literary examples of the automaton and the marionette and their staging in the Quay's film, the question arises as to who is 'pulling the strings' to enable the spectator's *anthropomorphic leap*, that shift from the perception of movement in the inanimate figure to motion in human life.

I

In 'The Sandman' (1817), a story by the German Romantic E.T.A. Hoffmann,[1] the student protagonist Nathaniel falls for a female automaton called Olympia. The puppet is a beauty and a brilliant dancer. Nathaniel is enamoured with an image he has invested with his own feelings. As spectators of an animated puppet film we resemble Nathaniel, unbothered by the fact that the puppet does not speak, not thinking of questioning her

Abstract: The article focuses on the *Street of Crocodiles* (1986) by the Brothers Quay as a prime example of puppet animation film set within live action. The viewer is presented with a marionette that is liberated seeing its strings cut loose – thereby embodying the principle of animation – alongside various forms of automata, most poignantly demonstrated by a ballet of screws that screw and unscrew themselves without the help of a screwdriver. By relating their film to literary examples of the automaton (E.T.A. Hoffmann) and the marionette (Heinrich von Kleist), the paper considers the question of how these diverse art forms present automotion as a principle of 'life'. What is the aesthetic status of marionette 'strings'? How is it that the puppet's decapitation in the Quays' film is perceived as an act of cruelty, evoking our compassion though we are viewing a realm of dead matter? How is the puppet's motion transformed into spectator emotion?

ontological status or examining whether she might be a lifeless puppet. What matters is her effect on us. We are fascinated by her movements. But for Nathaniel Olympia means even more. She is his perception of an ideal woman and he desires a relationship. In this case there is little difference between 'animation' and 'imagination'. Olympia exists on the same plane as Nathaniel's imaginary female idol.

2.

Nathaniel regarded as the quintessential spectator of any animation film, Olympia is thus the dancing automaton, the object of his desire and prototype of the animated figure – if only in literature. Olympia's body consists of inanimate material that produces motion, unable however to generate emotion of its own. Yet Nathaniel sees her as his love match. Even after all his declarations of love the puppet shows no signs of warming to him or becoming human in any way. As his beloved does not change, Nathaniel adopts her behavioural patterns. Thus he becomes increasingly mechanical, until he finally begins to rotate like a propeller. He leaps from a tower and not being a propeller, he crashes fatally.

3

Now let me turn from the automaton to the marionette. In his narrated dialogue 'On the marionette theatre' (1810) Heinrich von Kleist has his first-person-narrator and a dancer discuss the question, whether the lifeless marionette or the living human is the better dancer.[2] Surprisingly, the dancer argues in favour of the marionette, claiming that it has two significant advantages: firstly, it is suspended, therefore not weighed down by gravitation; secondly, it always remains perfectly in balance. The result is that the marionette appears more gracious than any human dancer impeded by the force of gravity, having to concentrate on maintaining his balance.

4

At this point one is tempted to ask, whether it is fair to compare the marionette to the dancer. Would it not be more appropriate to compare the dancer to the puppeteer? For the marionette is not an independent agent but the instrument of the puppet master, called the 'machinist' by Kleist to emphasise the technicality of his job.[3] Now if we were to compare the dancer to the puppeteer, a different aesthetic question would arise: Can the dancer express himself more gracefully with his own body or through employing a substitute non-human body under his control? Kleist's dancer has a clear-cut opinion; the dancing marionette's sole purpose is to convey beauty and grace, through a process that is fully controllable as a result of its purely technical nature.

5

Weightlessness is not a quality of the marionette. It is merely the impression it gives as it hangs on strings. Due to the force of gravity the marionette always hangs in plumb, looking beautifully poised. Kleist's contention is the following: It is the machinist's job to engage emphatically with the moving marionette. The marionette will then in turn seem 'animated' for the spectator. Thus the 'soul' (anima) is no psychological entity, but merely a 'moving force' which Kleist's dancer calls a 'vis motrix'.[4] The attention is thereby drawn from the marionette to the operator, for it is he who keeps a tight reign on everything and animates the anima.

6

Kleist's concept of the marionette theatre can provide us with a blueprint for the description of puppet animation. How do these two expressive forms compare? First, it seems obvious that in Kleist's set-up we can replace the 'machinist' by the 'animator' of an animation film, while the marionette is equivalent to the animated figure. But what about the *strings* of the marionette? For the puppeteer they are the technical device by which he controls the marionette's movements; in puppet animation these 'strings' are invisible, indeed, non-existent. Their function is replaced by the technique of frame-by-frame animation. Consequently we could go on from here and question whether the sculpted figure could be replaced by film trick or even the animator himself. Kleist's essay already entertains this concept. He alludes to a crank that could replace the operator and thus do away with 'the remains of the spirit'.[5] Thereby any direct human input may be excluded from the artistic performance, rendering it mathematically calculable. Calculations of this sort are essential in single-frame animation.

7

Kleist's marionette theatre contains a fundamental paradox that applies in the same way to puppet animation: The notion of liveliness is expressed by the absence of life itself. As in the illusionistic theatre of the 18th century that was eager to conceal stage technology, in puppet animation the agent of movement and the operative force remain invisible. In the marionette theatre it is the marionette that is moved by the pulling on the strings; in animation the puppet's position is altered for every new shot, manipulated step by step by the animator, in preparation for every new image. Frame-by-frame animation means that *differences* are recorded in single images.

8

The artistry of the animator lies in creating these differences and fixing them in images. Thus a puppet animation film is not filmed in real time, but photographed in individual, sequential frames. I would go even further and say that animation articulates itself essentially in the tension between the photographic image and film. The single frames represent specific arrangements in space. These are then shown as shot sequences, moving at twenty-four frames a second in order to appear as if they had been filmed or as if the puppet had moved on its own accord in front of the lense. When viewing the film, the different positions of the puppet merge and reproduce a fluid movement. This is when we describe animation as breathing life or movement into dead matter, creating the illusion of a 'soul' by means of a technique somewhere between photography and film that exploits a specific mode of perception. Unlike live action film, no living objects are filmed that move independent of any manipulator or animator.

9

Animation film, I would argue, is less concerned with what is shown than how it is shown. More important than plot is imitation of human movement and behaviour. Animation employs the spectator's imagination. The craftsmanship of the animator does not produce any complete illusion of life, while it is up to the spectator to complement the visual impressions and conceive of the animated figure as a living being displaying human traits. The art of enabling the spectator to envision the dead as alive is a characteristic feature of animation. In this respect animation film seems paradigmatic of film as such the premise of which is the spectator's willing acceptance of the moving image as a representation of 'life'.

10

I mentioned the word 'manipulation'. The term seems central to the concept of animation film. In 18th-century literature the automaton becomes a prominent motif[6] at a time when philosophy debates whether the individual is autonomous or heteronomous, e.g. governed by external forces. Jan Švankmajer, the Czech puppet animator, has referred to 'manipulation' as his 'obsessive theme', adding: 'Manipulation is not just a principle of totalitarian regimes'.[7] In the light of this remark, it is perhaps no coincidence that in the last century puppet animation was primarily

Fig. 1: Street of Crocodiles, *film still: Screw ballet. [Image courtesy of the Quay Brothers.]*

connected with Eastern Europe. Without being outwardly political, it could develop a subversive political dimension quite unexpectedly.

II

I should like to illustrate the points I have made by an example, not from Eastern Europe, but from a London studio: the 21-minute colour animation film *Street of Crocodiles* by the Brothers Quay of 1986. It is worth noting that two years earlier the Quays had completed an animation film on Svankmajer entitled *The Cabinet of Jan Švankmajer*. Since then the Quays have worked almost exclusively in puppet animation. I say almost, because during the last years they have embarked on feature film projects and dance films with live actors too.

12

If animation endows dead matter with the illusion of automotion as a principle of life, then surely this becomes nowhere more apparent than in the short choreography of screws in *Street of Crocodiles*. We behold a seemingly antique cabinet of curiosities in vitrines. All of a sudden rusty screws wind themselves out of dirty floor-boards, whirl across the surface like

43

Fig. 2: Street of Crocodiles, *film still: The liberation ...*
[Image courtesy of the Quay Brothers.]

Fig. 3: Street of Crocodiles, *film still: ... of the marionette.*
[Image courtesy of the Quay Brothers.]

skaters, before gracefully re-turning into the wood elsewhere. Technically we know that every slight turn of the screw is recorded as a single image. What we behold, however, is a beautiful ballet of screws whose 'vis motrix' (Kleist) is in the objects themselves.

13

In aesthetic liberation the screw has abandoned its actual purpose to join two independent objects. It is shown in its essential 'screwyness' and observed merely for the sake of its specific grammar of movement – a left-hand turn means appearing as a shape, a right-hand turn means disappearing into the wood. In this scene, maybe more than in any other, the key role of music becomes apparent. As the Quays have stated, the music by Leszek Jankowski existed prior to the images.[8] The flow of the music represents the aspired aesthetic effect of the fragmented images shown as a sequence. The music does not imbue the image with emotion, it imposes its inherent rhythm on it. Thus it is the rhythm that connects the individual notes and likewise enhances the connection of the individual images.

14

The main figure in *The Street of Crocodiles* is a male puppet that – at least partially – starts out as a marionette.[9] The marionette slumbers in a strange construct called 'The Wooden Esophagus' that is set in motion by human saliva. At the beginning we see a live actor spitting into a rotating mill consisting of razor blades. What follows is then the story of the marionette's awakening and emancipation from its strings. The movement in its hand, produced by loosening the tension of the thread, awakens the figure. At this point the hand is still connected to a thread. Then the live actor standing by the esophagus cuts through the thread with scissors and henceforth the marionette is off its leash. While exploring the museum, however, the puppet repeatedly encounters a system of threads operating an intricate mechanism. These threads, I would argue, allude to the strings of the marionette. It is as if the entire cabinet is being 'manipulated' by strings just like an over-sized marionette, with the difference that the strings are running through the intestines of the marionette's dreams.

15

The camera then adopts the point of view of the puppet. This is no longer the situation of the marionette theatre with the spectator facing the stage. The puppet is endowed with subjectivity and the spectator is immersed in the film's action. We look upon a puppet world with the eyes of the puppet

Fig. 4: Street of Crocodiles, *film still: The decapitation ...*
[Image courtesy of the Quay Brothers.]

Fig. 5: Street of Crocodiles, *film still: ... of the puppet.*
[Image courtesy of the Quay Brothers.]

itself. We identify with it to such an extent, that its destruction and reconstruction by a group of other puppets draws our compassion. Obviously, these are all 'dead' forms, unable to suffer pain. Aptly the critic Jonathan Romney remarked that the Quays 'do not so much animate dead matter, as dramatise the deadness of matter'.[10] The dramatisation of deadness is achieved by showing that 'death' (the puppet's head is screwed off!) is of no importance to the puppet, just as life is not, because it does not exist. The appearance of red meat serves to emphasise the materiality and the deadness of the puppet and its surroundings.

16

The puppet moves in the miniature world of a puppet set, but in the film this appears as a real location. In publicity by 'Zeitgeist Films', the filmmakers' distributor, we read that the Brothers' Quay stage sets are 'suggestive of long-repressed childhood dreams',[11] while writing about Švankmajer Wendy Jackson comments, 'one could almost make a dictionary of objects as symbols in Švankmajer's films, something akin to Freund's *Interpretation of Dreams*'.[12] But what about this dream world in Švankmajer and the Quays? With the subjectivity of the puppet in *Street of Crocodiles* we adopt the dream viewpoint. Thus the Brothers Quay seem to decree – taking up the title of Bruno Schulz's essay – 'The Republic of Dreams', a 'sovereign territory of poetry', and I quote Bruno Schulz in the manner of a Quayian manifesto: 'The dream contains an appetite for reality, a demand that commits reality'.[13]

17

The animation film is not an 'interpretation of dreams' from the perspective of Freudian reality, but rather an interpretation of reality from the perspective of the dream. The puppet seems to be asking: What can I utilise from reality in order to constitute my dream? That is my life! – the puppet claims. As Ludwig Wittgenstein noted: 'It is one of the most deep-rooted mistakes of philosophy: to view possibility as a shadow of reality'.[14] If we look at animation in such a way, then possibility is not a shadow of reality, but reality is a shadow of possibility.[15] Accordingly, the hypothetical animated world seems more tangible to the viewer than so-called reality.

Notes

1. Ernst Theodor Amadeus Hoffmann, Der Sandmann, in Fantasie- und Nachtstücke (Munich: Winkler Verlag, 1976): 331–363 (Translated by the author).

2. Heinrich von Kleist, 'Über das Marionettentheater', in Sämtliche Werke und Briefe, vol. 2, ed. Helmut Sembdner (Munich: Deutscher Taschenbuch Verlag, 1984): 338–345 (All translated by the author).

3. Kleist, 'Über das Marionettentheater': 340, '[…] der Maschinist, der diese Puppen regierte …'.

4. Kleist, 'Über das Marionettentheater': 341.

5. Kleist, 'Über das Marionettentheater': 340, 'Inzwischen glaube er, dass auch dieser letzte Bruch von Geist, von dem er gesprochen, aus den Marionetten entfernt werden, dass ihr Tanz gänzlich ins Reich mechanischer Kräfte hinübergespielt, und vermittelst einer Kurbel, so wie ich es mir gedacht, hervorgebracht werden könne'.

6. See Karlheinz Daniels (ed.), Mensch und Maschine: Literarische Dokumente (Frankfurt am Main: Verlag Moritz Diesterweg, 1981); Rudolf Drux (ed.), Menschen aus Menschenhand: Zur Geschichte der Androiden (Stuttgart: Metzler, 1988); Rudolf Drux, Marionette Mensch, Ein Metaphernkomplex und sein Kontext von E.T.A. Hoffmann bis Georg Büchner (München: Fink, 1986); Peter Gendolla, Die lebenden Maschinen: Zur Geschichte der Maschinenmenschen bei Jean Paul, E.T.A. Hoffmann und Villiers de l'Isle Adam (Marburg/Lahn: Guttandin und Hoppe, 1980); Liselotte Sauer, Marionetten, Maschinen, Automaten: Der künstliche Mensch in der deutschen und englischen Romantik (Bonn: Bouvier, 1983).

7. Peter Hames (ed.), Dark alchemy: The films of Jan Švankmajer (Trowbridge: Flicks Books, 1995): 114.

8. Suzanne H. Buchan, The Metaphysical Playroom: The Puppet Animation Films of Stephen and Timothy Quay, Unpublished PhD thesis, University of Zurich, 2003: 232–233.

9. For a detailed analysis of The Street of Crocodiles see Suzanne H. Buchan, The Metaphysical Playroom: The Puppet Animation Films of Stephen and Timothy Quay, Unpublished PhD thesis, University of Zurich, 2003.

10. Jonathan Romney, 'The Same Dark Drift', in Sight and Sound, vol. 1, no. 11, March 1992: 24–27 (25).

11. See Maureen Furniss, Art in motion: Animation aesthetics (London: John Libbey, 1998): 170.

12. Quoted in Furniss, 1998: 171.

13. Bruno Schulz, Gesammelte Werke in zwei Bänden, vol. 1 (Munich: Carl Hanser Verlag, 1992): 340, 'das souveräne Gebiet der Poesie'; 'Im Traum ist ein Hunger nach Wirklichkeit beschlossen, eine Forderung, welche die Wirklichkeit verpflichtet, unmerklich zur Glaubwürdigkeit und zu einem Postulat heranwächst, zu einem fälligen Wechsel, der nach Deckung verlangt' (Translated by the author).

14. Ludwig Wittgenstein, VII. Bemerkungen zur Philosophie: Wiener Ausgabe (Vienna: Springer, 1995): 24, remark 9, 'Es ist einer der tiefstwurzelnden Fehler der Philosophie: die Möglichkeit als ein Schatten der Wirklichkeit./einen Schatten der Wirklichkeit zu sehen./' (Translated by the author).

15. Siegfried Zielinski, Archäologie der Medien (Hamburg: Rowohlt, 2002): 41.

Resident in Zurich, **Richard E. Weihe**, M.Litt. Oxford University, PhD in Comparative Literature, University of Zurich, Habilitation in Theatre Studies at the Private University of Witten/Herdecke, Germany. Freelance writer, researcher and Lecturer (Privatdozent) in Drama and Theatre at the Universities of Zurich and Witten/Herdecke. Recent publications: Meer der Tusche. Erzählung mit zehn Bildern, Zurich: Nagel & Kimche/Hanser, 2003 (prose); Die Paradoxie der Maske. Geschichte einer Form, München: Fink Verlag, 2004; Weg des Vergessens (novel), Zurich: Dörlemann, 2006.

Chapter 4

Gesturing toward Olympia

Heather Crow

The outside is not a fixed limit but a moving matter animated by peristaltic movements, folds and foldings that altogether make up an inside: they are not something other than the outside, but precisely the inside *of* the outside.
Gilles Deleuze

Bodies in motion

‘Gestures are performed individually’, writes film scholar Lesley Stern, ‘but they are not possessed by individuals’.[1] Even though a turn of the head or the slow raising of a shoulder can be isolated and attributed to an individual subject, it cannot be owned by that subject, whose corporeal articulations are themselves subject to the systems of representation which render those articulations intelligible, to the bodies which make those movements possible, to what Stern calls ‘the conditions of performability’ which regulate the circulation and repetition of gestures on film, on stage, and in ‘social milieux’.[2] She likens gestures to ‘wandering homeless ghosts [that] take up residence in alien bodies, there to play out the repetition that is their destiny’.[3]

To say that gestures are ghosts is not to say that their haunting is an intrusion. For our gestures are some of our most intimate performances of

Abstract: ‘Gesturing toward Olympia’ examines the dynamics of bodily movement in two films by Stephen and Timothy Quay: *The Comb (From the Museums of Sleep)*, a short film which combines puppet animation and live-action, and *The Sandman* (co-directed by choreographer Will Tuckett), a dance film adapted from E.T.A. Hoffmann’s short story of the same name. These films bring to light (or rather, to life) the uncanniness of gesture and of the gesturing body by invoking two overdetermined figures, the hysteric and the automaton. Exploring the uncanny choreography of embodied subjectivity through gesturing puppets and mechanised female bodies, *The Comb* and *The Sandman* question the familiarity, stability, and animateness of the living body.

identity, and though we cannot own them, they are somehow our own nonetheless. They are foreign yet familiar; public yet private; they are *unheimlich*, in Sigmund Freud's sense of the word. Developed in Freud's 1919 essay 'Das "Unheimliche"' (The 'Uncanny'), the concept of the uncanny represents the anxious imbrication of the strange and the familiar; as Nicholas Royle explains, 'it disturbs any straightforward sense of what is inside and what is outside' and what is Self and what is Other.[4] In this sense, gesture itself is uncanny – a performative enactment of the slipperiness of boundaries and the ambivalence of moving bodies. Though not explicitly identified, the concept of the uncanny haunts Stern's exposition of the 'after-life of gesture', shadowing her discussion of the compulsive repetition of cinematic gesturality.[5]

Emerging in the 1970s and 1980s as a key concept in post-structuralist thought, the uncanny continues to have a profound influence on film studies, gender studies, and art history (among other disciplines), shaping notions of space, corporeality, and identity. It has been approached psychoanalytically, phenomenologically, cinematically, even architecturally, informing contemporary image-making practices and the theoretical paradigms that structure their interpretation. Despite the influence of the uncanny on contemporary theories of embodied subjectivity, however, its relationship to notions of gesturality remains underdeveloped. While Freud does not discuss gesturality explicitly in his text, *'das Unheimliche'* – which can be translated literally as 'the unhomely' – elucidates the yet undertheorised relationship between the wandering ghost of gesture and the alien body which is its unhomely home. The gestural uncanny designates the instability and ambivalence of the body in motion, turned inside out and outside in by (un)familiar corporeal articulations embraced as constitutive of embodied identity.

Possessed by the strange inside-outside force of the gestural uncanny, moving bodies are unstable, mutable, and processual, subject to the gestural specters that circulate among social and aesthetic milieux. They are moved – in other words, *animated* – by this dynamic choreography, the meanings of which are determined by the shifting identities, desires, and contexts that give gestures (and bodies) their shapes. To say that bodies are animated by gesture is not just to say that they are 'put in motion' (which, of course, they are). When interpreted conceptually, gesture's animation of the body points to the role of corporeal movement in the discursive construction of the live body; that is, live bodies are intelligible as such, in part, because they move.

My own understanding and application of animation as a concept derives from animation film scholarship. Most definitions of animation film position animation as a group of frame-by-frame filmic techniques that endow figures and objects with motion. Still drawings and inanimate matter are enlivened through the illusion of movement painstakingly created through techniques of animation. Sergei Eisenstein, great lover of Walt Disney's films, explains the principle of animation as 'if it moves, *then* it's alive; i.e. moved by an innate, independent, volitional impulse'.[6] The effect of autonomous volition, however, is produced while simultaneously called into question, for animated film as a set of techniques foregrounds the artificiality of its cinematic illusion. The reality of animation announces itself as fabricated – a virtual world of paint or plasticine, of moving bodies which are not really bodies at all. Producing live bodies by binding movement to an unstable 'animacy' (a term I use throughout this article to mean 'the state of being animate'), animation provides a particularly useful paradigm for exploring the complex relationships between bodies and the uncanny gestures that animate them. Gesture participates in the illusion of autonomous volition and self-identity of the individualised subject, whose animacy is epistemologically produced, in part, through corporeal movement.

The bodies constructed cinematically, graphically, and sculpturally through animation techniques unsettle conventional notions of a stable, bounded, coherent body. Animated film is characterised by shapeshifting bodies: bodies squashed and stretched, organs that jump out of the skin, human figures that transform into animals or objects. As Paul Wells writes, 'the body in animation is a form constantly in flux, always subject to redetermination and reconstruction'.[7] The animated body has political, social, and cultural implications, challenging corporeal normativity, rendering the boundaries between bodies and environments (as well as between bodies and other bodies) malleable and elastic. Animation creates bodies not once, but with every film frame, suggesting that every construction of embodiment is always a reconstruction, every animation is a reanimation, and that bodies are rendered intelligible through repetition and multiplicity.

Relying on the dynamism of animated embodiment, I will explore the gestural uncanny through two films by Stephen and Timothy Quay: *The Comb (From the Museums of Sleep)* (United Kingdom 1991), a short which combines puppet animation and live-action, and *The Sandman* (United Kingdom 2000), a dance film adapted from E.T.A. Hoffmann's short story of the same name. Although predominantly live-action, *The Sandman* opens with a brief animated sequence revealing the moving internal clockwork of the film's female automaton character. This sequence, depicting a tiny hammer falling amid metal gears, establishes animation as the film's central theme (if not its central technique), and positions the automaton's movement as an effect of the uncanny animation of the female body.

The Sandman and *The Comb* bring to light (or rather, to life) the uncanniness of gesture and of the gesturing body, itself. If gesture is a ghost, they claim, then the gesturing bodies in these films are machines, uncanny automata moved both internally and externally, and – like ghosts – trembling on the border between life and death. I do mean, literally, trembling, for the films of the Quay brothers are characterised by the twitchy, shuddering, and repetitive movements of figures who are, somehow, both alive and dead. The animated world of the Quays is, writes Laura Marks, 'full of ghosts, life in things that ought to be dead', and, I would add, gestures in bodies and objects that ought to be still.[8]

Positioning *The Comb* alongside *The Sandman*, I am responding to Paul Wells' compelling provocation: despite 'the prominence of the dynamics of movement itself as a narrative principle' of animated film, Wells writes, 'this obvious choreography, a direct extension of theatrical staging, has not been properly allied to theories of dance, an anomaly made even more strange given the proliferation of animated films which directly use dance'.[9] *The Sandman* (co-directed by choreographer Will Tuckett) illuminates the dynamics of movement manifested by *The Comb*'s puppets and live actor. My intention is not to collapse one artistic form into the other, but to reveal the uncanny convergences between dance and animated film, and to render analogous the dynamics of animacy presented in *The Sandman* and *The Comb*.

Sleeping beauty

The Comb is loosely based on several texts by Swiss author Robert Walser, including his 1908 novella *Jakob von Gunten*. In fact, the film was originally intended as a brief pilot for the Quays' *Jakob von Gunten* feature film project (1996's *Institute Benjamenta, or This Dream People Call Human Life*).[10] While *Institute Benjamenta* is almost entirely live-action, *The Comb* deals more explicitly with animation as a concept and a cinematic technique, exploring the inanimacy and animacy of bodies by alternating between a live actor and animated puppets. Less adapted from than inspired by Walser's texts, *The Comb* has only a tenuous narrative: a sleeping woman dreams of an animated puppet, then awakes and combs her hair, remembering a fragment of her dream. The simplicity of this narrative veils the complexity of its visual presentation; live-action sequences alternate with stop-motion, architectural spaces shift and give way to reveal stagey landscapes, cryptic figures enact a mysterious gestural choreography.

Played by actress Joy Constaninides, the sleeper twitches and tosses as she dreams of a crumbling figure, himself twitching and tossing in a vertiginous landscape of ladders. As Michael Atkinson summarises the film:

> Intercut with an anonymous woman's 'troubled sleep', a blistered doll jour-

neys through a skyless, uterine-red maze/forest by way of a ladder, which often leaves him in a narcoleptic daze and carries on itself, the doll's detached hands fluttering around it like gnats.[11]

A relationship between the sleeping woman and the 'blistered doll' of her dream is established by what the Quays call 'analogic gestures': the woman and the doll each have a disturbingly spastic, twitching finger.[12] The repetitiveness and automatism of this gesture call into question the agency of the sleeping woman's gesturing body. Does she move her hand because the figure in her dream does, or does the doll follow the gestures of the woman who dreams him into existence? For that matter, do we possess our dreams, or do they possess us?

Perhaps I was too quick to use the generic pronoun 'us', for the gender of the sleeper ('a sleeping beauty', as distributor Zeitgeist Films calls her), is significant here.[13] Lying on a spare, institutional-style bed, filmed in dingy, chiaroscuric black-and-white, she resembles the 19th century female hysterics photographed at Dr. Jean-Martin Charcot's Salpêtrière clinic in Paris. Charcot's favorite patient was fifteen and a half year old Augustine, whose troubled body was the subject of numerous nosological images.[14] These photographs and the medical discourse surrounding them were widely circulated in their time and after. Turn of the century cabarets staged hysteria-influenced song-and-dance routines, early film comedies spoofed the contemporary fascination with neurological disorder, and in 1928, surrealists Louis Aragon and André Breton proclaimed, 'we … like nothing so much as youthful hysterics'.[15] Lauded by these surrealists as 'the greatest poetic discovery of the end of the nineteenth century', hysteria is now infamous in feminist discourse concerned with the pathologisation of women's bodies.

One of the classic and most identifiable symptoms of hysteria is what Rae Beth Gordon calls 'hysterical gesture' – tics, grimaces, epileptoid convulsions, and mechanical, seemingly involuntary movements of the limbs or torso.[16] These gestures are characterised not only by their repetition (the same gesture was often repeated many times during an hysterical attack), but also by their reiterability: patients at the Salpêtrière would reenact their hysterical symptoms in front of audiences at Charcot's weekly public lectures. Performing hysterical gesture at Charcot's provocation (the doctor would induce hysterical attacks through hypnosis or pressure on certain areas of his patients' bodies), Charcot's hysterics were exhibited as animated machines 'turned on' by the doctor's animating touch. As Elisabeth Bronfen asserts:

> Charcot's innovation, one could say, was that he gave life, or rather body, to a psychosomatic disturbance, and this revivification fed off the aptitude, on the

part of the actresses, to perform their deformities, their contortions, paralyses, and hallucinations – their language of hysteria – as a public spectacle.[17]

The spectacle of hysterical gesture is that of the automatic body, moved not only by the internal mechanisms of unconscious desire and psychic trauma, but also by the external pressure of audience expectation (the fashionable Parisians who attended Charcot's lectures were there, of course, to see a show, just as Charcot was intent on giving them one). Furthermore, as both Gordon and Bronfen have noted, the performance of hysteria was shaped externally by other kinds of performance and visual iconography. Augustine's hysterical gestures imitate 'the iconography of visual representations of possession with modes of theatrical acting popular at the time'.[18] Bronfen continues: 'Augustine appears to alternate representing intimate scenes from her own biography [performed in gestural pantomime] and imitating foreign narratives and gestures imposed on her from outside, determined by others'.[19] Her 'hybrid self-representation' underscores the uncanniness of gestural embodiment, challenging the cohesiveness and the homogeneity of corporeal identity.[20]

Exhibited by Charcot, captured by his camera, the gesturing hysteric is a persistent and insistent icon of pathological feminine embodiment. She is an automaton of her passions, her nerves, her nightmares, her traumas. Fetishised by the surrealists, she is compulsive and convulsive in her beauty sleep. She is the uncanny incarnate.

The Comb is part of this iconographic genealogy of hysteria. It is ghosted by the multitude of hysterical figures that figure so prominently in surrealist art; French cabaret; early cinema; and now post-modern film, theatre, and critical theory. A contemporary performance of hysteria, *The Comb* relies on the overdetermined uncanniness of the gesturing female hysteric in order to stage the body as automaton. Embodiment itself becomes fraught with anxiety, becomes a kind of madness, in which the 'mine-ness' of one's own body is simultaneously an 'otherness' and corporeality is both possessed and dispossessed. Put differently, the body 'prove[s] capable of independent activity', to borrow a phrase from Freud, and like the feet which dance by themselves to which he is directly referring, the body is uncanny.[21] *The Comb* presents the mechanical, hysterical movement symptomatic of the gestural uncanny in order to question the familiarity, stability, even the animacy of the living body.

Body double

While Disney's Sleeping Beauty lay still and pretty in her slumber of suspended animation, her immobility inviting the prince's animating kiss, the so-called sleeping beauty of *The Comb* trembles and writhes in her 'troubled sleep'. She is doubled by the blistered doll of her dreams, whose twitching finger doubles her own. She is doubled, tripled even, for though Michael Atkinson mentions only one doll in his summary of *The Comb*, I see two – the wandering doll, ladder in hand, and another figure, sleeping and less battered than the first. Her pose echoes the pose of our sleeping beauty, but while the latter is troubled in her sleep, the former lies still. She looks like a corpse in her stillness, she has the uncanniness of a dead body, except for the twitching of a piece of dirty lace moved by her regular breaths. The twitching lace becomes an externalised materialisation of an internal movement we cannot see – the expansion of the lungs – drawing attention to the materiality of her body, and by extension, her body double, the dreaming woman. Our sleeping beauty is bound to her material doubles through analogic gestures that complicate the autonomy of bodies in motion.

The dreamer is uncanny in her multiplied and divided subjectivity. She and her other selves demonstrate the 'doubling, dividing, and interchanging of the self' that Freud associates with the uncanny Double, a figure which harkens back 'to a time when the ego had not yet marked itself off sharply from the external world and from other people'.[22] What is familiar to the infant – that is, the fluidity of the boundary between self and other, or self and mother – returns as frightening to the adult, who has staked his individuation and thus his selfhood on clearly demarcated boundaries. The dreaming woman returns, in a sense, to early childhood – she plays with dolls – and her play calls into question the stability and boundedness of her subjectivity as it recalls the multiplicity of her identity. The uncanny designates the strange force of repetition in the construction and decon-struction of subjectivity.

What hysterical gesture performs quite literally is this strange force of repetition. The convulsions, tics, and grimaces of the gesturing hysteric are uncanny in their excessive and successive reiteration and their repetition in contexts that do not seem to support them. Sometimes, the pathologised body of the hysteric seemed to enact, in solo pantomime, a traumatic experience: some of Augustine's gestural behavior was interpreted by Charcot as a reenactment of the rape she suffered as a child. The hysteric cannot, or *does not want to*, stop gesturing – she repeatedly strikes at invisible attackers, she mechanically contracts and releases her arm or her foot or her face. The hysterical subject's compulsion to repeat is performed as a compulsion to gesture, which, in turn, performs the body as puppet, moved by the outside/inside force of traumatic experience, and the body as ma-chine, twitching with mechanical repetition. This body performs a kind of subjectivity that constructs and deconstructs the embodied subject, demonstrating the repetition compulsion as '*an urge inherent in organic life to restore an earlier state of things*', especially 'the inanimate state'.[23]

The other story of The Sandman

The mechanical, automatic body – prized by surrealists who desired to transform themselves into writing machines moved by unconscious forces – is a profoundly gendered body. This body suggests the pathologised corporeality and gesturality of the hysteric, almost always female. It suggests the automaton, itself a gendered figure, especially since Freud's analysis in 'The "Uncanny"' of E.T.A. Hoffmann's 'The Sandman'. Olympia, the automaton of Hoffmann's story, haunts Freud's text; she is present despite Freud's attempts to absent her. Ultimately, she is the most uncanny thing of all.

Freud's 'The "Uncanny"' begins as a response to Ernst Jentsch, another critic of the uncanny who explains the uncanniness of Hoffmann's 'The Sandman' as the effect of the reader's intellectual uncertainty as to whether Olympia is living or inanimate. Freud rejects this explanation in favor of his theory of repetition: Olympia is uncanny, he writes, because she reminds us of the infantile desire to see our dolls come to life, and this desire is threatening when it comes back to life after a long repression. In fact, he claims that Olympia is not the only uncanny figure in 'The Sandman', nor is she the most striking or the most important. Freud takes great pains to return to 'The Sandman' its rightful centre – the figure of its namesake – and to assert the irrelevance of Jentsch's uncertainty.

In Hélène Cixous' deconstruction of 'The "Uncanny"', 'Fiction and its Phantoms', Olympia is privileged as the uncanny itself, as that which is repressed in Freud's text, yet returns to haunt the reader and writer, as the female body displaced by patriarchal logic. In response to her own provocation – 'And what if the doll became a woman? What if she *were* alive? What if, in looking at her, we animated her?' – Cixous brings Olympia out of the dark margins of Freud's text.[24] However, like all animation, Cixous' deconstruction produces an equivocal animacy: 'Olympia is not inanimate', but she is 'neither dead nor alive'.[25] For Cixous, automata are like ghosts – both are tainted by the strangeness of the in-between, both threaten the patriarchal subject by 'the insidious movement, through which opposites communicate'.[26] Cixous' text engages metaphors of movement (of 'revolving', 'push[ing] forth', 'dodging' and 'turn[ing]') to turn 'The "Uncanny"' on its side, aligning deconstruction with choreography and revealing the powerful push and pull of repression and recurrence barely concealed within Freud's work.[27]

And who, or what, is this automaton at the heart of Cixous' deconstruction?

Moved by Cixous, I have returned to Hoffmann's text, and have felt a strange gesturality ghosting his portrayal of Olympia. Nathaniel first sees her through a glass door in the house of his neighbor and professor of physics, Dr. Spalanzani. Pulled by curiosity toward a loosely drawn curtain covering the door, Nathaniel spies 'a woman, tall, very slim, perfectly proportioned and gorgeously dressed' sitting 'with her hands folded'. 'She seemed not to notice me', he continues, 'and her eyes had in general something fixed and staring about them … It made me feel quite uncanny, and I crept softly away into the neighboring lecture-room'.[28] Later, Nathaniel moves to a new lodging across from Spalanzani's apartment, and is fortunate to be able to gaze at her, stalker-fashion, through a window in his room. Noting that she sits alone and immobile for hours, her stare unmoving (like his own, perhaps?), Nathaniel nonetheless determines that she is looking back at him and that 'he had never seen a lovelier figure'.[29] She is the 'stiff, rigid Olympia', yet she is a 'beautiful statue' and, of course, a 'seductive sight'.[30] When Nathaniel finally meets Olympia and develops a relationship with her, he finds her stillness no longer uncanny, but appealing. A marvelous listener, a captive audience, 'she did not feed a cage bird, she did not play with a lapdog or with a favourite cat, she did not fiddle with a handkerchief or with anything else' – that is to say, she sits gloriously motionless.[31]

His schoolmates are not completely fooled by their professor's daughter. Olympia's debut at her coming-out party is met with mixed reviews. One of Nathaniel's friends says to him:

> She walks with a curiously measured gait; every movement seems as if controlled by clockwork. When she plays and sings it is with the unpleasant soulless regularity of a machine, and she dances the same way. We have come to find this Olympia quite uncanny; we would like to have nothing to do with her; it seems to us that she is only acting like a living creature, and yet there is some reason for that which we cannot fathom.[32]

Seductive in stillness – sitting for hours on end with her hands folded – Olympia is uncanny again in motion. When Nathaniel happens upon a violent row between Olympia's creators (Coppola, who provides the artificial eyes, and Spalanzani, responsible for everything else), he sees her yanked to and fro. 'Puppet', he cries in realisation, 'ha, lovely puppet, spin, spin!' And he cries 'Spin, puppet, spin!' all the way to the madhouse.[33]

Olympia's difference is marked gesturally; Nathaniel's friend notices that she moves as if controlled by an internal mechanism and Nathaniel observes her 'spinning' by external control. She is too external: no substance, all surface, moved by forces outside of her self. But she is also too internal; she is a dissembling woman with a deeply hidden secret, an automaton moved by a concealed mechanism. Olympia's gesturality takes on qualities of the mask; it conceals as it reveals, it asserts the success of Spalanzani's illusion and it also destroys the illusion. The word 'mask' is etymologically related, perhaps, to the post-classical Latin 'masca', meaning 'evil spirit' or 'spectre', which may be related to a group of Romance forms meaning 'to smear' or 'to blacken' (that is, to disguise the face with make-up). 'Mask' contains within it an admission of a very material method of illusion (make-up) and an occlusion of that illusion in favor of the eschatological (the performer possessed by a ghost). Related to the word 'mascara', 'mask' alludes to the relationship between femininity, dissemblance, sexuality, and performance. Olympia is, after all, doubly a performer: she is a charade, a sham who debuts at her coming-out party with operatic singing, playing the piano, and dancing.[34]

Like a continuous surface folded in on itself, Olympia's internality assumes only the dimensions of the patriarchal subject's sense of interiority. Her internality mocks the individuality and intentionality of the interiorised subject. Hers is the internal crossed with the external – as Deleuze writes in another context, 'the inside of the outside'. This topography brings to light the 'peristaltic movements' concealed within immobility: Olympia has always been a puppet, she has always been spinning to and fro, despite her frozen posture and still hands.[35] The gloriously still auditor is also a performer whose clockwork mechanism spins underneath a placid exterior. Immobility, Nathaniel discovers, is a form of spinning held (temporarily) in place.

An adaptation of Hoffmann's short story, the dance film *The Sandman* offers a productive commentary on Olympia's gestural alterity through a complex choreography of (im)mobility and (de)animation. The uncanniness of her gesturing body is not presented through the clockwork regularity and mad spinning of Hoffmann's Olympia or the twitchiness which characterises many of the Quays' films. Instead, Tuckett and the Quays explore hysterical gesture through shifting qualities of movement. Performed by Tamara Rojo, this Olympia moves with both mechanical rigidity and dollish limpness.[36] Her dancing is punctuated by frozen poses and momentary swoons. Before her first dance (with her father-creator, a villainous combination of Coppola, Spalanzani, and the Sandman), Olympia is given life when her father inserts her artificial eyes and removes her lace veil. Once animated, Olympia's body is a reminder of the stubborn inanimacy at the heart of animation. She acts as if she is learning to move like a living creature, yet cannot, or does not want to, shed her mechanical origins. Lifted by her father, she repeatedly poses with her arms stiff and outstretched, her body performing the complex dynamics of autonomy we see in the moving machine (which, though automated, requires some kind of human intervention). Olympia's gesturality becomes a kind of navel, an originary inscription of continuing paternal creation. Her mechanical movement anxiously suggests not only the inanimacy of live bodies, but the mechanicality of assuming and possessing a body.

Her limpness and rigidity take on new meaning, however, during her final *pas de deux* with her father, in which he dances his incestual desire for his creation. This moving scene transforms her limpness and rigidity into gestures of resistance. Stiff, muscles contracted, Olympia refuses to 'fall' for his sexual advances; limp, cold, and lifeless, she does not respond to his aggressive embraces and slips through his arms. This Olympia cannot be held – in other words, cannot be possessed (completely) – yet nonetheless is moved, quite literally, by the gestures of her father, creator of a body he cannot have. Frustrated, the Sandman drops her to the ground (or, perhaps, she drops herself), leaving Olympia apparently lifeless, her body prostrate, but her leg bent at the knee and jutting stiffly into the air. This immobile pose is that of death (it is suggestive of rigor mortis or the death pose of an insect), yet it is also a defensive manoeuvre: playing dead, she once again refuses his advances; one stiff limb in the air, she raises her leg like a phallic weapon to defend her body. And though her leg is stiff and still, it is also, in a way, rising: dancer Tamara Rojo pushes upward against the downward force of gravity, her leg held temporarily and uncannily in place.

Tuckett and the Quays' *The Sandman* ends in abandonment. Leaving her alone in his apartment-workshop, Olympia's father disappears after the unsuccessful seduction of his daughter. In a touching moment, a mysterious older woman (a middle-aged Clara, perhaps?) enters Olympia's final resting place and discovers her lying on her stomach, one stiff leg still bent at the knee and jutting into the air. The woman gently turns Olympia onto her back and tenderly carresses Olympia's forehead with her palm. She leaves. Orphaned, Olympia remains supine, with one arm rigidly extended above her. Once again, Rojo's upward movement against gravity is inscribed within a deathly immobility.

Insect dreams

Animation as a film form has a long-standing relationship with death and (im)mobility. One of the first stop-motion animators, Wladyslaw Starewicz, resorted to single-frame animation to recreate the fighting of stag beetles that were too stunned by the intense lighting needed for filming to spar naturally. As Starewicz describes:

> In the mating season, beetles fight. Their jaws remind one of deers' horns. I wished to film them but since their fighting is nocturnal, the light I used would freeze them into total immobility. By using embalmed beetles, I reconstructed the different phases of that fight, frame by frame, with progressive changes; more than five hundred frames for thirty seconds of projection. The result

surpassed my hopes: 1910 – Lucanus Cervus (10 metres long) – the first three-dimensional animated film.[37]

Starewicz's narrative of the birth of stop-motion puppet animated film (a spurious genesis, considering stop-motion techniques had been employed before 1910) ascribes to animation a restorative power – that is, the power to restore movement to stilled bodies. For these bodies to move naturally, however, they must be moved artificially; they must be killed, embalmed, and turned into animated performers in an unusual kind of 'stag' film. Deeming himself the patriarchal father-creator of a cinematic technique, Starewicz produced a cast of automata articulating instinctual insect movement shaped by the animator's own gestures. The slightly jerky quality of Starewicz's animation announces itself as a gestural after-life, an uncanny life within death.

Twitchy, jerky, doll-like, and mechanical – this is the movement of Starewicz's and the Quays' animations. This movement constructs and deconstructs gesturing bodies; like the 'stop-and-go flicker' of a zootrope (a Victorian optical toy which can be considered a precursor to animation film), its rhythm 'will simultaneously construct the gestalt and threaten it with dissolution, with a breakup into its separate, impotent fragments'.[38] In other words, this movement is convulsive; as Steve Connor reminds us, the word 'convulse' comes from the Latin '*convellere*', a strange word which literally means 'together' (con) + 'to pull apart' (vellere).[39] Animated movement in the Quays' and Starewicz's films is convulsive in that it permits the uncanny coexistence of opposites and the hysterical holding together-pulling apart that characterises gesture. Drawing on the relationship between animated film and death established by Starewicz, the Quays' works exploit and make explicit the peculiar capabilities of the medium, elucidating the uncanny choreography of embodiment.

The animated bodies which are brought to life in the Quays' puppet animation films are radically heterogeneous. Unable or unwilling to be held together without pulling apart, these bodies remain open to sympathetic vibrations from other bodies, both animate and inanimate. They are unstable assemblages of organic and inorganic matter haunted by the movements that vivify them. These bodies illuminate a collective cultural dream of the body as animated automaton, a dream which relies on certain overdetermined figures – the gesturing female hysteric, the immobile and alluring sleeping beauty, the little girl who desires to see her dolls spring to life, and the living doll, herself – as representatives of the uncanniness of embodiment. Animated film is particularly suited to explore the uncanniness of this dream, which is real and unreal, present and past, familiar, and very, very strange at the same time.

Notes

1. Lesley Stern, 'Putting on a Show, or The Ghostliness of Gesture', *Senses of Cinema* (July–August 2002), http://www.sensesofcinema.com/contents/02/21/sd_stern.html

2. Stern http://www.sensesofcinema.com/contents/02/21/sd_stern.html

3. Stern http://www.sensesofcinema.com/contents/02/21/sd_stern.html

4. Nicholas Royle, *The Uncanny* (New York: Routledge, 2003): 2.

5. Stern http://www.sensesofcinema.com/contents/02/21/sd_stern.html

6. Jay Leyda, ed., *Eisenstein on Disney* (London: Methuen, 1988): 54.

7. Paul Wells, *Understanding Animation* (London: Routledge, 1998): 213.

8. Laura U. Marks, *Touch: Sensuous Theory and Multisensory Media* (Minneapolis: University of Minnesota Press, 2002): 136.

9. Wells, 111.

10. 'Five Letters from the Brothers Quay and Still from The Comb', *The Review of Contemporary Fiction* 12.1 (Spring 1992): 58.

11. Michael Atkinson, 'The Night Countries of the Brothers Quay', *Film Comment* 30.5 (September–October 1994): 40.

12. Quoted in Atkinson: 38.

13. http://www.zeitgeistfilms.com/film.php?directoryname=comb Accessed 25 October 2004.

14. Aragon and Breton, 'The Quinquagenary of Hysteria (1878–1928)', in Patrick Waldberg, *Surrealism* (New York: McGraw Hill Book Company): 61.

15. Aragon and Breton: 61.

16. *Why the French Love Jerry Lewis: From Cabaret to Early Cinema* (Stanford: Stanford Unversity Press, 2001) throughout, see pages 2 and 7.

17. Elisabeth Bronfen, *The Knotted Subject: Hysteria and its Discontents* (Princeton, NJ: Princeton University Press, 1998): 182.

18. Bronfen: 196.

19. Bronfen:Ibid.

20. Bronfen: Ibid.

21. Sigmund Freud, 'The "Uncanny"', *Sigmund Freud: Psychological Writings and Letters*, ed. Sander L. Gilman (New York: Continuum, 1995): 144–145.

22. Freud: 135, 137.

23. Sigmund Freud, *Beyond the Pleasure Principle* (New York: W.W. Norton & Company, 1988): 43, 46.

24. Hélène Cixous, 'Fiction and its Phantoms: A Reading of Freud's Das Unheimliche (The "Uncanny")', *New Literary History* (Spring 1976): 538.

25. Cixous: 543, 540.

26. Cixous: 543.

27. Cixous: 533, 545, 536, 548.

28. E.T.A. Hoffmann, 'The Sandman', *Tales of Hoffmann* (London: Penguin Books, 1982): 99.

29. Hoffmann: 109.

30. Hoffmann: 109, 109, 111.

31. Hoffmann: 117.

32. Hoffmann: 116.

33. Hoffmann: 120.

34. All etymological information is from the Oxford English dictionary online.

35. Gilles Deleuze, *Foucault* (Minneapolis: University of Minnesota Press, 2000): 96–97.

36. Though the characters of Tuckett and the Quays' *The Sandman* are not identified in the credits by name, I call the film's automaton character Olympia after the Hoffmann character on which she is obviously based.

37. Quoted in Giannalberto Bendazzi, *Cartoons: One Hundred Years of Cinema Animation* (London: John Libbey, 1994): 35.

38. Rosalind E. Krauss, *The Optical Unconscious* (5th edn.) (Cambridge, MA: The MIT Press, 1998): 206, 209.

39. Connor, Steve, 'The Shakes: Conditions of Tremor', Available from: http://www.bbk.ac.uk/eh/eng/skc/shakes/ Accessed 24 October 2004.

Heather Crow is a doctoral candidate in Performance Studies at the University of California at Berkeley. She is completing a dissertation entitled *POSSESSIONS: Animated Bodies in Mediated Performance*. Her areas of research include theories of corporeality and materiality as they relate to contemporary animated film, theater, and architecture. She is also a puppeteer, actor, and theatrical designer.

Chapter 5

Literary Len: Trade Tattoo and Len Lye's Link with the Literary Avant-Garde

Miriam Harris

Len Lye's interests and creative output are an embodiment of the multifarious disciplines that may inspire the independent animator working within the fine arts realm. Sculpture, dance, jazz, tribal rhythms, Oceanic and African art, and modernist painting all played a vital role in Lye's ebullient animations. The media theorist Söke Dinkla has pointed out that certain literary innovations, such as the writings of James Joyce, have shaped narrative structures within contemporary digital interactive media.[1] Similarly, Lye's close connection with avant-garde literature – as a writer, admirer of the work of James Joyce, Gertrude Stein, and Arthur Rimbaud, and as a close friend of Laura Riding and Robert Graves – manifests itself within his animation, and is particularly evident in his film *Trade Tattoo* (1937).

At the end of 1926, after eight turbulent weeks crossing the Pacific and Atlantic Oceans, the New Zealand artist Len Lye disembarked in London. His joyful, off-beat personality, uniquely egg-shaped bald pate and the striking originality of his work quickly endeared him to a lively community

Abstract: This essay explores the multidisciplinary world of Len Lye's animated film *Trade Tattoo*, which was created in 1937 from rejected documentary takes from the General Post Office Film Unit in Great Britain, and merged with stencil patterns, direct animation and Cuban dance music. The essay begins by foregrounding the permeable boundaries between avant-garde literature and the visual arts in the 1920s and 30s, as outlined by modernist poetry theorist Charles Altieri, and goes on to examine the influence of writers such as Laura Riding, Robert Graves, Gertrude Stein, and James Joyce upon Len Lye's writing. Having established the unique characteristics of Lye's aesthetic and symbolic literary innovations, the essay closely examines these elements in relation to *Trade Tattoo*.

of artists and writers in Hammersmith who were in thrall to the creative possibilities of Modernism. Lye's passage from Sydney to London had been paid by stoking the ship's furnaces, and the motifs of journeying, motion, and manual labour repeatedly reverberate ten years later in his 1937 film *Trade Tattoo*.

Trade Tattoo is a multidisciplinary explosion of ideas and approaches created from rejected documentary takes from the General Post Office Film Unit and merged with stencil patterns, direct animation and Cuban dance music. From a technical perspective, it is a virtuoso mastery of colour film printing processes, but the most resounding innovations reside in the relationship between text and images. Constantly animated, in a perpetual state of flux, Lye's words and visuals, together with their rhythmic structure, can be traced to an avant-garde interest in disciplinary permeability and a departure from realism. His text and images endow the film with a poetic cohesiveness, allowing for the emergence of rich symbolic allusions, that would otherwise be stymied by a conservative approach to narrative.

This essay explores the poetic structure of *Trade Tattoo*, and its relationship with modernist poetry and painting of the 1920s and 1930s, and with Lye's own writing. Music is another vital strand in Lye's animated film, and cannot be ignored. Music, words, and pictures all contribute to Lye's overriding concern with rhythm, movement, and an exhilarating bodily energy. It is impossible to discuss his treatment of words and form without considering their relationship to sound and movement, and this was a concern shared by modernist writers. Text and image are intertwined in *Trade Tattoo* in a manner that differs from Lye's previous animations, and it is the implications of this dynamic coupling that I wish to focus upon.

In Lye's earlier animated films, such as *A Colour Box* (1935), *Kaleidoscope* (1935), and *Rainbow Dance* (1936), text introduces the film and then makes a surprise reappearance at the end in the form of a commercial advertisement. While Lye integrates the text stylistically with the preceding visuals and exhibits a textual playfulness that echoes modernist concerns, these segments can still be perceived as a comical, incongruous addition. Lye seems to wink at us, laughingly acknowledging the forces that made the film financially viable, with this leap into the prosaic. In *Trade Tattoo* however, image and text dance, chase each other, and attain sublime levels for the entire duration of the film. The rhythm is informed not only by the music, but also the movement of textual and imagistic passages, which may be compared to the structure of Lye's own poetry (Fig. 1).

It is useful to refer to the writings of the modernist poetry theorist Charles Altieri, in which he explores the work of poets such as Gertrude Stein and Ezra Pound, and their incorporation of the groundbreaking innovations of Paul Cézanne and Pablo Picasso. Altieri analyses Stein's writing, such as

Fig. 1: Len Lye at Work. [Courtesy of the Len Lye Foundation.]

'Portrait of Picasso', from a Cubist perspective, in which she translates into literature Cubism's attention to multiple spatial planes.[2] Through slight shifts in the structure of sentences, Stein created multifaceted modes of meaning:

> One who some were certainly following was one who was completely charming. One whom some were certainly following was one who was charming. One whom some were following was one who was completely charming. One whom some were following was one who was certainly completely charming.[3]

Such an approach was a radical departure from literature's previous efforts to differentiate itself from the visual arts. As the text and image theoretician, W.J.T. Mitchell, observes in connection to these earlier attitudes:

> Painting sees itself as uniquely fitted for the representation of the visible world, whereas poetry is primarily concerned with the invisible realm of ideas and feelings. Poetry is an art of time, motion, and action; painting an art of space, stasis, and arrested action.[4]

Altieri's analyses foreground the osmotic relationship between the visual arts and literature during the early heady days of modernism. The earlier attitudes toward painting and poetry, as outlined by Mitchell, were regarded as suspect by avant-garde circles enraged by Victorian hypocrisy, and the inadequacies of the ideals of Romanticism and the Enlightenment amidst the carnage of war. Altieri writes that the modernist poets 'sought alternative models of agency in the study of literary history, in the new ways of looking at the psyche being developed in their own time, and in the countercultural gestures elaborated by the visual arts'.[5] The visual arts had been moving away from 'mimetic values' and avant-garde literature followed suit.

This interflowing of ideas between the visual and literary arts is reflected in both Len Lye's life and his work. Isolated in New Zealand from the creative ferment and galleries of Europe, he latched on to the potentialities of Modernism through a book by Ezra Pound, about a young sculptor killed during the First World War. The book was named after the artist, *Gaudier-Brzeska*, and contained his manifesto attacking the Western art tradition, proffering in its stead a celebration of cave art and the tribal arts of Africa and the Pacific. Len Lye had already begun to venture into this alternative territory, finding the Maori and Pacific carvings in the Canterbury museum in Christchurch an irresistible lure. Lye valued their close link with kinetic sensation and the unconscious, or what he termed the 'Old Brain', as a refreshing contrast to Western rationalism.[6]

The composition of Len Lye's social milieu in Hammersmith also reflects the intermingling of visual artists and writers, together with the subversion of social conventions that Altieri has outlined. Lye became a member of the 'Seven and Five Society', a hotbed of Modernist visual innovation, which included the painter Ben Nicholson and the sculptors Henry Moore and Barbara Hepworth. Amongst Lye's closest friends were the writers Laura Riding, Robert Graves, and Norman Cameron. Riding had been involved in the United States with an influential modernist group known as the 'Fugitives' – one of her published poems caught the eye of Robert Graves, who invited her to visit. Riding wound up living with Graves as his lover, while his wife Nancy Nicholson (the sister of Ben Nicholson) lived in a barge on the Thames with their children. The arrangement was regarded as a 'trinity', and for a time at least, was successful.[7] It certainly illustrates the questioning of conventions that was a strong feature of the circle.

Graves and Riding were pivotal figures of the London Modernist scene, their flat in St Peter's Square a lively magnet for writers and artists, and their ideas an alternative to those of the Bloomsbury set. Robert Graves had been deeply traumatised by his experience of trench warfare from 1914–16, and was searching for alternatives to the Western society that had fostered such a catastrophe. He read Freud, and researched into myth and early civilisations. Lye's passion for tribal or 'Old Brain' art ignited Graves' interest and prompted a close connection; in 1978 Lye reminisced that Graves had told him 'we're the only two myth men I know'.[8]

Lye's writer friends introduced him to a new world of literature. In an interview with Wystan Curnow, Lye described the jolt he received upon reading Norman Cameron's translation of Rimbaud's poetry: 'I woke up'.[9] The writing was profoundly visual and sensuous, and 'each word was as if it was cut out of marble. Not cut out, incised.'[10] Lye had initially thought poetry 'was a lot of romanticised junk. I'd got this feeling as a kid, coming across Ella Wheeler Wilcox, and that level of maudlin stuff'.[11] It was only when he met Graves and Riding that his interest in poetry was sparked as 'here were these two sensible people immersed in poetry'.[12] Riding introduced Lye to further writers, and recognising talent in Lye's own writing, she encouraged his literary output. Her literary experience was considerable – in 1927 Riding and Graves co-authored a book, *A Survey of Modernist Poetry*, which had a huge impact on the way poetry was written and read. Her literary taste extended to the works of Gertrude Stein and James Joyce rather than Virginia Woolf and T.S. Eliot. Riding had a close association with Gertrude Stein, and Lye designed a frontispiece for one of Stein's works; Stein in turn admired the freshness of Lye's writing. In Riding's own poetry, she shared Stein's and Joyce's concern with alternatives to a description of linear time. She wrote that poetry 'must make the present period not so much the next one of a series as a resume of periods'.[13]

Altieri writes of the Modernist quest to develop new modes of thinking; boundaries between artists and writers were consequently lowered and revolutionary ideas shared around. Laura Riding and Gertrude Stein, for example, both sought textual equivalents to Cubism's evocation of simultaneous realities. In Lye's case, the concept driving the work was also the essential ingredient – issues such as energy, temporality, and tapping into the 'Old Brain' remained predominant concerns, whether he was using painting, sculpture, filmmaking, or writing as a vehicle for their expression.

Before embarking upon a close analysis of *Trade Tattoo*, it would be helpful to consider Lye's concerns as a writer, so that his approach to using animated text might be further illuminated. Over the next few paragraphs, comparisons will be made with the innovations of peers who influenced Lye. Since Lye was a unique spirit, chartering new territory in a largely unexplored realm, qualities that are intrinsically his own will also be foregrounded. These features will then be explored in relation to the merger of text and image in *Trade Tattoo*, and the impact of this aesthetic union upon the structure of the film.

One of Lye's dominant creative concerns was the embodiment of a kinetic energy, suffused with a 'heart quality of resonance – as distinct from your bloody skull resonance'.[14] In painting and sculpture, the technique of doodling provided an access route into the 'Old Brain'; Lye wrote that 'I doodled to assuage my hunger for some hypnotic image I'd never seen before'.[15] His sketchbooks, held in archives at the Len Lye Foundation in New Plymouth, New Zealand, are filled with pulsating lines and symbols, sometimes transforming into shapes that resemble wobbly amoebas, stars, or an exotic alphabet. Similarly, in writing, Lye valued a doodling style that bypassed rational logic and collapsed conventions of punctuation and grammar. The following segment appears in the book *No Trouble*, a compilation of Lye's letters to friends and family that was edited by Laura Riding in 1930, and published by Graves' and Riding's Seizin Press. The lack of punctuation hastens the stream of consciousness flow, from which markers intermittently appear that the reader might start to shape into images and narratives. This excerpt comes from a letter addressed to Ben Nicholson:

> Only just the weather now A? Outside in the sun buy a yacht and go for a swim around the world easy jazz all sunburnt to working in the shade to mean nothing to do the most kind of work in the world this is the most important world to me so after nothing follows important work.[16]

This passage transports the reader in a fashion that is freewheeling, and it constantly takes one by surprise. Stylistically, there are echoes in Lye's letter of the subconscious meanderings and rapid changes in register that permeate Joyce's prose. Lye enthusiastically described James Joyce's language in *Finnegan's Wake* as being 'beautifully intactly lifted right from spontaneous mind-level first thought'.[17] *Finnegan's Wake* was published in 1939, two years after *Trade Tattoo*'s completion, but instalments appeared prior to publication in *Transition*, a Parisian avant-garde magazine with which Laura Riding was closely connected. In this excerpt from Joyce's *Ulysses*, the flow of consciousness parallels Lye's unfettered prose: 'Two sheets cream vellum paper on reserve two envelopes when I was in Wisdom Hely's wise Bloom in Daly's Henry Flower bought'.[18]

Lye and Joyce both discard traditional devices of punctuation, and grammatical subversions and ambiguities draw attention to words as images and sounds, and as slippery agents of meaning. This self-reflexivity and assertion of the visual in the textual was an aspect of modernist literary experimentation, and a result of a closer relationship with developments in the visual arts. In the excerpt from his letter, Lye playfully transforms the colloquial expression 'eh' into both a letter ('A') and an image, a polymorphous representation evinced also in the work of e.e. cummings, Guillaume Apollinaire, the concrete poets, and the painter Joan Miro.

One can draw parallels between Joyce and Lye's subversion of grammatical conventions and the exuberant suspension of traditional modes of editing in *Trade Tattoo*. Links between the two artists' approaches were also made by reviewers in the 1930s; a review of Joyce's *Finnegan's Wake* in the Glasgow Herald lamented the writing's lack of clarity and that 'one has to submit to Mr Joyce's flow of words as one submits to Len Lye's films of abstract motion, to Shelley's play with celestial images, and to counterpoint in Bach'.[19] Lye was disinterested in conventional literary narratives, and *Trade Tattoo* combines a wild melange of approaches, ranging from rapid jump cuts to motifs that creep along at a snail's pace. In an essay entitled 'Film-Making' that he co-wrote with Riding in 1935, Lye proclaimed that:

The language of the cinema is movement. When it attempts to make of movement a literary language the result is a physical-intellectual caricature-language which furnishes stories of life as something half-true, half-ridiculous (the result of such films as *Henry VIII, Catherine the Great, Christina of Sweden*).[20]

In his drive to privilege movement over a linear literary narrative, Lye created startling twists and changes in register. Meaning is established in *Trade Tattoo* through the juxtaposition of colours, lines, forms, and sounds, and the speed at which elements travel or the length of their duration on the screen. Here comparisons can again be made with Joyce and Stein. Through the use of juxtaposition, puns, onomatopoeia and the repetition of words, Stein drew attention to language's formal features, rhythm, and unconscious associations. Meaning is generated through neighbouring words and the context of elements, rather than narrative description. For instance, in the collection *Tender Buttons*, under the heading 'Eating', Stein enlists repetition, alliteration, and truncation to suggest masticating jaws and chopped up food:

> Eel us eel us with no no pea no pea cool, no pea cool cooler, no pea cooler with a land a land cost in, with a land cost in stretches.
>
> Eating he heat eating he heat it eating, he heat it heat eating. He heat eating.[21]

In a prose piece called 'Grass Clippings', Lye employed evocative words, rich in their sensory response to the writers that he admired. He described Gertrude Stein's writing as 'an oak word bank scrubbed clean and strata built pure Bach fugue stitched with buttons sewn in a big Dutch of a room full of daylight'.[22] In the last line of Lye's prose poem 'Chair in Your Hair', he playfully reshapes the infamous segment from Gertrude Stein's poem 'Sacred Emily': 'Rose is a rose is a rose is a rose'. The whole poem adopts the rhythm of a nursery rhyme – Lye's writing, like Stein's, often uses rhythm and aural devices to extend the range of associations – and he refers to the father of modernist painting, Cézanne, with the affectionate collo-quial 'poppa'.

> Painting painting where is thy mind sting: there there under the chair: not *under* the chair says poppa Cézanne in the legs of the chair says poppa Cézanne: that old chair? Chair in your hair Cézanne Cézanne. A chair in the mind is worth none in the bush. A chair is a chair so leave it there.[23]

There is a spirited irreverence at work here, yet also a well-intentioned homage to Cézanne's painting and his interest in subjective and objective reality. The chair is a constant motif that travels throughout the piece, taking on different incarnations depending on the context within which it is placed. Such a device can be compared to collage's interest in the multifaceted nature of signs, where elements denote different readings depending upon their representation and context. Braque, Picasso, and the Dadaists used collage to play with this semiotic flexibility, so that a torn

Fig. 2: Lye's Letter to Yancy. [Courtesy of the Len Lye Foundation.]

fragment with letters also stood in for a newspaper, or five lines denoted a guitar.

Trade Tattoo is awash in a variety of signs and signifiers that gleefully don different guises, avoiding categorisation. In the course of the film, written signs are also images, kinetic beats, sounds, associative streams of consciousness. Just as Joyce and Stein demonstrated that words lacked the powers of specificity with which they had been previously endowed by the tradition of narrative literature, Lye exposes their chameleon-like propensities. This fascination with the malleable nature of signs is keenly expressed in a later letter to his daughter Yancy.[24] Exemplifying Lye's visual/verbal doodling proclivities, an assortment of signs represent 'spring'. There are written letters, the textual signifier for 'spring'. Below these markings one sees a rapid tangle of loops that suggest the wire bouncy object rather than the season – both signs share the same written and aural signifier. Adjacent to this swirling line is a linear daffodil, a true motif for spring (Fig. 2).

In concluding this brief appraisal of Len Lye's writing concerns, I am struck by the extent to which Lye's texts already embrace the imagistic, aural, and kinetic realms. *Trade Tattoo* embodies such plurality; it can be interpreted as a semiotic soup, a site in which disciplinary boundaries have been lowered and the visual and textual readily leak into each other. The combination of painting, stencils, live footage, and Cuban dance music on a stretch of vibrantly edited celluloid film is a natural extension of Lye's textual innovations. Söke Dinkla has written that one of interactive digital media's unique abilities is the unfolding of multiple simultaneous narratives; if Joyce was working today, the medium would offer a superb articulation of his interests. The multisensory nature of animation is likewise an ideal medium for Len Lye.

Intrinsic to animation's properties as a medium is its ability to evoke a gamut of signs. Animation enables Lye to enlist the senses of sight and sound, and even tactility is suggested with the rapid changes from photography to drawings to cut-out shapes which stress the materiality of their composition. A vast spectrum of modes of denotation can be employed through animation; drawing, painting, collage, typography, and photography can adopt a naturalistic style of representation or veer towards the abstract. Words can be read, but also viewed as images. Similarly, because animation is not a static medium, images are imbued with temporal powers that allow them to not only be seen, but also read according to their movement and placement within a sequence, and their relationship with sound.

The remainder of this essay will discuss the implications of the mutability of signs in *Trade Tattoo*, and will make comparisons with the visual/textual fluidity in Len Lye's writing. Elements in the film will be explored in chronological order, despite Lye's challenging of naturalistic narrative conventions. Superficially, the momentum of *Trade Tattoo* is steered by a conventional narrative, in which words and images create an industrious picture of Britain at work, thanks to the indispensable presence of the postal service. Biographer and Len Lye authority Roger Horrocks believes that Lye was given the script by the General Post Office: 'The rhythm of work-a-day Britain / The furnaces are fired / Cargoes are loaded / Markets are found / By the power of correspondence / The rhythm of trade is maintained by the mails / Keep in rhythm by posting early / You must post early to keep in rhythm / Before 2 p.m.'[25]

Trade Tattoo commences with a title, opening credits and the pulsating rhythms of the Cuban Lecuona band. The viewer is subsequently taken on a journey that echoes the chronology of the script, in which words, drawing, painting, and cut-outs are interspersed with processed live footage of welders, ship loaders, and mail sorters. Lye wrote in a letter that he wanted to express 'a romanticism about the work of the everyday', and the film translates mundane, repetitive activities into stretches of vibrant kineticism.[26] In the opening sequence, for instance, a mood of vitality is introduced with a series of rapid shifts and explosions of colour, pulsing stencil patterns and darting dots that move in tandem with the music, but also twitch and bounce, due to some striking jump cuts. A graphic of a piece of film enters from the sidelines and is subject to the same kind of spasmodic motion. Just as the writing of Lye, Joyce and Stein exposes the physicality of language through the subversion of grammar and the use of repetition, the sprocket edges of the film graphic expose the material basis of what we otherwise perceive as animated forms.

The title 'Trade Tattoo by Len Lye' jumps and abruptly jerks as if it had got caught in a film projector. In contrast to the German experimental animators Hans Richter and Oskar Fischinger, who strove for a seamless animation of abstract forms, Lye delighted in the energetic jitter that arose as a consequence of each frame being manually painted, scratched, or stencilled. This feature can again be compared to the willingness of Lye and other modernist writers to revel in the intrinsic properties of their chosen medium, rather than create a smooth veneer governed by naturalistic representation.

The issue of textual and visual interchangeability is established early on in *Trade Tattoo*. Words take on the properties of images due to variations in size, font, and colour. Letters and their backgrounds change their chromatic and proportional dimensions with the same rapidity as the abstract patterns whizzing behind them. In his writing, Lye draws attention to words as images and sounds by abandoning traditional grammar and punctuation, and a similar effect is achieved in the film by feeding us the sentence 'the rhythm of work-a-day Britain' in increments, so that meaning is postponed and our attention is focused upon aspects such as shape and colour. The words gracefully swerve and pulsate in response to the percussive rhythm of the dance music, which imbues them with a kinetic energy that further enhances the connotations of the words 'rhythm of work-a-day Britain'.

A dynamic coupling between image and text occurs in the next sentence that appears: 'the furnaces are fired'. Flickering lines, painted at great speed, suggest flames but also become fiery text. This is also reminiscent of Lye's paintings and later animations such as *Free Radicals*, in which he reaches into what he called his 'Old Brain' or primordial collective consciousness, and relinquishes himself to the lines and shapes that emerge. There are lines

Fig. 3: Trade Tattoo *images. [Courtesy of the Len Lye Foundation.]*

that teeter on the edge of bursting into the symbolic with the suggestion of letters, and lines forming vibrant motifs that seem intent on communication, but to which we need to respond intuitively as we lack the conventional decoders. This alternation between the semiotic and the symbolic, and abstraction and representation echoes the fluid moment between image and text. Subsequent to the sentence 'the furnaces are fired', Lye introduces processed documentary footage of searingly hot furnaces and welders producing sparks. However, these images of 'reality' are intertwined with abstraction because they are processed with a technique that creates vivid, surreal colorations. The grids of diamonds, dots, and lozenge shapes that whirl over the documentary footage therefore bear a resemblance to the photographic imagery in terms of colour and form (Fig. 3).

An important issue is raised here concerning signs and the immense consequence of context in conveying meaning. Gertrude Stein demonstrated how meaning shifts through the rearrangement of sentence structures, and Lye's chair in 'Chair in Your Hair' absorbs different qualities according to its neighbouring elements. Similarly, in *Trade Tattoo*, abstract symbols acquire further resonance through their juxtaposition with other motifs. For instance, the dancing circles, dots and rectangles, that can be initially read as purely abstract pattern, develop different associations in the course of the film due to their formal similarities with adjacent motifs. When juxtaposed with photographic images of clock faces, circles turn into timepieces. Diagonal lines are intercut with footage of ropes lowering cargo onto a ship, and thereby acquire a new reading. Rectangles and lozenge shapes transmute into the sprocket holes of a film strip, and later a swarm of painted envelopes heading towards their destination.

This method of juxtaposition can be related to Sergei Eisenstein's montage technique, but there is also a significant difference. Eisenstein's use of interrelationships, for example in the classic 'Odessa Steps' sequence in *Battleship Potemkin* (1925), employs purely live footage, and formal and rhythmic juxtapositions serve to add deeper resonance to the narrative's momentum, rather than expose the materiality of the medium of film. Lye's metamorphosing forms reflect movement and the multifaceted nature of visual and textual communication. Lye emphasises semiotic flexibility; disciplinary boundaries are lowered and there is a promotion of fluid travel between all the signifying camps. This strategy lends weight to an overarching theme that permeates the film – a relishing of self-reflexivity, movement, and communication.

Both Eisenstein and Len Lye published their theories about filmmaking, and it is intriguing to absorb Lye's ideas about linking colour, speech, text and sound. His interest in poetry led to the film *Full Fathom Five* (1935) which has unfortunately been lost, in which John Gielgud's voice, eloquently reading from Shakespeare's 'The Tempest', is accompanied by 'a pouring out of image and association which leaves a feeling of magic, an underlit, underwater quality, which the verse has …'.[27] Lye's interest in the interchangeability of signs, where a word can also be a number, is clearly apparent in this description of *Full Fathom Five* by Robert Herring: 'It is not true to say that it is an illustration of Shakespeare – unless you are willing to concede that a figure five floating across the screen is an illustration of the opening line …'.[28] The original approaches required for the interaction of a variety of media compelled Lye to articulate his theories in an essay written the following year, 'Voice and Colour'. This essay is a profound testimony to Lye's concern with the associative layers of signs, and lays the groundwork for *Trade Tattoo* in 1937. An excerpt illustrates these issues: 'If simple colour variations followed the grammatical pattern of speech, they could help the descriptive or significant sense of the words. Nouns, verbs, adjectives, etc, even punctuation, each could have their pictorial treatment'.[29]

In returning to an analysis of *Trade Tattoo*, in accordance with its sequential order, one observes a continued exploration of the many-sided nature of signs. The live footage of fiery furnaces is followed by a series of documentary clips featuring ship workers. A representation of a ship that is stylistically unexpected – cartoon-like ropes gliding past goofy cut-out clouds – is inserted at this point, and enlarges the semiotic repertoire.[30] The sentence 'Cargoes are loaded' appears in typewritten capitals, one word at a time. The typewriter font adds further weight to the developing theme of postal correspondence, and this notion of travel is supported by the subsequent footage of ships being loaded, and the panning motion of the camera.

Typewritten capitals also convey the next sentence, 'Markets are found'. The words appear jerkily and 'markets' is repeated several times, in the fashion of Joyce and Stein. Rapidly cut, chromatically varied footage of mail sorters is then interspersed with images of a darting painted envelope, and the hand-drawn words 'By the power of correspondence'. 'Correspondence' is playfully fed to the viewer in hyphenated portions, 'Corres-pon-dence', enticing the viewer to employ both reading and looking, in the act of piecing together each visual fragment. Typewritten words, illegible, but denoting written communication, swoop in from the sidelines and circle over footage of exotic locations. This sequence accentuates how animation enables Lye to evoke an extraordinarily rich range of associations. Whereas Joyce and Stein are confined to black typeset words on a white page, Lye enlists colour, typography, drawing, painting, movement, and sound to explore the materiality of communication and motion.

The next passage also epitomises the richness of Lye's semiotic approach. The music becomes resoundingly percussive, and the editing features rapid cutting between a variety of aesthetic modes; the omnipresent grids of whirring stencil patterns are cut with footage of transportation. Railway tracks are echoed by diagonal rectangles, while white rectangles suggesting envelopes find their live footage equivalent in the lights of a train shooting through the night. The typewritten words, 'The rhythm of trade is maintained by the mails', are repeated three times. Just as the rhythm of Stein's words in her poem 'Eating' reflects the concept of chewing, Lye's use of repetition literally reinforces the words 'The rhythm of trade'.

Lye's semiotic soup becomes brimful in the last segment of *Trade Tattoo* with an outpouring of signs denoting temporality and rhythm. These motifs range from the photographically realistic to cartoon-like representations and abstract mark-making. Footage of real clocks, cartoon sketches of frantic pendulums, marks in a circle representing minutes, ticking drawn clock hands, stencils of envelopes and patterns darting to and fro, all denote time. Their exuberant spontaneity and individuality however stress the importance and the freshness of the present moment, and the editing, which incorporates jump cuts together with longer stretches, further demands our immediate attention, and emphasises that time is a sequence of vital, sensory moments. At the film's conclusion, Lye focuses on a real envelope surrounded by black space, with curvilinear handwriting that announces 'The End'. It too, like all of the text and images in *Trade Tattoo*, is susceptible to transmutation, and it is transformed into a rectangular shape as it recedes into limitless space.

In an interview with Ray Thorburn that appeared in 'Art International' in 1974, Len Lye reminisced that in the 1930s, 'somebody once said that *Trade Tattoo* in one hundred years would look as fresh and frisky as anything going on then and that was nice'.[31] It is now seventy years since *Trade Tattoo* was created, and it still looks and feels startlingly vivid and fresh. Few films can surpass it for aesthetic and conceptual richness. It represents the culmination of Len Lye's exploration of modernist writing in the 1920s and 1930s, and manifests his dexterity in intertwining images and text.

Notes

1. Söke Dinkla, 'The Art of Narrative – Towards the Floating Work of Art'. Martin Reiser & Andrea Zapp, eds. *New Screen Media, Cinema/Art/Narrative* (London: British Film Institute, 2002): 27–41.

2. Charles Altieri, *Painterly Abstraction in Modernist American Poetry: The Contemporaneity of Modernism* (Cambridge: University Press, 1989): 240–248.

3. Ibid.: 241.

4. W.J.T. Mitchell, *Iconology: Image, Text, Ideology* (Chicago: University of Chicago Press, 1987): 48.

5. Altieri, 1989: 4.

6. Wystan Curnow, 'An Interview with Len Lye' in *Art New Zealand*, vol. 17, 1980: 61.

7. Deborah Baker, *In Extremis: The Life of Laura Riding* (London: Hamish Hamilton Ltd, 1993):154.

8. Wystan Curnow, 1980: 60.

9. Ibid: 61.

10. Ibid: 61.

11. Ibid: 61.

12. Ibid: 61.

13. Baker: 183.

14. Wystan Curnow, 1980: 61.

15. Roger Horrocks, *Len Lye* (Auckland: Auckland University Press, 2000): 91.

16. Wystan Curnow and Roger Horrocks, *Figures of Motion: Len Lye Selected Writings* (Auckland: Auckland University Press, 1984): 99.

17. Roger Horrocks, 'My Word My World', *Landfall 205* (Otago: University of Otago Press, 2003): 181.

18. James Joyce, *Ulysses* (New York: Vintage Books, 1961): 263.

19. 'Reflections from Mr Joyce's Distorting Mirrors', *The Glasgow Herald* (4 May 1939), held in the Len Lye Archive, New Plymouth, New Zealand.

20. Curnow and Horrocks, 1984: 40.

21. Gertrude Stein, *Look at Me Now and Here I Am* (Harmondsworth: Penguin, 1984): 193.

22. Roger Horrocks, 'My Word My World', *Landfall 205* (Otago: University of Otago Press, 2003): 181.

23. Curnow and Horrocks, 1984: 114.

24. This image appears courtesy of Roger Horrocks and the Len Lye Foundation.

25. Roger Horrocks, *Len Lye* (Auckland: Auckland University Press, 2000): 151.

26. Ibid: 151.

27. Ibid: 135.

28. Ibid: 135.

29. Curnow and Horrocks: 43.

30. I wish to acknowledge Roger Horrocks for this observation, in a conversation with the author, April 2003.

31. 'Ray Thorburn Interviews Len Lye', *Art International*, (Vol. XIX April, 1975): 66.

Miriam Harris is a lecturer in Media Design and Animation at the Unitec Institute of Technology, Auckland, New Zealand. She is an artist and animator, and a graduate of the Post Graduate Diploma programme in Digital Animation and Visual Effects at Sheridan College, Canada. She is nearing completion on a PhD that explores the intertwining of text, image, and narrative.

Chapter 6

Literary Theory, Animation and the 'Subjective Correlative': Defining the Narrative 'World' in Brit-lit Animation

Paul Wells

N ovelists and poets, John Updike, Italo Calvino, E.M. Forster and e.e. cummings, among others, profoundly admired the animated film. For them, animated cartoons embodied a model of visualisation each desired to capture in their poetry and prose. For them, too, there was a recognition that 'animated worlds' were conjured with the kind of brevity, intensity and affect that transcends words, yet communicates so powerfully. While it is clear that all art forms connect and integrate in some way, the space between the classical status of 'the novel' and the claims of 'the animated film' remain distant in the sense that even with the post-modern elevation of popular culture, and clear evidence of the aesthetic, technical and progressive quality of animation throughout its history, it still seems a less regarded form of expression. Part of the reason for this is straightfor-ward. As illustrator and graphic novelist Raymond Briggs notes:

In this country [the UK] there is a hierarchy of snobbery in the arts. Opera,

Abstract: This essay explores the pertinence of modernist literary theory in the critical evaluation of animated literary adaptations. Beginning with an address of the relationship between word and image in the practice of contemporary artists embracing mneumonic idioms, and the role of the illustrated Victorian novel, the discussion draws together theoretical perspectives on modernist literature, including work by Forster, Woolf, Eliot and Calvino, as well as critics, Kempson and Ruskin; and the terms and conditions of the animation *langue*, to create the critical concept of the 'subjective correlative' which is then used as a tool for the analysis of literary adaptations.

of course, is at the top, then theatre (count the knighthoods), next literature, with poetry hovering uncertainly in the background. Below that comes film, followed by painting, which few people understand. Below that comes illustration and respectable political cartooning such as that of David Low. Further down comes very *un*respectable cartooning such as Steve Bell's, and then right at the bottom, in the gutter, is the strip cartoon, a medium for children and the simple minded.[1]

Animated film does not even appear in this hierarchy, though ironically it is clearly affiliated to and has embraced all the arts cited here. There is no surprise in this. All the art forms mentioned here do not merely have a longevity and an enduring social presence; they also have a canon of criticism which has sustained their credibility and growth in academic and cultural life.

Work in Animation Studies is still largely an act of recovery and excavation: moving the margins into the mainstream; playing out ideas about the distinctiveness of animation in its own right; mapping its relationship to other arts and other fields and disciplines, and to modes of critical theory drawn from a variety of perspectives. In my view, this essentially remains a struggle to find the language which best describes the technical apparatus of the animated form, its on-screen effects and outcomes, and its deducible meanings. While it is clear that no essentialist or determinist critical language is supportable given the variety and breadth of animated texts, it also remains the case that this is exactly the same for many fields in the arts. Consequently, the critical tools drawn from other disciplines may be just as pertinent as those which seek to define the essentialist specificity of the animated *langue*.[2] I return then to my novelists and poets, and the critics who have engaged with them, to explore two issues. Firstly, to evaluate how novelists and poets relate to the animated form; secondly, to use the theoretical premises of modernist criticism, in the construction of an interrogative approach to animation, which I am terming the 'subjective correlative'.

Novelist John Updike notes:

> I can't remember the moment when I fell in love with cartoons, I was so young. I still have a Donald Duck book, on oilclothy paper in big print format, and remember a smaller cardboard-covered book based on the animated cartoon, *Three Little Pigs* (Walt Disney, USA, 1933). It was the intense stylisation of those images, with their finely brushed outlines and their rounded buttony furniture and their faces so curiously amalgamated of human and animal elements, that drew me in, into a world where I, child though I was, loomed as a king, and where my parents and other grownups were strangers.[3]

Updike's perspective here is revealing, in that he embraces the relationship between the animated cartoon and 'reading', through an illustrated book in which he recognises his own omnipotence as participant and mediator of the text. His later love for cartooning, comic strips and animation of all sorts led to him wanting to be a cartoonist; while that career never materialised, it is clear that this influence informs his literary work, in what Heer calls 'mnemonic lyricism', essentially an art of creating imagery which stimulates memory and recollection.[4] Curiously, this chimes with the view and approach of political cartoonist and animator, Gerald Scarfe, who says:

> Drawing with clarity helps me to recall things. I had to do a caricature of Arnold Schwarzenegger, and so I observed him, making lots of brief sketches to get an immediate sense of him, and those coupled with some photographs I had, enabled me to do the work. The sketches are like brief words in a diary – everything comes back to you because of those few jottings, and you are able to proceed with the final drawings knowing that you have got a sense of the individual as they are and the creative way in which you want to depict them.[5]

This 'mnemonic' tendency – which operates as a tension between words and images, observation and imagination, control and creativity – is fundamental to the ways in which animation might be understood through the filter of literary criticism. Updike, long a champion of the modernist novel and the cartoon, suggests 'I see no intrinsic reason why a doubly talented artist might not arise and create a comic strip novel masterpiece', adding 'one can continue to cartoon, in a way, with words, for whatever crispness and animation my writing has I give some credit to the cartoonist manqué'.[6] Clearly, Art Spiegelman's *Maus* (1986/1991) or Chris Ware's *Jimmy Corrigan, The Smartest Kid On Earth* (2001) speak to his earlier prediction. However, it is Updike's latter observation that is most useful here, as the desire *not* to draw a distinction between the words and their suggested images enables an engagement with the *deconstruction* of a literary text as a pertinent vehicle for the *reconstruction* of a set of critical tools to address the 'animation' imbued both in words and images.

In this respect, I have written elsewhere, for example, about the process of adaptation from literary sources, considering the capacity of animation to embrace the most complex of linguistic and imaginary propositions. Using the Barthesian concepts of 'anchorage' and 'relay' as tools by which to engage with animation's intrinsic capacity to both *literally* translate and *abstract* – a capacity which speaks readily to the tensions cited above – I suggested that 'above all other film-making practices … animation transfigures the literary intention and transubstantiates the reader/viewer's imagination into a visual mode that ultimately speaks louder than the words that inspired it'.[7] In this essay, I wish to extend this point of view, by looking at the pertinence of using modernist literary theory as a tool to address and describe the uniqueness and affect of the animated narrative space, with some reference to a range of British 'literary' animations. The emphasis here though is to trace a theoretical position that allows such analysis.

As I have suggested, novelists and poets have been attracted to the animated form and, in a way similar to Updike, sought to theorise it as a tool to understand their own practice in prose or poetry. For example, Italo Calvino notes:

> If any part of cinema has in fact influenced some of my work, it is the animated cartoon. The world of drawing has always been closer to me than that of photography, and I find that the art of moving cartoon figures about on a static background is not so different from that of telling a story with words arranged in lines on a blank sheet of paper. The animated cartoon has a lot to teach the writer, above all how to define characters and objects with a few strokes. It is a metaphorical and a metonymic art at one and the same time; it is the art of metamorphosis … and of anthropomorphism.[8]

This observation alone recognises the material quality of both words and images as potential 'texts' in their own right above and beyond their apparent meanings and associations. Furthermore, Calvino's point about the minimalism-yet-intensity of suggestion in the construction of characters and objects in the animated form works as a comment about the potential specificity-yet-openness of particular linguistic choices and constructions in literary texts. The point also works as an implied critique of length and density without purpose in the written form. His insight, too, concerning the flux of representational potential in animation is one made in a spirit of recognising the uniqueness of the form, and the desire to echo its structures and outcomes in his own writing. In reading words against images in this way, Calvino, like Updike and Scarfe, recognises the mutuality of the 'text' as a synthesised whole.

There is an obvious early link in this chain, where such interdisciplinary synthesis was made literal in the illustrated novel. Serialisations of novels by Charles Dickens like *Dombey and Son* (1846–48) were accompanied by illustrations by Hablot K. Browne, known as 'Phiz'. These illustrations were in the tradition of satirical caricature and inevitably veered towards the grotesque. Concerned by the ways in which an image could 'fix' a character or situation in the public imagination, Dickens requested seeing a proto- 'model sheet' for Dombey before agreeing to the illustrations. More pertinent, though, was not the specific design of the characters, but the way in which a particular kind of caricature carried with it serio-comic overtones, and a certain degree of sentimentality, sometimes undermining harder-edged critique, or indeed, the particularity of the narrative. Such caricature had done much to introduce new subject matter to the public sphere, and often spoke for the voiceless social classes, but its sheer 'difference' and anti-realist agenda once more undermined its authenticity. Indeed, hardened Dickensians were forthright in their criticism. W.A Fraser, writing in 1906, asserts 'Hablot Browne was not a genius or even a great artist, and George Cruickshank was a mere caricaturist of the bad old school of Gilray and Rowlandson'.[9] Interestingly, it took a novelist, G. K. Chesterton, to recognise how the implications and suggestions of the words could be imbued seamlessly into the illustration, and suggest the possibilities of a new art form:

> There was about Cruickshank's art a kind of cramped energy which is almost the definition of the criminal mind. His drawings have a dark strength: yet he does not only draw morbidly, he draws meanly. In the doubled up figure and frightful eyes of Fagin in a condemned cell there is not only a baseness of subject; there is a kind of baseness in the very technique of it. It is not drawn with the free lines of a free man; it has the half-witted secrecies of a hunted thief. It does not look merely like a picture of Fagin; it looks like a picture by Fagin.[10]

This kind of caricature – the 'low culture' of its time, and now intrinsic to the understanding of contemporary satirical animation – was not seen to have aesthetic legitimacy on its own terms, and supposedly served to undermine the credibility of the literature. Only the 'naturalism' of established history painting and its conventions carried with it the gravitas of properly representing English 'literary' achievement – for example, Joseph Highmore's twelve scenes from Samuel Richardson's novel *Pamela* (1741). The inevitable meeting of these styles – a more naturalised, quasi-photographic, mode of visual abstraction – equally inevitably resulted in the banality of much illustrative imagery, epitomised, for example, in John Millais' frontispiece to Anthony Trollope's *Orley Farm* (1883). Crucial then, though partially accidental, was the intervention of John Tenniel, whose illustrations for Lewis Carroll's *Alice's Adventures in Wonderland* (1865) signalled a specific kind of illustration that proved especially apposite to the symbolic logic and surrealist tendencies at the heart of Carroll's text. As Martin Seymour-Smith has noted:

> Tenniel submitted rather vague drawings to the engraver, and they were fleshed out with the stiff, dead lines of the wood-block procedure at its most automatic. The resulting images are marvellously apt for the spirit of the books – holding Carroll's thing-persons poised between animate and inanimate, and his dream-monsters, like the Jabberwock, between the poles of terror and comedy.[11]

This, then, was the recovery of the synthesis between word and image: illustration which almost made literal the tension between configuration and abstraction; and which played out the 'fantastical' in a fashion that maintained the authenticity of its own 'inner logic', as if indeed this was observed and literal. It was this condition that Russian film-maker and formalist critic Sergei Eisenstein engaged with, apropos of his discussion of Disney's *Silly Symphonies*, as the fullest recognition of a 'plasmatic' condition intrinsic to the animated form.[12] Crucially, though, what such a recognition confirmed was the way in which word and image constructed the specific terms and conditions of an imagined 'world'. Such a world operated purely through its own codes and conventions, and through a fidelity to its own inner logic. This is the fundamental condition of the animated film. This condition also embraces a polarity and a flux between 'seriousness' and 'comic effects' – a tension that I will call 'wit' – which may also be viewed as an endemic aspect of animation informed by this 'plasmatic' state.[13] This aesthetic model invites further definition though, through the way it moves beyond the specificity of how word transmutes to image, and reaches synthesis in a state which may be termed *word as image*.

Novelist E.M. Forster's eulogy to Mickey Mouse, 'Mickey and Minnie'[14] served as a provocateur for one of his most enduring and publicly embraced theories – the notion of 'flat' and 'rounded' characters – drawing on his literal understanding of the cartoon, and the ways that this degree of 'minimalist' suggestion related to the changing construction of character in the modernist novel. He says: 'Flat characters were called "humours" in the 17th century, and are sometimes called types, and sometimes caricatures. In their purest form they are constructed round a single idea or quality: when there is more than one factor in them, we get the beginning of the curve towards the round'.[15] What is important here is not so much the derivation of the concept in Forster's enjoyment and understanding of animation, but the ways in which there was a recognition that the modernist novel wanted to re-configure character, moving away from the literalness of a realist idiom, and into a more experimental mode, predicated on psychological and emotional states and, crucially, mnemonic idioms. e.e.cummings embraced this modernism in George Herriman's 'Krazy Kat' comic strip and Warner Bros. cartoons, suggesting that they subverted the 'monotonous mobility' of live action, and contained 'in a single inimitable sequence, several hundred volumes of psychology'.[16] This sense of experimentation was intrinsically linked to the modernity of the evolving language of cinema. Ironically, but perhaps inevitably, it was particularly related to the already established predominance of the *live action* form; little attention was given to the already marginalised, yet always progressive modernities of the animated film, when the relationship between the modernist novel (indeed, modernity itself) and the condition of animation had more obvious purchase.[17]

This only becomes important, though, because works by James Joyce, for example – with his stream of consciousness technique and his solipsistic 'epiphanies' in characters – were criticised and disparaged because of this connection to both a visual apparatus and a popular form. Commenting at the Soviet Writers' Congress in 1934, Karl Radek brutally critiqued Joyce by saying, 'A Heap of Dung, crawling with worms, photographed by a cinema apparatus through a microscope – such is Joyce's work'.[18] Rather than contradict this point of view, it is important to revise its insight, and suggest that it is this very detailed, 'close-up', constantly moving picture which might lead to the view that specific kinds of modernist literature speak very closely to the imperatives and conditions of animation, bringing together the synthesis implied in illustrated novels, and texts predicated on highly visualised pictorial suggestion. The capacity for metamorphosis (the ability to facilitate the change from one form into another without edit); condensation (the maximum degree of suggestion in the minimum of imagery); anthropomorphism (the imposition of human traits on animals, objects and environments); fabrication (the physical creation of imaginary figures and spaces); penetration (the visualisation of unimaginable psychological/physical/technical 'interiors'); and symbolic association (the use of abstract visual signs and their related meanings) has enabled animators to embrace the minutiae of the 'stream of consciousness' text. *To literally* depict states of consciousness – dreams, visions, fantasies, memories, hallucinations, and mere interiority of a more mundane kind – has allied the process of creative thought with the process of thinking and feeling itself, and further has synthesised word and imagery in the art practice implied by Chesterton as early as 1906. This is perhaps best described by Virginia Woolf's remarks upon the works of Dostoyevsky, which simultaneously, in my view, describe the procedural minutiae by which animation 'records' its process and outcome:

> From the crowd of objects pressing upon our attention we select now this one, now that one, weaving them inconsequently into our thought; the associations of a word perhaps make another loop on the line, from which we spring back again to a different section of our main thought, and the whole process seems both inevitable and perfectly lucid. But if we try to construct our mental processes later, we find that the links between one thought and another submerged. The chain is sunk out of sight and only the leading points emerge to mark the course. Alone among writers Dostoevsky [sic] has the power of reconstructing these most swift and complicated states of mind, of re-thinking the whole train of thought in all its speed, now as it flashes into light, now as it lapses into darkness; for he is able to follow not only the vivid streak of achieved thought but to suggest the dim and populous underworld of the mind's consciousness where desires and impulses are moving blindly beneath the sod …This is the exact opposite of the method adopted, perforce, by most of our novelists. They reproduce all the external appearances – tricks of manner, landscape, dress, and the effect of the hero upon his friends – but very rarely, and only for an instant, penetrate to the tumult of thought which rages within his own mind.[19]

It is this sense of construction and re-construction following the complex dynamics of consciousness that animation can readily embrace, and – in works like Alison DeVere's *The Black Dog* (UK, 1987) or David Anderson's *Deadsy* (UK, 1990) or John Canemaker's *A MidSummer Night's Dream*

(USA, 1983) – can be readily seen; DeVere, from the point of view of a dream; Anderson from the perspective of a corrupted bedtime story narrative-cum-nightmare scenario and Canemaker, from the rich suggestion of the Shakespearian text.[20]

Such a model is enabling in recognising how the literary text can echo the very process and outcome of its own construction in the execution of an animated text, and while in some senses persuasive, it doesn't wholly explain the particular appropriateness of a certain kind of quasi-modernist writing to the animated form. It is now, therefore, that I turn to William Empson, whose work engaged with a core 'truth' in the English language, and its construction in a variety of forms. Empson saw the deep 'ambiguity' at the heart of the English language itself as a result of the accruing propositions that language accommodated in its extensive plenitude of uses. 'Ambiguity' was therefore the condition of the language:

> 'Ambiguity' itself can mean an indecision as to what you mean, an intention to mean several things, a probability that one or the other or both of two things has been meant, and the fact that a statement has several meanings.[21]

He adds:

> English prepositions ... from being used in so many ways and in combination with so many verbs, have acquired not so much a number of meanings as a body of meaning continuous in several dimensions.[22]

This 'body of meaning' and its expression effectively renders the novel (for example, Orwell's *Animal Farm* (1945) or Melville's *Moby Dick* (1851)), the poem (perhaps Plath's *Winter Trees* (1962) or Chaucer's *The Canterbury Tales* (1478) or Motion's *The Lines* (2000)), or the radio text (most notably, *Under Milkwood* (1954)), as multi-dimensional infrastructures. They are *not* readily reducible to a 'narrative', but rather a 'narrative space' – a *world* – which animators and animation engage with at the primary level of aesthetic expression, before the secondary level of 'story'. Empson also stresses that the English language is full of 'dead metaphors', or rather dormant metaphors meaningful in their time and context, which disappear or are forgotten, to be recovered under other terms and conditions.[23] Linked to these metaphors is what John Ruskin called 'the pathetic fallacy' – the imposition of animate characteristics on the inanimate – a particularly pertinent concept in this context. What Ruskin considers a variable poetic device, as useful and incisive as it is without value (in some senses 'a pathetic fallacy'; in another an intuitive and valuable interrogation), becomes a core criterion in the literal enactment of the animator's interpretation of the text.[24] Empson also comments on the importance of what he calls 'the symbolism of sound'; again, hugely apposite in relation to animation, yet more a reminder in his text of the value of sound in the vocal execution or performance of words.[25] This aesthetic primacy insists upon using 'the body of meaning' and the constructive 'ambiguity' as its substantive premise because it is this which is most apposite to the mutability and flux of animation, and *not* the demands of classical narrative.

Sometimes this aesthetic literally and effectively pictorialises its own structure. For example, after the fashion of concrete poetry – a form which illustrates itself by placing the words on the page to visualise the poem's intended meanings and affects – and is described in the words of Guillaume Apollinaire, as 'something syncretic, an object between a poem and a picture'.[26] More significantly, however, in his estimation:

> psychologically, it is of no importance that this visible image be composed of broken language, for the bond between these fragments is no longer the logic of grammar but an ideographic logic, culminating in an order of spatial disposition totally opposed to discursive juxtaposition – it is the opposite of narration.[27]

The concepts of 'ideographic logic' and 'spatial disposition' are especially useful in the sense that they point to the ways that the 'text' – literary or animated – resists the dominant processes of narrativisation and adaptation in live action films. Rather, the primacy of the aesthetic is being used to liberate the ambiguity and multiplicity of the text into a form which can actually accommodate it. The process of mediation between the two requires some further consideration though, because it embraces the view that animation remains the most *auteurist* of media; even in its most collaborative of modes, the animation *auteur* effectively re-presents both the author and the model of authorship in the literary text played out through such an aesthetic formulation.

T.S. Eliot maintained that the most 'achieved' art-form succeeded in distancing itself from its creator, and was an art-work in its own right, seemingly when untainted by the less pure or less successful elements, or one might say, less human aspects of expression. This led to Eliot's theoretical formulation of the 'objective correlative':

> The only way of expressing in the form of art is by finding an 'objective correlative'; in other words, a set of objects, a situation, a chain of events which shall be the formula of that particular emotion; such that when the external facts, which must terminate in sensory experience, are given, the emotion is immediately evoked.[28]

While this may be the premise of particular kinds of prose and poetry, there is some irony in the way that it has been literally constructed within the pre-determined 'emotive' aspects of classical cinema. There is no failure in the 'concept' here, nor in its use in more pertinent literary contexts; but in relation to the way I am suggesting the literary text works in animation, Eliot's position points towards a concept which might be termed the '*subjective* correlative'. This effectively determines how and in what ways, and with what outcomes, the animator 'transmutes' the literary source, by:

- Embracing and re-interpreting textual sources for 'plasmatic potential';
- Enunciating the conflicts and tensions in the serio-comic (simultaneously a tension between the literal and the abstract);
- Literally creating the process of interiority/exteriority as an illustrative outcome;
- Using 'ambiguity' as a mode of continuity and revelation;
- Adopting an 'ideographic logic' (simultaneously, the 'inner logic' of the world);
- Evoking a 'self-figurative' perspective as an aesthetic outcome.

Figs. 1–5: The Lines (Suzie Hanna & Hayley Winter, UK, 2001). A sequence showing how a textual pun from the poem becomes a visual pun in the animated film. Words litera'ly become images. [Images used by permission of Suzie Hanna.]

The 'self-figurative' is especially important as it 'personalises' the material as it translates it while acknowledging the multiple infrastructures and meanings of the source. Consequently, the animator, and animation as a form, intrinsically signals this formation of the 'subjective correlative' because the presence of the *auteur* within the animated text in turn insists upon the recognition of 'subjectivity', and both invokes and provokes the 'correlative'. Such 'subjective correlative' defines a process which views any 'text' – linguistic or visual – as a model of transmutation which must account for: its execution ('plasmaticness'); its wit (the 'serio-comic'); its solipsism (the illustration of the 'interior' creative premise – the space where animation *auteur* and literary author simulate each other); its simultaneity of the literal and the abstract ('ambiguity'); its spatial discourse (the 'ideographic logic'); and its intended affect (the emotional outcome). Consequently, it is my view that only animation can properly facilitate the fullest proposition of the literary text, *and* evidence its defining theoretical legacy within a modernist context. It remains, then, to look at two examples of 'Brit-Lit' animation to illustrate this perspective.

Suzie Hanna and Hayley Winter's adaptation of Andrew Motion's poem, *The Lines*, works well as an example of the 'subjective correlative'. The adaptation is played out by looking for 'plasmatic potential' in the suggestion offered up by 'lines' of poetry; the 'lines' which constitute the 'drawing' and pictorial abstraction of the piece, and the railway 'lines' which are the central context for the poetic narrative. The animation and multi-media forms and the symbolic use of sound serve to respond to the nuanced stimuli of each of the words and phrases. The words of the poem are shown as typographic images, as they are read by Motion himself; his voice ebbing and flowing in the sound mix, sometimes half-heard, sometimes distorted. Letters are used as 'hard unbroken rain'; sound waves are literally represented as a radio playing; and spoken lines temporarily reduced to an uncertain soundscape represent the serpentine flow of heat haze. The enunciative quality of the piece lies in its interpretive wit as the theme of loss and grief is localised in the anxiety of a man (the poet) journeying on the railway to see his terminally ill mother, while recalling a lost history embedded in the construction of the railway he travels on. At one and the same time this is a literal journey and an emotional journey, recorded in the images of moving through the countryside on the train, but also in the extrapolation of a creative solipsism as the images embrace the consciousness of the poet physically typing his poem. The creative act *is* the capturing of emotional experience while being portrayed *as* an emotional experience. The whole film works as a mode of 'interiority'; again, a stream of consciousness embracing sense memory, contemplation and absence. The ambiguity the film calls upon is at once literal and a reinforcement of the psycho-somatic presence of the poet. A line of navigators becomes a graphic pun as a human alligator, but the real ambiguity here is in the lack of distinction between what is felt, imagined or known. The ontological equivalence of the animated imagery is matched and echoed in the onto- logical equivalence of human feeling and expression. This readily fits the ideographic logic of the piece as the typographic text – almost a version of concrete poetry – is rendered freely as a fragmented, sometimes seemingly incoherent form representing the discontinuities of grief, while at the same time maintaining the linear 'inner logic' of the poem through its over- arching structure and purpose. The sense of evocation is powerful; a journey undertaken as a rite of passage, ritual, and release. Consequently, Hanna and Winter succeed in their self-figurative presence as the mediators of empathy and identification, as the poet 'line by line' brings his mother's death to 'lonely hidden villages, red tiled farms, helpless women and timid men'. The synthesis of word and image is complete, speaking both to the completion of the creative enterprise by animator and poet, and the release of meaning to the listener, the viewer, and participant.

Richard Williams' adaptation of Charles Dickens' celebrated Christmas story also works within the parameters of the 'subjective correlative'. Williams' sense of the 'plasmatic potential' in the story is facilitated by two key aspects. First, the opportunity to evoke Victorian London through references to the pages of 'The Illustrated London News', and the carica- turial work of Tenniel, and Leech, whose work he had also successfully used in his animated sequences for Tony Richardson's *The Charge of the Light Brigade* (UK, 1968). Second, through the scale and extent of the 'supernatu- ral' imagery, which lends itself readily to the mutability and liminal aspects of animated metamorphosis. This particularly underpins the enunciative tension between Scrooge's lived and perceived reality – simultaneously literal and abstract, and part of the 'wit' of Dickensian moral didacticism – and Williams' presentation of the story in the tradition of satirical caricature. The story, too, lends itself to a narrative and aesthetic ambiguity, in the sense that the whole episode of Scrooge's visitation by the ghosts of Christmas Past, Present and Future could indeed 'be more of gravy than of grave', if this is a figurative illustration of psychological and emotional transition in the light of guilt, insecurity and fear. The whole narrative could be taking place in his head; his solipsism a stream of consciousness rendered visible as memory, projection and selective thinking. The very 'ambiguity' of Scrooge's status is compounded by the absent presence of the phantoms, who lead him through different spaces in time. The ideographic logic of the film is bound up in its use of metamorphoses of people and places as Scrooge must understand the changes he has experienced and learn to change from the embittered, inhuman soul he has become, and whom he ultimately sees reflected in the spectral presences before him. The 'inner logic' of the piece is bound up with Scrooge's alienation and the depressing series of animated 'snapshots' which show his demise, his gratuitous ambition and greed, and his own sense of loss, constantly juxtaposed with Williams' vigour in the depiction of the human fortitude in the face of adversity, especially in the figures of miners, a lighthouse keeper and sailors as they sing 'God Rest Ye Merry Gentlemen'. Williams' knowledge of caricature recalls Browne and Cruickshank, the great Dickensian illustrators, who were the first to achieve a synthesis with the Dickens text because their visual imaginations, *like Dickens'*, had been shaped by the much deeper heritage and influence of Hogarth. Williams' self-figuration is present in his use of animation to create an aesthetic that embraces all of this tradition, and simultaneously, make claims for the quasi-cartoonal form as a key associative language.

These examples serve to show that the 'subjective correlative' constructed and determined by the symbiosis of literary theory and the animation *langue*, is an effective critical tool in the evaluation of animated literary adaptation, but perhaps most importantly, as a vehicle which demonstrates and advances Updike's desire to 'cartoon in words'. More significantly, they are a demonstration of the specific and particular 'world' of the literary text as it is made animate, not merely in the imagination, but in a visual language most pertinent to its apprehension and exhibition.

Notes

1. Raymond Briggs, 'The Genius of Jimmy', *The Guardian Saturday Review*, (8/12/2001): 9.
2. See John Canemaker (ed.), *Storytelling in Animation*, (Los Angeles, AFI, 1988); Alan Cholodenko, *The Illusion of Life* (Sydney: Power Publications: 1991); Jayne Pilling, (ed.) *A Reader in Animation Studies* (London & Sydney: John Libbey, 1997); Paul Wells, *Understanding Animation* (London & New York : Routledge, 1998); Maureen Furniss, *Art in Motion: Animation Aesthetics* (London : John Libbey, 1998); Esther Leslie, *Hollywood Flatlands : Animation, Critical Theory and the Avant Garde* (London & New York: Verso, 2002).
3. Quoted in Jeet Heer, 'Animated Ambitions', *The Guardian*, (20/3/2004): 34–35
4. Ibid, 2004: 35
5. Interview with the Author, October 2004
6. Quoted in Heer, 2004, op. cit., 2004: 35
7. See Paul Wells, 'Thou Art Translated' : Analysing Animated Adaptation' in Cartmell, Deborah, & Whelehan, Imelda, (eds), *Adaptations* (London & New York: Routledge, 1999): 199–213
8. Italo Calvino, 'Cinema and the Novel: Problems of Narrative', in *The Literature Machine* (London: Secker & Warburg, 1997): 79–80.
9. Quoted in John Charles Olmsted & Jeffrey Egan Welch, *Victorian Novel Illustration: A Selected Checklist, 1900–1976*, (New York & London: Garland Publishing, 1979): xi.
10. Quoted in Ibid, 1979: xii
11. Martin Seymour-Smith, (ed.) *Novels and Novelists*, (London: Windward, 1980): 244.
12. See Jay Leyda (ed.), *Eisenstein on Disney* (London: Methuen, 1988).
13. I explore the concept of 'wit' further in its British context in Paul Wells, *British Animation: A Critical Survey* (London: BFI, 2006): Forthcoming.

14. E.M. Forster 'Mickey and Minnie' in Danny Peary & Gerald Peary (eds), *The American Animated Cartoon* (New York: E.P. Dutton, 1980): 238–240.

15. Quoted in Martin Seymour-Smith, (ed.), op. cit., 1980: 25.

16. E.E. Cummings, 'Miracles and Dreams' in Ibid., 1980: 43–45.

17. See Paul Wells, *Animation and America* (New Brunswick, New Jersey: Rutgers University Press, 2002); Esther Leslie, *Hollywood Flatlands: Animation, Critical Theory and the Avant Garde* (London & New York: Verso, 2002).

18. Quoted in Esther Leslie, *Hollywood Flatlands: Animation, Critical Theory and the Avant Garde* (London & New York: Verso, 2002): 228.

19. Mary Lyon (ed.), Woolf, Virginia, 'More Dostoyevsky', *Books and Portraits* (London: Triad Granada, 1979): 142.

20. See Paul Wells, op. cit., 1999: 210–213; and Laurie E. Osborne, 'Poetry in Motion: Animating Shakespeare', in Lynda E. Boose & Richard Burt, (eds) *Shakespeare the Movie* (London & New York: Routledge, 1997): 103–120.

21. W. Empson *Seven Types of Ambiguity* (London: Peregrine, 1961): 5.

22. Op. cit., 1961: 5.

23. Op. cit., 1961: 25.

24. Op. cit., 1961: 40.

25. Op. cit., 1961: 15.

26. Quoted in Esther Leslie, op. cit., 2002: 23.

27. Ibid: 23.

28. T.S. Eliot 'Hamlet' in Frank Kermode (ed.) *Selected Prose of T.S. Eliot* (London & Boston: Faber & Faber, 1980): 45.

Professor **Paul Wells** is Director of Animation at The Animation Academy in the School of Art and Design at Loughborough University, UK. He has published widely in the field of animation, including 'Animation and America' (Rutgers 2002), 'Animation : Genre and Authorship' (Wallflower 2002) and 'Fundamentals of Animation' (2005). He is currently completing a history of the Halas & Batchelor Studio with Vivien Halas (Forthcoming 2006), and working on a second edition of 'Understanding Animation' (first published,1998), and an Animation scriptwriting project.

Chapter 7

Animated Fathers: Representations of Masculinity in The Simpsons and King of the Hill

Suzanne Williams-Rautiola

As one of the central characters in the longest-running sitcom in the history of American television (*The Simpsons*, created by Matt Groening, 1989 to present), Homer Simpson is an enduring and controversial male figure. The appeal of the show is varied and is in part explained by clever writing, a socially insightful critique delivered by an excellent voice cast, and an animated visualisation that complements the writing with rich detail in its visual jokes. However, it is the complex personalities of the characters that provide the continuing connection to the audience and the fertile ground for its stories.

When one looks at Homer, he seems to have few of the characteristics that would make him a staple in homes week after week. Unlike Hank Hill of *King of the Hill* (created by Michael Judge and Greg Daniels, 1997), Homer is not the 'culturally idealized form of masculine character' termed by sociologists 'hegemonic masculinity'.[1] He is a character with significant

Abstract: In animated television programming where masculine characters are often portrayed as super heroes with easy answers to life's challenges, Homer Simpson and Hank Hill offer two very different and complex animated worlds of masculinity. *The Simpsons* is an example of Roland Barthes' 'writerly text' with a drawing style and open narrative that provide a 'discursive reserve', allowing Homer to recreate himself with each challenge to explore a variety of both positive and negative masculinities. In the 'readerly' text of *King of the Hill* the drawing style and cultural references tie the text to small town Texas where the hegemonic masculine values of Hank Hill meet modern social and ethical dilemmas, often generated by his son, Bobby. The animated text takes the contrasts and dilemmas to their extremes, challenging and interrogating the simplistic answers offered by Hank's hegemonic definition of masculinity.

flaws and appetites who has moments of transcendence that critic Carl Matheson characterises as 'the thirty seconds or so of apparent redemption ... there mainly to allow us to soldier on for twenty-one and a half minutes of maniacal cruelty'.[2] David Arnold argues that although *The Simpsons* could be classified as an example of Roland Barthes' 'writerly' text, it is 'an "irresponsible" text, one rich in associations and connotations and perversely unwilling to have those connotations pinned down'.[3]

This essay takes as its beginning the suggestion by Arnold that *The Simpsons* is a 'writerly' text. However, it goes beyond Arnold's discussion of signifiers to suggest how multiple entrances to the open, animated narrative provide a discursive reserve that offers the viewer an expansive rather than irresponsible vision of masculinity. This depiction of expansive masculinities is contrasted with the readerly text of *King of the Hill* – a narrative that allows the hegemonic ideals of masculinity to be taken to their limits through animation in order to expose both their strengths and weaknesses. In the modern world of animation in which masculine characters (particularly in animation developed for children) are often portrayed as super heroes, Homer Simpson and Hank Hill offer two very different and complex animated worlds of masculinity.

Hank Hill vs. Homer Simpson – hegemonic masculinity meets the buffoon

As is evident in both series, masculinity comes in a variety of forms. Sociologist Michael Kimmel notes:

> We think of manhood as eternal, a timeless essence that resides deep in the heart of every man ... We think of manhood as innate, residing in the particular biological composition of the human male, the result of androgens or the possession of a penis ... I view masculinity as a constantly changing collection of meanings that we construct through our relationships with ourselves, with each other, and with our world.[4]

There are several important issues that recur throughout the literature on masculinity. First, masculinity is a process; gender is created and recreated through an internalisation of relationships and ongoing interaction with the external world. Second, masculinity is a 'collection of meanings' that encompasses such a wide range of characteristics and behaviours that it is arguably more accurate to think of *masculinities* rather than *masculinity*.[5]

While recognising the multiplicity of masculinities, sociologists and communication theorists have also identified several cultural ideals related to masculinity. According to Nick Trujillo, 'hegemonic masculinity' is characterised in the literature as (1) 'physical force and control', (2) 'occupational achievement in an industrialized, capitalistic society', (3) 'patriarchy', which includes being 'breadwinners', 'family protectors', and 'strong father figures', (4) 'frontiersmanship', including the daring and romance of the past and the outdoorsman of today, and (5) 'heterosexuality'.[6] However, the television representation of the working class American father is often very different. Richard Butsch writes, '[Working class fathers] are dumb, immature, irresponsible or lacking in common sense ... [They are] typically well-intentioned, even lovable, but no one to respect or emulate'.[7]

As a working-class father, Hank Hill embodies all of the identified hegemonic ideals of masculinity with few of the buffoonish characteristics described by Butsch. Although Hank does not have a stereotypically muscular body, he is a man who is defined by his physical abilities, often referring to his high school prowess as a member of the football team and introducing his abusive football coach as a role model for his son, Bobby ('Three Coaches and a Bobby'). Further, his occupation is of paramount importance to Hank. When he introduces himself, he always notes in a somewhat breathy, awe-filled voice that he sells 'propane and propane accessories'. The importance he places on work can be found in the number of times that he attempts to interest Bobby in the propane business ('Snow Job', 'Rodeo Days', and 'Meet the Propaniacs') and his attempts to get Bobby and his niece, Luanne, jobs ('The Buck Stops Here', 'Life in the Fast Lane, Bobby's Saga', and 'Jon Vitti Presents: "Return to La Grunta"'). Although his wife, Peggy, works as a substitute teacher, he is the family protector and breadwinner, eagerly encouraging Peggy to quit her job ('Peggy's Turtle Song'). In addition, he is a strong father to his son, as even his combative father, Cotton, and antagonistic neighbour, Kahn Souphanousinphone, have to agree ('Next of Shin' and 'Aisle 8'). Hank is an accomplished outdoorsman, taking Bobby and his friends camping ('The Order of the Straight Arrow') and Bobby hunting ('Good Hill Hunting'). Thoroughly heterosexual, Hank often worries that Bobby is too effeminate, implying that he fears Bobby is gay ('Bobby Goes Nuts', 'Rodeo Days' and 'Sleight of Hank').

Homer Simpson has few of the characteristics of 'hegemonic masculinity' and all of the buffoonish characteristics enumerated by Butsch. An early critic of *The Simpsons*, Butsch writes, 'While Bart may at first appear refreshingly antiauthoritarian, the contrasting buffoonery of his father repeats an insidious anti-working-class theme ... In [*Good Times, All in the Family, The Life of Riley*, and *I Remember Mama*] the children outdistance the blue-collar father. At best, father is benign but inferior, at worst, an embarrassment'.[8] Homer is overweight because of his voracious appetite for fattening food and Duff beer. Far from being physically forceful, he is generally found at home on the couch watching television or seated on a barstool at Moe's Tavern. Further, occupational achievement is not a motivating force for Homer. Although he does not want to lose his job as a safety inspector for the nuclear power plant, he is always pictured as sleeping, eating doughnuts, or loafing on the job – a fact that is regularly observed by his boss, C. Montgomery Burns. Although Homer is the breadwinner and at times the family protector, he cannot be described as a strong father figure. Homer is at a loss to know what to do when wife Marge asks him to take care of their infant daughter, Maggie ('Homer Alone'). He is so self-centered that his eight-year-old daughter, Lisa, has to find ways to relate to him, rather than vice versa ('Lisa the Greek'). And, when he buys a cheap trampoline, Lisa remarks, 'Dad, this one gesture almost makes up for all those years of shaky fathering' ('Bart's Inner Child'). The only hegemonic characteristic he possesses is heterosexuality, regularly ending the show in bed with Marge.

In contrast he possesses all of the buffoonish characteristics observed by Butsch. Homer is not very bright and is often corrected by Lisa or Bart when he makes errors. Although he is 'street wise' and often lucky in his decisions, the only time Homer becomes truly intelligent is after a crayon that is up his nose and lodged in his brain is removed. While his new-found intelligence allows him to communicate meaningfully for the first time with his highly intelligent daughter Lisa, it negatively affects most of his other relationships. Eventually he chooses to have the crayon reinserted into his brain to go back to being dumb again ('HOMR'). His immature behaviour not only gets him into trouble with his family (for example, when he gets drunk and insults their friends at a party in 'The War of the Simpsons'), but his irresponsibility also at times places his family in great jeopardy (such as when he abandons childcare duties to attempt to win a prize offered by a radio station, leaving Bart and Milhouse, who get into trouble in 'The Parent Rap').

Dismissing Homer as another example of buffoonish masculinity or Hank Hill as another example of hegemonic masculinity, however, does not adequately explain the impact of these characters or their role in making their primetime animated programs successful. Both series offer the audience rich expressions of masculinity coupled with striking contradictions. In *The Simpsons*, Homer recreates himself each episode exploring the plurality of masculinities, while the hegemonic masculinity of Hank is interrogated by a changing society and by his son.

Homer Simpson: a multiplicity of masculinities in a writerly text

Homer escapes easy categorisation through what Roland Barthes has characterised as a writerly text. For Barthes 'the goal of literary work (of literature as work) is to make the reader no longer a consumer, but a producer of the text ... the writerly text is *ourselves writing*, before the infinite play of the world'. The model of the writerly text is 'a productive (and no longer a representative) one'.[9] The writerly text is juxtaposed against what Barthes calls a readerly text. He states, 'As we might expect, the readerly is controlled by the principle of non-contradiction, by multiplying solidarities, by stressing at every opportunity the *compatible* nature of circumstances, by attaching narrated events together with a kind of logical "paste"'.[10] According to Kaja Silverman, 'the readerly approach stresses all of the values implicit in the paradigmatic classic text – unity, realism, and transparency'.[11]

In contrast, John Fiske characterises the writerly text as 'multiple and full of contradictions; it foregrounds its own nature as discourse and resists coherence or unity'.[12] According to Barthes, the ideal writerly text is made of networks which

> are many and interact, without any one of them being able to surpass the rest; this text is a galaxy of signifiers, not a structure of signifieds; it has no beginning; it is reversible; we gain access to it by several entrances, none of which can be authoritatively declared to be the main one ... the systems of meaning can take over this absolutely plural text, but their number is never closed ... it is not a question of conceding some meanings, of magnanimously acknowledging that each one has its share of truth; it is a question, against all in-difference, of asserting the very existence of plurality.[13]

Since the segmentation of the television text by commercials works to disrupt textual unity and foregrounds its inherent discourse, Fiske suggests that television could be writerly, except for the fact that the writerly texts that Barthes was addressing were typically avant-garde with a minority appeal. Fiske wishes to call the television text 'producerly' because it 'combines the televisual characteristics of a writerly text with the easy accessibility of the readerly'.[14]

If the model for a writerly text is one that is productive and encourages the audience to share in its creation, then the writerly text is not necessarily avant-garde for a minority audience. In *The Pleasure of the Text*, Barthes notes,

> There are those who want a text ... without a shadow, without 'the dominant ideology'; but this is to want a text without fecundity, without productivity, a sterile text ... The text needs its shadow: this shadow is *a bit* of ideology, *a bit* of representation, *a bit* of subject: ghosts, pockets, traces, necessary clouds: subversion must produce its own chiaroscuro.[15]

Thus, a text that is productive and by extension writerly can be connected to the dominant ideology and representation through its galaxy of signifiers and multilevel narrative.

Also, as noted by Alex Ben Block, *The Simpsons* was created to be 'alternative' television, something very different from the mainstream in order to attract young, urban viewers to the fledgling FOX network.[16] The most noticeable of the differences was the development of sitcom content in animated form, what Jason Mittell calls 'genre mixing'.[17] When it first aired, critics contrasted *The Simpsons* with sitcom ancestors such as *Father Knows Best* because of its 'anti-family' stance and compared it to other anti-family sitcoms of the early 1990s (such as *Married ... with Children* or *Roseanne*).[18] As noted by Vincent Brook, '*The Simpsons* ... is both parody and homage. It preserves the blue-collar setting of *The Flintstones* and the family constellations are similar, but the "warmedy" *Flintstone* world is turned on its ear'.[19] Critics also lauded its reinvigoration of the 'cartoon' genre, although as noted by Mittell 'the cartoon's pejorative qualities and low cultural status are never far from the surface'.[20] As noted by Paul Wells:

> The very language of comedy, like animation, is an intrinsically alternative one, speaking to a revisionist engagement with the 'taken-for-granted'. In the American context, it is especially the case that animation in all its forms, not merely those played for laughs, has served to operate as a distorting and re-positioning parallel genre both to established live-action film and television texts (and their predominantly conservative codes of representation), but more importantly, to society in general.[21]

Thus, *The Simpsons* was immediately recognised as different from other television comedies as the first primetime animated sitcom since *The Flintstones* and utilised the subversive qualities of animation to challenge the 'taken-for-granted' representation of the family and masculinity to capture a young audience.

In discussing *The Simpsons* as a writerly text, Arnold notes, '*The Simpsons* gets its energy precisely from the conflict between our recognition of the signifiers as highly mediated, as un-realistic, and our understanding that they nonetheless resemble a reality we recognize'.[22] *The Simpsons* is populated with an idealised, intact family, including father (Homer), mother (Marge), and two-and-a-half children – Bart, Lisa, and Maggie (who is an infant). While the Simpson family is human in its appearance, the show's creator Matt Groening also employs signifiers in the characters' animated design to bring to the forefront their constructed nature. Their skin is bright yellow, because as Groening has stated, he wants the viewers to think that their television needs adjusting when watching the show.[23] In addition, some of their features are more symbolic than realistic – particularly their eyes which are bulging, round orbs and the representations of their heads and hair. For example the hair on Homer's oversized head is represented by only a few lines. Further, the characters have three fingers and a thumb – an animation standard for human and anthropomorphic characters. Finally, most of the characters on *The Simpsons* are stylistically similar, with little to no chin, a recessed lower jaw, and a large protruding upper lip. Thus, while the characters are definitely human, they resist easy connections to real world people, bringing to the forefront their constructed nature and establishing a world of characters that is identifiable but set apart from the real and from other cartoon or live action worlds.

Although the signifiers are unrealistic, simplified, and representative, the text develops what Robert Ferguson calls a large 'discursive reserve' through an open setting, large cast of characters, and intertextual connections. In writing about representations of race, Ferguson has drawn upon the work of Teun Van Dijk, who uses the pyramid as a metaphor for the way complex issues are represented in the press. Complex issues such as those involving race and gender, are often represented by abbreviated means such as captions or headlines (the tip of the pyramid), 'discursive reserve' remaining below the surface (the base of the pyramid), providing a galaxy of signifiers and additional entrances to the text.[24]

The setting for *The Simpsons* has generated fan debate over the long run of the show, because it is also more open than is that of *King of the Hill*. The Simpsons inhabit the town of Springfield; however, the exact state in which the town is located is never identified. Springfield was the setting of the 1950s sitcom *Father Knows Best*; however, there are numerous cities and towns named Springfield throughout the United States. Also, the geographical references that might identify the location of the town are contradictory. Thus, though the physical space is suggestive of 'small-town America', where people know each other and kids freely move about the town, *The Simpsons* is not tied to a cultural tradition in a particular area of the country. Also, as reported by critic Tom Shales, Executive Producer James L. Brooks has exploited the flexibility of the animated form to change locations as well as to add characters (which for a live-action sitcom is very costly).[25] Thus, the Simpson family has packed up and moved to a new locale on numerous occasions only to return to Springfield by the next episode.

Discursive reserve is also developed by numerous references to other texts (films, television shows, books, cartoons, personalities, etc.), making *The Simpsons* what many critics define as a postmodern text. The narrative space shifts from such widely divergent connections as Amy Tan's *Joy Luck Club* to singer Michael Jackson to the movie *Psycho*. As noted by Matthew Henry, *The Simpsons* 'operates like a "mobile game of trivia" for its adult fans'.[26] There is so much textual complexity that recording the show in order to watch it again or to catch cultural references that go by too quickly has been part of the pleasure in watching from the beginning.[27] These references serve not only to pluralise the narrative but also to allow Homer Simpson to occupy a much more pluralistic stance within the text than does Hank Hill.

Unlike Hank and the Marketplace Man described by Kimmel, who derives his identity from success in the capitalist marketplace – 'a male-only world in which he pits himself against other men'[28] – Homer does not define himself by his job as a safety inspector at the nuclear power plant. He rarely refers to his work life, other than plotting to get out of work. In addition to his primary job, Homer has often inexplicably taken on other full-time jobs with no mention of being fired from or quitting his job at the power plant, and he returns to work at the power plant without formally being rehired. Some of the different jobs that Homer has had over the years include voice talent in a cartoon ('The Itchy and Scratchy and Poochie Show'), head of a security company ('Poppa's Got a Brand New Badge'), a music promoter ('Colonel Homer'), a Hollywood producer ('Beyond Blunderdome'), and many more. Through the writerly text, Homer continually reinvents himself through his work.

While males still maintain the greatest share of power in American society, according to Kimmel they do not feel powerful. He notes that they are bossed around at work, but they also feel bossed around at home.[29] Although by most standards Homer is not powerful, he does not wait for others to empower him nor does he rely on traditional cultural values. When motivated, his responses to the problems of life are inventive and action-oriented. In 'Homer the Vigilante', he states, 'We don't need a thinker, we need a doer. Someone who will act without thinking'. For example, Homer leads his neighbours in a revolt against the phone company ('A Tale of Two Springfields'), helps to form a neighbourhood security force when burglary is rampant in Springfield ('Homer, the Vigilante'), and is elected President of the union when he stands up to Mr Burns who wants to cut their dental plan ('Last Exit to Springfield').

Further, sociologist Vicki Nobel notes that when asked what they feared most, men reported that their greatest fear was being laughed at.[30] Homer spends little time worrying about what others think and much of the humour in the show results from Homer's running into trouble because he also spends little time planning his actions or choosing his words. Whether from lack of social awareness or stupidity, he generally speaks his mind and often other characters respond positively to his honesty. For example, when Homer writes a scathing review of Mel Gibson's film on an audience survey card, Gibson hires Homer to help correct the problems he has identified with the film. Unfortunately, the movie that results from the Simpson-Gibson collaboration is panned by the premiere audience. Undaunted, Homer optimistically suggests other films that they might do together, before Gibson pushes him out the door ('Beyond Blunderdome').

Homer's optimism generally does not follow from past success. Unlike Hank Hill, who is the family protector and generally saves his family and neighbours from their follies, most of Homer's schemes turn out disastrously as did the Gibson-Simpson movie. For example, Homer discovers he has a half brother, Herb, who owns an automobile manufacturing plant that is losing market share to the Japanese. When they meet, Homer makes some design suggestions, and Herb hires him to design a new car for the common man. Homer's outlandish ideas result in a car that costs $82,000, causing Herb to declare bankruptcy and lose his business, home, and all his possessions. Lisa remarks, 'His life was an unbridled success until he found out he was a Simpson'. When told the news, Homer's dad adds, 'I knew you'd blow it'. However, Homer is only momentarily slowed by this failure and immediately brightens when Bart tells him that he thought his car was 'really cool' ('Oh, Brother, Where Art Thou?').

In *The Simpsons*, animation is also utilised to tap into the discursive reserve of emotional expression that would be unacceptable in a live-action sitcom. Communication theorist Muriel Cantor notes that no sitcom on television would portray child abuse.[31] She is correct in that no *live-action* sitcom does; however, when Homer is frustrated, he strangles Bart. This reaches its zenith in 'I'm Furious Yellow' as the frequency and intensity of Homer's emotional outbursts increases each time Bart goads him into getting angry. Why is it that a viewer might accept such an immoral action and even consider it humorous? One could read Homer's strangling Bart as child abuse and object to the family dynamics depicted on the show (and some do).[32] However, one might see this action as symbolic of parents' extreme inner frustrations with their children, and this interpretation is encouraged because the cartoony actions of the Simpsons are not very different from the slapstick actions of the animated characters of the past.

Brian Ott notes, 'since he has no real history, Homer can be radically multiple and contradictory ... . No matter how traumatic his experiences, Homer never learns anything, in part, because he is not a distinct, thinking subject ... and exemplifies a radical postmodern multiplicity – [quoting James M. Glass] "an extreme rejection of boundary, stability, historicity, and any concept of cohesive self".'[33] Whereas Ott suggests that this results in a decentered subject that is 'simply another product of the culture industry', this essay argues that as a writerly text, it opens the doors to a variety of entrances to masculinity without any one authoritatively being the main one.

What keeps the text from being lost in endless pluralities is what Mittell calls the 'paradox of animated realism'. While *The Simpsons* is representative in its depiction of characters and setting, Mittell argues that when compared to *The Cosby Show*, critics have found it to be more real.[34] Critic Laurel Shaper Walters quotes a street vendor who sells boot-legged Bart T-shirts as saying, '*Cosby* is the way it is supposed to be. *The Simpsons* is the way it really is – that's life'.[35] As noted by critic Joanna Elm, 'The lives of the

Conners and Bundys and Simpsons reflect the grimmer realities facing many families today. Family members often find themselves at the mercy of stronger, more powerful figures: like the bully who makes Bart's life miserable or the boss at the nuclear plant who decides on a whim to do away with the annual Christmas bonus'.[36] She notes that this is particularly true as the gap widens between rich and poor, citing Ella Taylor, author of *Prime-Time Families*, who states '*The Simpsons* goes further in articulating these difficulties than *Roseanne*. But because it's a cartoon it's safer. It seems less real.'[37]

As specialised, technical knowledge becomes the key to unlock the American Dream, Homer worries briefly that he is falling behind. He says, 'The saddest day of my life was when I realised I could beat my dad at most things, and Bart experienced that at the age of four' ('Moaning Lisa'). Further, he worries about whether his family is normal and even pawns their beloved TV in order to pay for counselling for them ('There's No Disgrace Like Home'). Thus, Homer's frustrations with his children, his inability to keep up with the changes in everyday life, his desire to have and give his family the advantages of life such as cable TV even if he has to get it illegally ('Homer Vs. Lisa and the 8th Commandment'), and his worries over the over the normalcy of his family provide the 'shadow of ideology' that links *The Simpsons* to their audience.

In addition to articulating some of the concerns of the audience, Homer is a likable character. Philosopher Raja Halwani believes that the best assessment of Homer is articulated by Marge in 'Scenes from the Class Struggle in Springfield' in which she states that the quality she likes most about Homer is his 'in-your-face humanity'. Halwani does not want to claim that Homer is an admirable person, only that he possesses an ethically admirable trait.

> Homer's love of life stands out as an important quality *especially* in our age, an age in which political correctness, over-politeness, lack of willingness to judge others, inflated obsession with physical health, and pessimism about what is good and enjoyable about life reign more or less supreme.[38]

Homer's thoughtless pursuit of the American dream has resulted in a great deal of criticism. Critic Harry Waters accuses the show of shamelessly pandering 'to a kid's-eye view of the world: parents dispense dopey advice, school is a drag and happiness can be attained only by subverting the system'.[39] One could view Homer as an attractive character because he does not spend a great deal of time obsessing (as does Hank Hill) over what others think or the negative things that happen in his life. Waters quotes Matt Groening as observing, 'The world kicks Homer in the ass but he doesn't resent it'.[40] However, some viewers see him as irresponsible and self-centred.[41] For Brook the 'true subversive potential' resides in the show's 'open-ended disruption', part of which he identifies as the 'punishment not fitting the crime' – for example Homer on numerous occasions trying to cheat the system only to be caught, and let off with a 'slap on the wrist' ('Bart Gets Hit by a Car').[42]

Theorists Michael Billig et al suggest that ideology is not a unified system of beliefs that operates in a linear fashion without contradiction nor do they view individuals as unthinking followers of ideological schemata. They suggest that a better way of conceptualising ideology is to stress its 'dilemmatic nature'.

> By assuming that there are contrary themes, a different image of the thinker can emerge. The person is not necessarily pushed into an unthinking obedience, in which conformity to ritual has replaced deliberation. Ideology may produce such conformity, but it can also provide the dilemmatic elements which enable deliberation to occur.[43]

As noted by Ferguson, 'This is an important conceptualisation because it suggests that audiences have to negotiate meaning in the face of often contradictory evidence or contradictory personal perceptions of a given situation'.[44] And, as Paul Wells suggests,

> Fundamentally ... animation in the United States has been characterized by a desire to express *difference* and otherness ... it has engaged with the contradictory conditions of American mores, reflected the anxieties within American culture, and offered insight into the mytho-political, and, indeed, mytho-poetic zeitgeist of a nation.[45]

Homer is emblematic of the process through which gender is created in an ongoing interaction with the external world that at times results in contradictions. Homer confronts many of the issues that sociologists have found modern males face – 'the reflected anxieties within the American culture'[46] – and he *acts* to overcome them. In the plural writerly text that is developed through the character of Homer, various masculinities are explored – both the good and the bad. He is the caring father, the angry father, the self-centred father, the anxious father. He is the thoughtless husband, and the tender, loving husband. He is the slovenly employee and the tireless entrepreneur. Through multiple entrances to the text the audience is introduced to the possible masculinities and left to discover what we will make of them. The evidence that such dilemmatic assessment occurs was reported by Brook. In a study of one episode ('Lisa the Iconoclast') he found that while participants in the study agreed on '*what* happened', there was marked disagreement in '*why* it happened and what should *be made* of it'.[47]

Hank Hill: interrogating hegemonic masculinity through a readerly text

Although *The Simpsons* has been called realistic in its depiction of the issues and contradictions surrounding the modern family, *King of the* Hill offers a realism that is very different. In its structure, it is an example of Barthes' readerly text as we see only an occasional example of contradiction within the character of Hank. Instead the narrative is controlled by 'multiplying solidarities' with events which are linked together 'with a kind of logical "paste"'.[48]

Unlike *The Simpsons*, the entry into the text is well defined. *King of the Hill* has been described by co-creator Mike Judge as 'very simple and realistic, not showing off'.[49] The characters are much closer to a human look and proportion, with few cartoony characteristics to separate them from live-action actors (including having all their fingers). Their eyes are normal size and shape for their faces, and their body proportions and hair styles are easily identifiable as characteristics that could be duplicated with live actors. The conventions of animation add little to the characterisation of the Hill family or to Hank. Also, in the development of the setting and the narrative, *King of the Hill* is closer to live-action sitcoms than the more symbolic world developed in *The Simpsons*. In *King of the Hill* what executive producers Mike Judge and Greg Daniels have created is, in the experience of this Texas native, a fairly realistic depiction of life in a Texas town which they call Arlen. Arlen is not clearly established as a suburban part of the Dallas Metroplex as its purported inspiration Garland, Texas; however, its tie to small-town Texan culture is unmistakable with numerous references to Texas traditions – for example the yearly game between the University of Texas at Austin and University of Oklahoma – its use of colloquial phrases by Hank and the other characters, and numerous connections to Texas locations.

As with the Simpsons, the Hills are a nuclear family and include father (Hank), mother (Peggy), and son (Bobby) – although their niece (Luanne) lives with them at varying times throughout the series. Both Homer and Hank have extended families that appear throughout the show, jobs that they have held for the duration of the show, and male friends with whom they regularly meet to drink beer. However, this is where the structural similarities end. According to Daniels, 'The idea of the show is that common-sense Americans are smarter than people who live on the coasts'.[50] Thus, a contrast is established between a clearly defined, working-class man from Texas and the forces of change within the society – chief of which are educated liberals from the coasts.

Much of the humour in *King of the Hill* comes from Hank Hill's struggle to adjust to modern American life. Hank clings to traditional, hegemonic male values and traits identified by Trujillo, including resistance to all things deemed to be feminine, highlighting his clear definitions of gender based upon hegemonic values. Hank is supremely confident in his knowledge of and ability to use tools, regularly fixing his son's and his friends' mistakes ('The Buck Stops Here' and 'A Firefighting We Will Go'). He is a man who loves his family, friends, home, job, lawn, and Lady Bird, his hunting dog, however not necessarily in that order. Always in control of himself, Hank is only flustered when he attempts to deal with his emotions (such as telling his son that he loves him). Hank is a modest man, who is easily embarrassed by his niece's presence in his home (Pilot Episode) and by any medical condition that marks him as different – his narrow urethra ('Hank's Unmentionable Problem'), low sperm count ('Next of Shin'), or back trouble ('Hank's Back Story'). Hank so completely identifies himself with his job as a propane salesman that he believes it is sacrilege to use anything else but propane in his home and in his barbeque pit. His devotion to the company is so strong that when the owner, Buck Strickland, has a heart attack and chooses MBA-educated Lloyd Vickers to run the company, while relegating Hank to feed the dogs, he becomes depressed. He is further disillusioned when he finds out that Mr. Strickland uses electricity instead of propane in his home. While one can understand his frustration at being passed over in favour of a younger, less experienced employee; however, instead of seizing other opportunities, a very traditional answer comes to Hank in a small country store – go back to basics and deliver 'service with a smile'. Hank returns to work with a smile and finds that Vickers has so enraged the drivers with his business methods that they have all walked off the job. Hank saves their customers from freezing and the company from going bankrupt as he figures out a way to deliver the propane to those who need it ('Snow Job').

On the rare occasions when Hank acts outside of hegemonic values, his actions are often in service to a higher value. For example, when Hank's friend, Bill Dauterive, who is distraught over the break-up of his marriage to Lenore, arrives at a party wearing women's clothing, in order to save his friend from physical harm from the other men at the party Hank also dons a dress. By pretending to be Lenore, Hank is able to bring Bill back to reality ('Pretty, Pretty Dresses').

Within the readerly text with its multiplying solidarities, according to Barthes, the reader is 'left with no more than the poor freedom either to accept or reject the text: reading is nothing more than a referendum'.[51] This might be true for *King of the Hill* if it were not for the other males on the show. His three friends – Dale Gribble, the paranoid, incompetent exterminator; Bill Dauterive, the overweight, naïve Armed Forces barber; and Boomhauer the self-absorbed ladies' man – combine to represent Butsch's male buffoon. Since he is surrounded by incompetence, Hank's careful attention to detail and slow methodical actions seem very prudent. And, indeed, in the Hill's world Hank's emotional development is a definite improvement over that of his father, Cotton, who is emotionally abusive and distant from his second wife, Didi, and from other members of his family, including his son, Hank. Further, the series' critique of the hyper-educated, condescending liberal while at times strident strikes a chord. As noted by critic Kevin Michael Grace, '*King of the Hill* provokes a shock of recognition – it was only two generations ago that most American men were just like Hank. After four decades of unrelieved "progress", who would argue that our "sophistication" is healthier than Hank's prudery?'[52]

What allows this readerly text to interrogate hegemonic masculinity is Bobby's exploration of non-traditional forms of masculinity. Bobby who is in middle school is different from Hank in almost every way. He is overweight but is unwilling to curb his appetite. His ambition is to be an entertainer, an occupation to which Hank feels no 'real man' should aspire. Undeterred, Bobby practices magic, pursues comedy, etc., while Hank gets him part-time jobs as a caddy at the local country club ('The Buck Stops Here') and a soda vendor at the racetrack ('Life in the Fast Lane, Bobby's Saga'). While Hank often relives the glory days of his football career, Bobby has little interest in sports. Although Hank loves Bobby, it is clear that Hank views Bobby's overweight physique, his desire to be an entertainer, and his lack of ability at sports as failures. Although Homer is an experimenter and a doer without regard for the consequences, Hank is driven and limited by hegemonic concerns and his fear of what others will think. Hank so often worries about Bobby's feminine characteristics that one might be tempted to read him as homophobic. However, he does not appear upset when he and Dale Gribble discover that Dale's father is gay ('My Own Private Rodeo'). There is no overt homophobia, rather Bobby's interest in what Hank deems to be feminine is a threat to Hank's definition of masculinity.

The Hills are hard working, God-fearing, church-going people, who live by most of the moral guidelines that Homer eschews. It is Hank's steadfast avowal of these platitudes in the face of a changing society and the inability of these rules to provide his son, Bobby, an adequate guide by which to live that marks much of the humour in the show and begins to open the text. Most of the time, one can see the error of these simplistic platitudes, because the dogmatic adherence to traditional principles rarely turns out as positively for Hank as it did for Jim Anderson in *Father Knows Best*, and Hank is forced to adjust. Thus, when Bobby gets a job selling soft drinks at the racetrack, Hank urges him to give it 110%. Hank is so proud that his son is following his advice that he fails to detect the abuse by Bobby's boss until Bobby's life is placed in jeopardy ('Life in the Fast Lane, Bobby's Saga').

The effect of *King of the Hill* is often to walk a fine line between comedy and tragedy. For example, as Bobby tries to give 110%, he is urged by his boss to cross a racetrack to deliver some sodas while the race is in progress. While it would be very uncomfortable for an audience to see a real child in that situation, animation allows the multiplying solidarities to continue to their extreme conclusion, so that the true consequences of the mindless adherence to cultural platitudes are explored.

Finally, *King of the Hill* also unflinchingly explores the dilemmatic nature of some of the modern issues. A good example is in the episode entitled 'Husky Bobby'. Although Bobby does not control his eating, he also does not feel good about his body until Peggy discovers a new store that carries clothes for 'husky' children. Bobby is so delighted that he cannot contain himself, wearing the clothes with such flair that the store's owner asks him to be a model in the store's next advertisement. Bobby is thrilled, gets an agent, rises to the top as a model, and is invited to participate in a fashion show at a local mall. However, Hank is appalled. Although he does not tell anyone, his major objection arises from the fact that in his youth, Hank made fun of overweight kids. He also views modelling as a feminine activity, particularly when he goes to a photo session in which the photographer is depicted as stereotypically and flamboyantly gay. Bobby defies Hank and goes to the show, but as Hank fears, the show is disrupted by a gang of youths who throw food at the kids on stage. Hank arrives on the scene, and 'rescues' Bobby by carrying him to safety from the stage. So while Bobby reaches out toward new definitions of masculinity and self-worth, this is contrasted to Hank's narrow outlook, which prevails in the end. Rather than continue to resist Hank's narrow-minded assessment of the situation, Bobby responds by thanking him, stating that he realises that Hank was right all along. While one might be disappointed with this hegemonic conclusion and be tempted to evaluate this as the multiplying solidarities of the readerly text, the narrative offers another explanation. Hank is acting in part from an understanding of his own prejudices. He understands his son's tormentors and perhaps may still understand their point of view, because the reality is that his son is overweight. Hank saves the day, and Bobby is grateful; however, the dilemma is not neatly solved. It is up to the audience to decide 'what it means'.

Conclusion

Barthes suggests:

> [The text] produces, in me, the best pleasure if it manages to make itself heard indirectly; if, reading it, I am led to look up often, to listen to something else. In the text of pleasure, the opposing forces are no longer repressed but in a state of becoming: nothing is really antagonistic, everything is plural.[53]

Both shows invite the audience to interact with the text but in very different ways.

While *The Simpsons* maintains a shadow of the dominant ideology in the traditional structure of the nuclear family, it discards most of the traditional ideals of the how members of a family should relate to each other, other than to care about one another. It opens a space where a father's fears are articulated without easy, simplistic, or always appealing answers but provides ambiguous role models, opening moral and ethical dilemmas that the audience must then negotiate. What Homer unequivocally demonstrates is an enjoyment of life and an enthusiasm for what he decides to do however difficult it might be to predict what he will do. In *The Simpsons'* open animated world, we find possibilities for masculinities that are far different from the limitations of live-action sitcoms, and the enjoyment is seeing how Homer will react to and expand these possibilities week to week.

With *King of the Hill* we return to the idyllic family of the 1950s only to find that the simplistic answers that did not work back then truly do not work in the new millennium. Through the 'multiplying solidarities' of Hank's work ethic, his religious faith, his articulated value structure about what it is to be a man, and his confrontation with the forces of change in modern life, the audience sees the limitations of hegemonic ideology. However, in the animated world of *King of the Hill*, contrasts can be sharply drawn and taken to their extreme, so that the viewer moves beyond a simple referendum to consider some of the dilemmas we all face in modern life.

Notes

1. R.W. Connell, 'An Iron Man: The Body and Some Contradictions of Hegemonic Masculinity', in Michael A. Messner and Don F. Sabo (eds) *Sport, Men and the Gender Order: Critical Feminist Perspectives* (Champaign, IL: Human Kinetics, 1990): 83–95.

2. Carl Matheson, '*The Simpsons*, Hyper-Irony, and the Meaning of Life', in William Irwin, Mark T. Conard, and Aeon J. Skoble (eds) *The Simpsons and Philosophy: The D'oh! of Homer* (Chicago, IL: Open Court, 2001): 124.

3. David L.G. Arnold, '"And the Rest Writes Itself": Roland Barthes watches *The Simpsons*', in William Irwin, Mark T. Conard, and Aeon J. Skoble (eds) *The Simpsons and Philosophy: The D'oh! of Homer* (Chicago, IL: Open Court, 2001): 264.

4. Michael S. Kimmel, 'Masculinity as Homophobia: Fear, Shame, Silence in the Construction of Gender Identity', in Harry Brod and Michael Kaufman (eds) *Theorizing Masculinities* (Thousand Oaks, CA: Sage, 1994): 119–121.

5. See Michael Kaufman, ' Men, Feminism, and Men's Contradictory Experiences of Power' and Jeff Hearn, and David L. Collinson, 'Theorizing Unities and Differences between Men and between Masculinities', in Harry Brod and Michael Kaufman (eds) *Theorizing Masculinities* (Thousand Oaks, CA: Sage, 1994) and Diana Saco, 'Masculinity as Signs: Poststructuralist Feminist Approaches to the Study of Gender', in Steve Craig (ed.) *Men, Masculinity, and the Media* (Newbury Park, CA: Sage Publications, 1992): 23–39.

6. Nick Trujillo, 'Hegemonic Masculinity on the Mound: Media Representations of Nolan Ryan

and American Sports Culture', *Critical Studies in Mass Communication* 8, 3 (September, 1991): 291–292.

7. Richard Butsch, 'Ralph, Fred, Archie and Homer: Why Television Keeps Recreating the White Male Working-Class Buffoon', in Gail Dines and Jean M. Humez (eds) *Gender, Race and Class in Media* (Thousand Oaks, CA: Sage Publications, 1995): 404.

8. Richard Butsch, '*The Simpsons*: A breath of fresh air mixed with old pollutants', *In These Times* (18–31 July 1990): 19.

9. Roland Barthes, *S/Z*, trans. by Richard Miller (New York: Hill & Wang, 1974): 4–5.

10. Ibid.: 156.

11. Kaja Silverman, *The Subject of Semiotics* (Oxford: Oxford University Press, 1983): 144

12. John Fiske, *Television Culture* (New York: Routledge, 1997): 94.

13. Barthes, op.cit.: 5–6.

14. Fiske, op.cit.: 95.

15. Roland Barthes, *The Pleasure of the Text*, trans. by Richard Miller (New York: Hill & Wang, 1975): 32.

16. Alex Ben Block, *Outfoxed: Marvin Davis, Barry Diller, Rupert Murdoch, Joan Rivers, and the Inside Story of America's Fourth Television Network* (New York: St. Martin's, 1990): 159.

17. Jason Mittell, 'Cartoon Realism: Genre Mixing and the Cultural Life of *The Simpsons*', *The Velvet Light Trap* 47 (Spring, 2001): 15–28.

18. See Joe Morgenstern, 'Bart Simpson's Real Father', *Los Angeles Times Magazine* 6, 17 (29 April 1990): 12–18, 20, 22; Josh Ozersky, 'TV's Anti-Families: Married ... with Malaise', *Tikkun* 6, 1 (1991): 11–14, 92–93; and Michael Reese, 'A Mutant *Ozzie and Harriet*', *Newsweek* (25 December 1989): 70.

19. Vincent Brook, 'Myth or Consequences: Ideological Fault Lines in *The Simpsons*' in John Alberti (ed.) *Leaving Springfield: The Simpsons and the Possibility of Oppositional Culture* (Detroit, MI: Wayne State University Press, 2004): 176.

20. Mittell, op. cit.: 19.

21. Paul Wells, *Animation and America* (New Brunswick, NJ: Rutgers University Press, 2002): 5.

22. Arnold, op. cit.: 259.

23. Andrew Billen, 'Groening Success', *New Statesman*, 129 (26 June 2000): 49–50.

24. Robert Ferguson, *Representing Race: Ideology, Identity and the Media* (London: Arnold Publishers, 1988): 129–132.

25. Tom Shales, 'The Primest Time: Sunday Night Television, from *The Ed Sullivan Show* to *The Simpsons*', *Washington Post* (11 March 1990): G1.

26. Matthew Henry, 'The Triumph of Popular Culture: Situation Comedy, Postmodernism, and *The Simpsons*' in Joanne Morreale (ed.) *Critiquing the Sitcom* (Syracuse, NY: Syracuse University Press, 2003): 264.

27. Brad Chisholm, 'Difficult Viewing: The Pleasures of Complex Screen Narratives', *Critical Studies in Mass Communication* 8, 4 (December, 1991): 389–403.

28. Kimmel, op. cit.: 123.

29. Kimmel: 135–136.

30. Vicki Nobel, 'A Helping Hand from the Guys', in Kay Leigh Hagan (ed.) *Women Respond to the Men's Movement* (San Francisco, CA: HarperCollins, 1992): 105–106.

31. Muriel G. Cantor, 'Prime-time Fathers: A Study in Continuity and Change', *Critical Studies in Mass Communication* 7, 3 (September 1990): 283.

32. See Diane F. Alters, '"We Hardly Watch That Rude, Crude Show": Class and Taste in *The Simpsons*', in Carol A. Stabile and Mark Harrison (eds) *Prime Time Animation: Television Animation and American Culture* (London: Routledge, 2003): 165–184.

III

33. Ott, op. cit.: 66.

34. Mittell, op. cit.: 23.

35. Laurel Shaper Walters, '"In" T-Shirts of Bart Simpson Are Out at Some Schools', *Christian Science Monitor* (27 September 1990):14.

36. Joanna Elm, 'Are the Simpsons America's TV family of the '90s?' *TV Guide* 38 (17 March 1990): 8.

37. Id.

38. Raja Halwani, 'Homer and Aristotle', in William Irwin, Mark T. Conard, and Aeon J. Skoble (eds) *The Simpsons and Philosophy: The D'oh! of Homer* (Chicago, IL: Open Court, 2001): 21–23.

39. Harry F. Waters, 'Family Feuds', *Newsweek* (23 April 1990): 60.

40. Id.

41. Alters, op. cit.

42. Brook, op. cit.: 183.

43. Michael Billig, Susan Condor, Derek Edwards, Mike Gane, David Middleton, and Alan Radley, *Ideological Dilemmas: A Social Psychology of Everyday Thinking* (London: Sage Publications, 1988): 31.

44. Ferguson, op. cit.: 54.

45. Wells, op. cit.: 1.

46. Id.

47. Brook, op. cit.: 192.

48. Barthes, *S/Z*, op. cit.: 5–6.

49. David Hill, 'I Need a Hill', *Rolling Stone*, 754 (20 February 1997): 79.

50. Id.

51. Barthes, op. cit.: 4.

52. Kevin Michael Grace, 'Surprise! A Hit Television Show Celebrates Patriotism, Decency and Decorum', *Western Report* 25, 42 (5 October 1998): 31.

53. Barthes, *The Pleasure of the Text*: 24–31.

Suzanne Williams-Rautiola, Ph.D., is an Associate Professor at Trinity University in the Department of Communication. She teaches courses in animation studies and history and has authored a book chapter and papers on the representation of values in prime time animation on television in the United States. She has also authored numerous articles and papers dealing with curricular and pedagogical issues in animation and television.

Chapter 8

Animated Interactions: Animation Aesthetics and the World of the 'Interactive' Documentary

Paul Ward

Introduction

In this essay, I wish to explore what might be called a sub-genre of both animation and documentary. These films take a real-life interview and then animate it by creatively interpreting the recorded sound of the interview with imaginative animated visuals. But films like the computer-rotoscoped film *Snack and Drink* (Bob Sabiston, USA 1999), or the Aardman clay animation film *Going Equipped* (Peter Lord, UK 1989) are actually playing with profound philosophical categories, and they make us think about animation and documentary's ability to represent things in a very important way. They exist on a boundary, a liminal space, between modes of representation. My discussion will offer a reading of these two exemplary films and how they mobilise a number of key debates for both

Abstract: This essay explores the relationship between two animated films – *Snack and Drink* (Bob Sabiston, 1999) and *Going Equipped* (Peter Lord, 1989) – and the real 'pro-filmic' interviews they re-present. With animated films there is a tension or contradiction between an attempt to represent a pre-existing reality (the autistic teenager in *Snack and Drink* for example) and the aesthetic and technological 'intervention' that animation techniques produce. Therefore, the construction of *a* world via animation techniques in order to re-present a real person from *the* world of actuality is the contradiction at the centre of these two films. The notion of an animated 'world' suggests one that is completely divorced from the indexical connection that is supposed to obtain in documentary representations. Yet these films demonstrate that animated documentaries are perfectly capable of re-pre-senting and 'embodying' knowledge about the real world.

Animation Studies and Documentary Studies. Both animation and documentary are diverse discursive categories rather than simple entities, and it is instructive to examine the points of contact between them. As I have stated in detail elsewhere, it is something of a myth that animation is a mode that somehow cannot be used by documentary practitioners. Such a way of thinking is based in naïve and simplistic notions of how documentary functions, and in a misguided belief that documentary is somehow 'capturing' reality rather than offering an *analysis* of it. Animation can do this just as well as live-action; in some cases, animation is in fact better suited to the job. This is the case with these two films.

It is necessary to start with a brief outline of what I mean by the term 'interactive' in relation to documentary. This has nothing to do with more recent meanings of interactive – that is, in the sense of digital media and how the user/spectator is given a level of ability to (apparently) interact with and somehow shape the text they are experiencing. Examples of such 'interactivity' are the plethora of viewer phone-ins, exhortations to press the red button while watching digital broadcasts, as well as notions of interactivity in gameplay. To my mind, much of the interaction in these cases is fiercely circumscribed and no real power is passed to the viewer/user/consumer/player. Certainly, recent developments in digital television allow for a good deal of viewer manipulation (ability to record, playback, pause ostensibly 'live' broadcasts), but I would argue that this is not the same as actual control over how and what is produced. The way that interaction or interactivity is rhetorically inflected in these contexts exaggerates the control that viewers are given. As we shall see, the interactive in the sense I am using it is borrowed from Bill Nichols' typology of documentary modes.[1] Once I have outlined this and how the interactive mode in animated documentary represents or 'embodies' knowledge in specific ways, I will say a little more about how the very idea of the 'bodily' is problematised by animation, and by these animated films in particular. A key point will be that it is the process of animating what are filmed or aural records of real people and their actual thoughts, feelings and situations that inflects the knowledge represented in such an intriguing way. The very idea of the pro-filmic event, for instance – the 'actuality' that is apparently captured in a documentary – is problematised by animation. There is a real sense here that these films are a stylised 'performance' of certain kinds of knowledge; knowledge that is in some sense hidden or masked by more conventional forms of documentary representation. Furthermore, both of these animated documentaries attempt to give voice to specific people and the worlds they inhabit, and to the ways they interact (or *fail* to interact) with the social. In other words, these films represent to viewers not some stylised fantasy world, but reveal something about *the* world of actuality. The animated worlds depicted are, actually, part and parcel of our world.

The interactive documentary and the embodiment of knowledge

Bill Nichols describes the interactive documentary as a category that 'stresses images of testimony or verbal exchange ... textual authority [therefore] shifts towards the social actors recruited [to speak in the films]... various forms of monologue and dialogue (real or apparent) predominate'.[2] The interesting thing about the interactive documentary is that it makes us think about the kinds of knowledge produced by interactions between people in the real world (including the interaction between the social actors in the documentary and the filmmakers); such interaction most commonly takes the form of an interview. As Nichols' 'real or apparent' aside suggests, though, there are many ways that such interaction can manifest itself on the screen. There are, of course, lots of different kinds of interview (vox pops, formal interrogation, talk show reminiscence) but Nichols' point is not so much to point to the range of interviews, but to the range of ways in which material can be *inflected* by the documentary form. So, a fairly straightforward filmed or taped question and answer interview can be edited in such a way as to make the questioner 'disappear', and the answers are re-presented as a kind of monologue, albeit probably intercut with material that 'illustrates' what the speaker is saying. Or the converse might be true, where what was a fairly monologue-like delivery is intercut with questions to impose the structure of a dialogue that was not originally present. These are commonplace conventions of documentary, and what is interesting about them is that they reveal the extent to which interaction can be either effaced from a text, or foregrounded, or even manufactured.

In the case of the animated films I am discussing, we have two distinct tendencies of interactive documentary. *Snack and Drink* is in the tradition of the 'roving reporter' in the sense that the interview, such as it is, is conducted 'on the hoof', and has a spur of the moment feel to it as befits the subject matter: the filmmakers are talking to an autistic teenager and they therefore have to grasp the opportunity when it comes along. In the case of the Aardman film, *Going Equipped*, we have a marriage of clay animation with a 'real' ambient soundtrack. This takes the form of a monologue by a man who has been in various penal institutions for half of his life, talking while he sits in a gloomy, sparsely furnished room. Although the form of his speech manifests itself as a monologue, it is actually pieced together from a considerably longer interview. The interview for *Going Equipped* was conducted by journalist Derek Robinson. The subject was interviewed at Robinson's house for approximately one hour. The interview was recorded. It consisted of a standard question and answer format, though Robinson stated that a good deal of his contributions were nods and prompting noises rather than direct, specific questions. The subject was lucid and reflective enough to be allowed to talk at some length. Nevertheless, the one hour of material that was recorded was reduced (by Aardman) to the five minutes for the film's soundtrack and, in the course of this editing, the obvious 'interaction' between interviewer and interviewee was effaced completely, giving the impression of a monologue.[3] In this respect, the actual interaction between the subject of the film and the filmmakers is minimised (as Nichols would put it, this is an 'apparent' rather than 'real' monologue) so as to emphasise the intimate, confessional aspects of the piece.

In *Snack and Drink*, the animation technique employed is the so-called Rotoshop software, developed by Bob Sabiston, and later seen to great effect in the feature-length *Waking Life* (Richard Linklater, USA 2001). This is a form of computerised rotoscoping, where live-action footage (in this case, shot using digital video cameras) is 'drawn over' by the animator. The live-action footage is saved to computer and converted to Quicktime files. The resulting files can then be viewed one frame at a time and 'drawn over' using the Rotoshop program. As the footage is viewed, the animation process is carried out via pressure-sensitive Wacom pads and pens, allowing for a wide variety of shades and relative hardness or softness of lines. The result is an eerie, fluid, mutable aesthetic, perfect for the representation of dreams, alternate realities and hallucinations.[4] The direct indexical link to a pro-filmic reality – the foundation upon which 'documentary' as a form apparently rests – is severed by Sabiston's outlandish animation (bulging eyes, blurring shapes). And yet, in my view, the film remains resolutely a documentary. The real person 'underneath' the overlaid rotoscoped imagery is still 'there'. Below I will return to the bodily 'presence' of real people in animated documentaries, but for the moment I would like to concentrate on the way that knowledge itself is embodied. In particular, we are presented with knowledge about the mindset of Ryan Power, who is autistic. *Snack and Drink* therefore offers us insight into the 'world' of autism, and does so in a way that live-action could not. This is a fascinating topic for discussion in relation to how the 'real world' is represented because someone with autism views the world in a markedly different way from the accepted norm. Aside from the tendency to be introverted and often obsessed with routines, people with autism and Asperger's Syndrome (AS) can exhibit near-miraculous 'savant' abilities. (By no means all people with autism/AS have these abilities, but a significantly higher proportion than in the general population.) Those autistic people who are able to articulate how their minds 'work' demonstrate an extraordinarily high level of visuality in the way they think about things, as well as a seeming inability to think in the abstract. This perhaps explains why people with autism are unable to deal with metaphors and figures of speech, as they tend to 'take everything literally'.

The film commences very suddenly with no credits. The shifting perspectives of Rotoshop, as well as what turns out to be rather skewed camerawork in the original live-action footage Rotoshopped for the film (Sabiston and Pallotta are running down the stairs in order to catch up with Ryan as he goes to the 7-Eleven convenience store and snack shop) make for a disorienting first few seconds. We hear a snatch of sound – a woman's voice saying something about the removal company U-Haul – to which Sabiston momentarily responds. All the time, he is trying to catch up with Ryan: 'Hey hold up! Wait, wait, wait!'. This seemingly random opening to the film sets some important markers in terms of its documentary status. We appear to stumble across the action, as if by accident, and the aesthetic rough edges are played up and exaggerated by the animation style. For example, one very brief shot of Ryan Power at the beginning of the film (just after the 'Wait!' moment) is of him standing stock-still but with Rotoshopped animated lines undulating around him, exaggerating his 'aliveness' even though he appears to have stopped dead. The soundtrack accompanying this shot is the typical noises one hears when a filmmaker is hurriedly shifting equipment – a muffled knocking of a microphone and additional ambient 'wild sound'. Once the filmmakers and their subject start moving down the road, with Pallotta taking charge of camera duties, while Sabiston can be heard – and occasionally seen – asking questions, Ryan Power launches into an apparently unprompted monologue (Fig. 1) about the television cartoon

Fig. 1: Snack and Drink, *Bob Sabiston.*
[Courtesy of Bob Sabiston, ©Flat Black Films 1999.]

series *Fievel's American Tails* (Larry Jacobs and Lawrence Jacobs, USA 1991). He lists the shows and their availability on video:

> Well, they're *Fievel's American Tails*, on six video cassettes with two episodes on each one, which, that features 'The Gift' and 'The Case of the Hiccups', 'The Legend of Mouse Hollow' and 'Babysitting Blues'

He goes on to list all twelve episodes as they are paired on the video series. Sabiston then asks 'How do you know about this?' to which Ryan replies 'Because I saw them before'. Sabiston: 'So what are you going to 7-Eleven for?' The reply is 'I'm going to get a snack and drink'. All of Ryan's speech is in the same monotone, whether he is listing TV shows or responding to direct questions from Sabiston.

One of the common misunderstandings of forms of autism is that all those afflicted with it are somehow *completely* unable to communicate with (or even recognise) the 'real' world and the 'ordinary' people in it. As *Snack and Drink* demonstrates, some autistic individuals can communicate but in ways that are not perhaps what most people would deem to be 'normal'.[5] There is often an obsession with detail and minutiae to the detriment of other things, including 'normal' communication and interaction with other people. An upset to a routine can cause untold torment. In *Snack and Drink*, the trip to the 7-Eleven that we actually see functions as what Brian Winston, using a term from Gerard Genette's narrative theory, refers to as the 'iterative' code. As Winston puts it, the iterative shows 'an event or activity which can be read as a *typical instance* of that event or activity'.[6] In other words, we see *one* instance of something happening, but it is clearly marked as something that actually happens all the time, is a *regular* occurrence. The iterative is crucial for documentary discourse as it 'anchors' what we see and emphasises its relation to the real world of actuality.

The importance of the iterative in relation to this film is that Ryan Power's trip to the 7-Eleven is clearly part of a cherished routine. This much comes across in his responses to Sabiston's questions – his interaction with the filmmakers – and is entirely characteristic of someone with autism. A number of the people interviewed in *A is for Autism* (Tim Webb, UK 1992) attest to this seeming obsession with routine and everything being in its place. In one sequence in Webb's film, a woman remembers that when she was a child she used to repeatedly ask around dusk 'Why are the streetlights going on?' or 'The streetlights are going on now, aren't they?' to which her mother would reply 'Yes, because it's getting dark'. The girl would then ask the same question again, and again, oblivious to her mother's increasing consternation. As the adult woman reflects 'I did this because it was pleasurable to hear the answer. If a particular topic intrigued me, I zeroed in on that subject and talked it into the ground'. Earlier in the film, the same woman talks about how she would often home in on a spinning top or coin,

Fig. 2: Snack and Drink, *Bob Sabiston.*
[Courtesy of Bob Sabiston, ©Flat Black Films 1999.]

and nothing would be able to distract her from watching it.[7] Such obsessive and repetitive thoughts and actions seem extraordinary to many people, but are commonplace for sufferers of autism. The most minor of details can become part of a highly cherished routine which can block out other aspects of the everyday world around them.

The prosaic nature of the title *Snack and Drink*, and the seeming mundanity of the events in the film, can therefore be contrasted with the importance of the routine to someone like Ryan Power. Once in the store, there is a relatively very long sequence (just under one minute out of a running time of three minutes forty seconds) devoted to Ryan obtaining his drink from a self-service set of dispensers (Fig. 2).

RP: I usually mix them all.

BS: What?

RP: I usually mix them all.

BS: All the different drinks?

RP: Yes, all the different drinks.

BS: Do you like that?

RP: Yes, I like that.

BS: Even Diet?

RP: Yes.

He grasps his Double Gulp cup and moves along the row of dispensers, adding a squirt from each so that he ends up with, as he puts it, 'all mixed flavours ... mixed drink'.

The single-minded and obsessive nature of his behaviour while serving himself his drink contrasts with the animation at this point. As Ryan moves along the dispensers, he seems oblivious to everything around him. His eyes are Rotoshopped to bulge unnaturally from their sockets to emphasise his concentration. Sabiston has also literally brought the dispensers to life by giving them little faces and arms that they wave about, in an apparent attempt to attract Ryan's attention. It is an amusing and strangely touching visual rendering of just how obsessively focused an autistic person can be. At the same time though, Ryan *does* respond to Sabiston's questions asking what he is doing; but it has to be said that this is only because those questions are firmly rooted in (and are about) the very routine he is carrying out. In many respects, Sabiston's and Pallotta's presence is an obvious break with routine, but Ryan seems more able to cope because they are there fitting in with *his* world. As the exchange above shows, Ryan will often respond to a question by repeating it, prefaced by 'Yes ...'. Any times that Sabiston asks him something he is less sure about, the response is more likely to be a simple 'Yes' with no repetition. Such communication is characteristic of autistic individuals – stilted, repetitive, awkward. Oliver Sacks has written astutely of the ways that autistic individuals can appear to learn how to interact with some semblance of 'normality' – as he puts it, such individuals can learn 'to create social surfaces they could present to the world'.[8] While hardly interacting with people in an 'ordinary' manner, there can be points of contact – the 'social surfaces' to which Sacks refers. Unlike non-autistic people, for whom social interaction is to a large extent intuitive and natural, autistic people, when they are able, have to *learn* how to interact at the simplest level. However, such points of contact can also revolve around an interest the autistic person has: Sacks writes of how he managed to communicate with twins who appeared only to 'speak' in prime numbers, or how latching onto their interest in theatre or music helped him to engage with certain individuals.[9] A similar thing is going on with Ryan Power and Sabiston: an interaction prompted to a great degree by an interest in cartoons (see below).

Peter Lord's *Going Equipped* differs from *Snack and Drink* in the sense that its speaker is anonymous – a man talking about his previous criminal behaviour (petty theft, followed by 'creeping' and then full-blown burglary, or the 'going equipped' of the title) – and he has a sense of self in what he is saying. His words on the soundtrack constitute a clear reflection on what he has done in the past. The film is one of a number of shorts made by Aardman Animation that explore the possibilities of animated repre-

Fig. 3: Going Equipped, *Peter Lord.*
[Courtesy of Aardman Animations Ltd, © Aardman Animations Ltd 1989.]

sentations of real or captured situations, with snatches of real conversation or speech of particular importance.[10] As Brian Sibley says of this loosely-connected set of films:

> Although the audio track suggests that the characters on screen have been accurately drawn from life, the truth is more complex since the animation is, in fact, an imaginative interpretation of what is heard. By hearing the dialogue 'performed' by a realistic puppet – who may or may not bear any resemblance to the real owner of the voice – the words seems [sic] more sharply focused and the passing banalities of life take on a new significance.[11]

Going Equipped has the power of a confessional; the memories of the man's childhood, how he got into crime and so on. It is also in the tradition of 'talking head' films – films that are structured around what Nichols calls 'cephalic knowledge'.[12] But the discrepancy of hearing an obviously authentic soundtrack accompanied by clay animation makes what is said, strangely, all the more poignant. Although using clay animation, *Going Equipped* manages a startlingly naturalistic verisimilitude – not only achieved by the accuracy and detail of the clay figure's facial expressions and body movement, but also through the plausible and atmospheric *mise en scène* (particularly the lighting) (Fig. 3). What was conducted as an interview (by journalist Derek Robinson) is actually presented as a stream-of-consciousness recollection. As Sibley points out, the animators then construct an 'imaginative interpretation of what is heard'. In other words, they construct 'a world' that will metaphorically emphasise (or ironically undermine) what the viewer is hearing on the soundtrack. The documentary status of this represented world therefore resides not in its direct, indexical link to an actual location, but rather to its symbolic and metaphorical resonance. In many respects, the striking naturalism of the voice on the soundtrack – complete with pauses, involuntary noises and repetitions – contrasts starkly with the deliberately atmospheric lighting effects. For example, there are moments when the raindrops that are trickling down the window panes can be seen in the light (mainly streetlights, with occasional headlamps of passing cars), as they trickle, like tears, down the animated character's face onto which their flowing shadows are thrown. It is moments of poetic licence like this that give the film its power, emphasising the importance of the protagonist's words.

Another Aardman film that explores language and reminiscence – albeit in relation to a very different subject matter – is Lord's *Palmy Days* (1981, part of the *Animated Conversations* series). The soundtrack here consists of the banal and rambling anecdotes and chit-chat of a group of four pensioners. Instead of the intensely focused remembrance of the man from *Going Equipped*, we find a good-naturedly overlapping set of conversations about nothing in particular. Again, though, the clay animation figures are very naturalistically portrayed and detailed, and poetic licence has been taken with the setting in which they are placed. Their clothes are ragged, their shelter is a sparse hut; the final shot of the film reveals that they are stranded on a desert island, a crashed plane in the background. The prosaic, banal nature of the anecdotes and snatches of conversation therefore take on a whole new resonance in the light of this. Instead of some old people merely rambling at each other, the soundtrack takes on new meaning as a record of a past life, the reminiscing juxtaposed with the stark change of circumstances. It is this juxtaposition of 'real', captured conversation with an imagined, visually represented location that gives the film its amusing (and yet very poignant) tone. *Palmy Days* might seem to be a fanciful, fictional construction, but I would suggest that its use of actual captured conversation, in all its ethnographic detail, interpreted by imaginative visuals, gives it considerable *documentary* power.

The way in which these films can be termed 'documentary' has therefore less to do with a direct indexical link to an external reality and more to do with the viewers' engagement and interaction with the signifying strategies. In short, *we respond to them* as documentaries. As Dai Vaughan proposes in his essay 'The Aesthetics of Ambiguity':

> The term 'documentary' properly describes not a style or method or a genre of filmmaking but a mode of response to film material ... the documentary response is one in which the image is perceived as signifying what it appears to record. ... A crucial fact about the definition of documentary as a mode of response is that it places the attribution of documentary significance squarely within the province of the viewer.[13]

Now, there are certainly potential problems with Vaughan's contention that 'the documentary response is one in which the image is perceived as signifying what it appears to record'; he acknowledges as much in another essay in the same anthology (delightfully entitled 'What Do We Mean by "What"?'), in which he states:

> To see a film as documentary is to see its meaning as pertinent to the events and objects which passed before the camera ... such a definition may run into theoretical difficulties. The objection may be made that record and significa- tion are not facts of the same order, and are not directly comparable. All the same, it does enable us to avoid the labyrinth of rules and exceptions, and exceptions to the exceptions, which awaits anyone who tries to identify documentary by generic or stylistic criteria.[14]

I would suggest that Vaughan's gambit here is ideal for those who wish to bring animated films into their discussion of documentary signification. It is also worth reiterating that it focuses attention on another kind of inter- action: that of the *viewer* with the documentary material, at the point of *viewing* it. In this respect we must consider how the 'world' represented on-screen measures up to the 'world' of the viewer (that is, the real world of actuality). Vivian Sobchack has outlined very clearly how viewers of nonfictional and documentary material relate to such material at the actual point of viewing it.[15] This phenomenology of nonfictional film experience is very useful for the purposes of thinking about animation in general and animated documentary in particular. From a phenomenological perspec- tive, the viewer of an animated documentary cannot 'take up' the viewed material as anything *other than* a complete creation on the part of the animator; it cannot be known to them in anything like the 'prior' ways that Sobchack notes in her essay. She talks of different 'states' of viewing existing on a continuum, and how they involve different levels of 'knowing'. One can 'know' what one looks at in an intimate prior way (Sobchack's example here is of the 'film-souvenir' or home movie); or at one remove (images of people we do not know personally, but recognise as having a real historical existence), or in purely fictional terms (that is, we know while watching that the world depicted is a fabricated diegesis rather than a pre-existing, pro-filmic world). The problem with these animated documentaries is that the viewer is caught in a paradoxical position – simultaneously knowing that what they are *seeing* is a complete fabrication, while what they are *hearing* is a record of a real interaction.[16]

It is important that we do not only attend to the relationship the viewer has to the film material. Another kind of interaction, manifested in *Snack and Drink*, is the fact that the filmmakers involved the subject and his family in the making of the film. Apparently, Bob Sabiston and Tommy Pallotta met Ryan's mother, and when she learned that they were making animated documentaries she said 'Oh, you should interview my son, he's obsessed with cartoons'.[17] Sabiston continues:

> She thought it would be interesting for him to see himself as a cartoon. When we arrived at his house, he was shy and did not want to be interviewed. We started interviewing his sister and his mother, when he came out from his bedroom and announced that he was going to '7-Eleven' for a snack and a drink. We asked if we could go along and film him, and he assented. Ryan's mother and aunt participated in animating a small section of the film. It took about a month to complete. When Ryan saw the completed animation, he watched it three times in a row and pronounced it 'pretty ok'.[18]

This is interesting because it shows that the techniques used are simple and accessible, while still offering a startling effect. The filmmakers are interacting with their subjects (and here I am including Ryan Power's family), arguably giving them some of the power over the representation. It is also interesting to note that Ryan's shyness is circumvented by being able to go out and interview him 'on the hoof' – the digital technology allowing the film to be made in this way – and the intriguing nature of the Rotoshop technique also perhaps encourages an interaction between Ryan and the filmmakers that might not otherwise have been there. For example, the manner in which real, live-action footage can be taken and transformed via Rotoshop, offering an exaggerated vision that is clearly linked to the notion of 'cartoons', mentioned earlier, almost certainly means that Ryan is more forthcoming than he might otherwise have been. Much of Sabiston's work is clearly documentary in tone and intention; and his fascination lies with the ways that his animation software can 'interpret' the complexities of everyday life. Even in the feature-length *Waking Life*, where Sabiston is credited for 'Art Direction' (even though he oversaw the entire Rotoshop process), we can see a kind of quasi-documentary intention at play – the picaresque narrative arc, such as it is, contains much quotidian detail. In addition to this, it is obvious that one of the key 'points' of the film is to explore the slippage between the different realities of the waking world and the dreaming world. As such, the Rotoshop animation technique is the perfect aesthetic device for accentuating the difference (and yet overlap) between these often conflicting realities.[19]

In general (i.e. when we are talking about live-action), the documentary has a great investment in real human beings laid out for us as spectators. Our ability to *see* someone and at the same time *learn something* (about them) fulfils both scopophilic and epistephilic drives (the desire to *look* and the desire to *know*, respectively). The somatic or bodily is to some extent problematised by representations such as the ones in question here: what we are seeing is not the person themselves but a representation of them. And not just a representation (which, after all, covers all live-action as well), but one that makes the viewer *interrogate* what they are actually looking at, and to think about the slippage between merely *looking* at something and *knowing* that something.[20] These films dwell on the presence of the body as a highly specific guarantee of a certain kind of knowledge, and it is the 'body-ness' or somatic aspect to which we now turn.

The performative and the somatic in animated documentary

Joanna Bouldin has written instructively about the use of the rotoscope (the forerunner of Rotoshop) and how it is implicated in the representation of gender and ethnicity in Betty Boop cartoons.[21] Part of her argument is concerned with the way that rotoscope techniques mobilise a form of 'realism' that is strongly imbricated on the body of the 'underlying' performers. Their body is the evidence of the real person that has been overlaid by the animation process. What we are talking about here is interpretation: the live-action footage is creatively interpreted by the animator, and certain aspects (an overly bulging eyeball, a seductive wiggle, Betty Boop performing a peculiarly 'ethnic' dance) are exaggerated for (usually) comic effect. In the case of *Snack and Drink*, such interpretation is strongly linked to an attempt to visualise (and thereby to help understand) an affliction such as autism. In this sense, the animation technique can of course be seen as a documentary technique, albeit a somewhat flamboyant one. Similarly, the clay animation rendering of captured conversations or monologues seen in the Aardman films are a creative interpretation of a specific portion of actuality.[22]

The performative and the bodily intersect in certain types of documentary. In these animated films, we have a 'thickening' of the presence of the body, as Bouldin refers to it in her analysis. Bouldin's argument stresses that although 'the real' has a different relationship to animated and live-action representations, with the latter having a privileged relationship by virtue of the indexical/conventional relationship noted earlier, we can never say that the real is completely absent or banished from animation. Indeed, Bouldin suggests:

> The material and sensuous connection between image and original is maintained in animation, albeit in a complicated, morphed and multiplied form. Rather than relying on the single, material body of the original, as in photography, the animated body draws upon multiple originals – from models to voice actors to the animators themselves.[23]

This is useful because it latches directly onto what is so interesting about what I have termed 'animated interactions'. It is the *multiplication* of what was originally *there* – the real people and the situations in which they are filmed – that generates meaning. The 'interaction' that is taking place is between the 'multiple originals' – the real person, the taped interview, the animated 'version' of the person, and so on.[24] It is, then, a reworking of the interactive in the sense that Nichols proposes. The dialogical relationship between real and animated, between real person and their avatar or re-inscription, means we as viewers have to re-evaluate our understanding of representations of the real. I would suggest that this phenomenon is particularly acute in the films I am talking about; it boils down, in one sense, to a *recognition* of the relationship between the profilmic material and what happens to it when it is treated by the filmmaker. My colleague, Mike Wayne, made this comment on the use of computer rotoscoping in *Waking Life*:

> The spectator is caught between acknowledging the raw material of the profilmic event *and* its subsequent transformation; they are perpetually reminded of that process instead of the raw material being folded invisibly into the finished product; it's like watching two films simultaneously and one is constantly aware of the gap as well as the relation between them.[25]

This paradox is also a classic case of 'present-absence', something that John Ellis marks out as a characteristic of the cinematic experience itself.[26] These people are absent and yet they are present. Nichols discusses the notions of 'presence' and 'absence' in relation to the conventions of the ethnographic film and draws upon phenomenology:

> The phenomenological tradition shares with ethnographic film a commitment to the appearance of things in their specificity. It takes considerable interest in the question of the body and how embodied action – performance – constitutes a sense of self in relation to others. Phenomenology addresses the issue of experience directly. It brings into focus the (largely absent) body of the filmmaker him- or herself as the organizing locus of knowledge.[27]

In this respect, the ethnographic films are a 'performing' or 'enactment' of a certain *kind* of knowledge, 'concrete and embodied, based on the specificities of personal experience'.[28] The way in which the animated films under scrutiny here inflect these issues is that the apparent certainties of documentary discourse (what Nichols has referred to as belonging to the 'discourses of sobriety') are filtered through animation aesthetics, and the mode of address is thereby 'made strange'.[29] We have real-life recordings of real people, but they are being performed – represented, if you will – by animated stand-ins.

The ways in which these animated documentaries represent their worlds has interesting philosophical ramifications that are only beginning to be critically evaluated. As I have suggested above, following Bouldin's arguments, the somatic or bodily presence of real, actual people, while attenuated in animation, is never entirely absent. Indeed, although their physical presence may be made problematic via the animation process (whether this is clay animation, rotoscoping, or any other type of animation), as Bouldin makes clear, their presence is multiplied in other ways. The character's 'being-ness' is therefore of considerable interest, especially in relation to the worlds depicted: what we might term (to use a Heideggerian terminology) their 'being-in-the-world-ness'. Heidegger coined the term 'Dasein' to refer to that specifically authentic sense of 'Being'; a rooted, socially-situated, *knowing* human being.[30] It is interesting to consider how such a concept applies to animated documentary in general and these two films in particular. The people depicted in *Snack and Drink* and *Going Equipped* are quite clearly real, existent beings, and aspects of their lives, their worlds, are 'documented' for us in the films. Arguably, however, the viewer of these films oscillates between knowing that what they are seeing is a depiction of someone that has a real world existence, while simultaneously knowing that what they are looking at and experiencing directly at the point of viewing, is a fabrication. The way in which the people depicted might be said to be authentic or have a valid 'being-ness' is thereby further problematised by the *animatedness* of the characters and the worlds they inhabit.

Notes

1. Bill Nichols, *Representing Reality* (Bloomington and Indianapolis: Indiana University Press, 1991): 32–75. His typology in this book includes: expository, observational, interactive and reflexive. More recently, Nichols expanded the typology to include what he terms the 'performative' mode of documentary. See Bill Nichols, *Blurred Boundaries* (Bloomington and Indianapolis: Indiana University Press, 1994): 92–106. More recently still, the notion of the interactive mode appears to have been replaced by the term 'participatory' to cover much of the same sorts of documentary (though participatory is a broader category, so perhaps it is more accurate to say that the participatory has subsumed the interactive). I have retained the term 'interactive' in the current discussion, as I believe that it better describes what is going on in these specific films, with their explicit exploration of the interview, and the attendant interaction between filmmaker and subject. The term interaction is also more accurate for describing how all the levels of signification (and viewer response) dialectically relate in these animated documentaries.

2. Nichols, *Representing Reality*: 44.

3. The details of the interview technique for *Going Equipped* were provided by Derek Robinson in a telephone conversation (October 2004).

4. For a more detailed account of Rotoshop and some of its applications see Paul Ward, 'Rotoshop in context: Computer rotoscoping and animation aesthetics', *Animation Journal*, volume 12 (2004): 32–52.

5. See Tim Webb's animated documentary *A is for Autism* (1992), which features a number of interviews with autistic individuals and uses their own drawings to provide the basis for the animation. The film demonstrates obsessions and problems with communication that autistic people have to deal with, but also shows that those with autism can reach a level of self-awareness and 'reflexivity'. The reason why *A is for Autism* is such a landmark film is that it succeeds in visually representing (to coin a phrase: 'documenting') what it might be like inside the mind of someone with autism. I feel that *Snack and Drink* also succeeds at this. A fictional work which also explores the mind of someone with autism – the story is told from the autistic protagonist's point of view – is Mark Haddon's remarkable novel *The Curious Incident of the Dog in the Night-Time* (London: Jonathan Cape, 2003).

6. Brian Winston, *Claiming the Real* (London: BFI, 1995): 101. Italics added.

7. The woman is Dr. Temple Grandin. She advised on the film *Rain Man*, is a Professor of Animal Sciences at Colorado State University in the US, and has written several books on autism, most notably her autobiography *Thinking in Pictures – and other reports from my life with autism* (New York: Vintage, 1996). She also features in Oliver Sacks' book *An Anthropologist on Mars: Seven Paradoxical Tales*, (London: Picador, 1995).

8. Sacks, *An Anthropologist on Mars*: 240.

9. See the chapters entitled 'The Twins' and 'Rebecca' respectively in Oliver Sacks, *The Man Who Mistook his Wife for a Hat* (London: Picador, 1986).

10. The films are: *Confessions of a Foyer Girl*, *Down and Out* (both under the title *Animated Conversations*, made for the BBC, 1978); *On Probation*, *Sales Pitch*, *Early Bird*, *Palmy Days*, *Late Edition* (*Conversation Pieces*, Channel 4, 1981). *Going Equipped* is part of 1989's *Lip Synch* series of films, which also includes *Creature Comforts* (Nick Park), *War Story* (Peter Lord), *Next!* (Barry Purves) and *Ident* (Richard Goleszowski). Of the *Lip Synch* series, the two Lord films and Park's most closely follow the template set up by the earlier two series of films.

11. Brian Sibley, [with Peter Lord] *Cracking Animation: The Aardman Book of 3-D Animation* (London: Thames and Hudson, 1998): 53.

12. Bill Nichols, *Blurred Boundaries*: 74.

13. Dai Vaughan, 'The Aesthetics of Ambiguity' in *For Documentary: Twelve Essays* (Berkeley: University of California Press, 1999): 58.

14. Dai Vaughan, 'What do we mean by "What"?' in *For Documentary*: 84–85.

15. Vivian Sobchack, 'Toward a Phenomenology of Nonfictional Film Experience' in Jane M. Gaines and Michael Renov (eds) *Collecting Visible Evidence* (Minneapolis: University of Minnesota Press, 1999): 241–254.

16. In this respect, we should emphasise here that the voices and the soundtrack are where the 'documentary' status of the films perhaps resides. More research is certainly needed into the role of the soundtrack in anchoring documentary meaning, but I do not have the space to go into this matter here.

17. Quoted in Sabiston's synopsis/preview of the film, from http://www.abm-medien.de/film-buero/snack_e.htm

18. Ibid.

19. For a discussion of how dreaming and reality are explored and figured in *Waking Life*, see Paul Ward, '"I was dreaming I was awake and then I woke up and found myself asleep": Dreaming, Spectacle and Reality in *Waking Life*', in Geoff King (ed.) *The Spectacle of the Real: From Hollywood to 'Reality' TV and Beyond* (Bristol: Intellect Press, 2005): 161–171.

20. Again, this takes us into the phenomenological realm. I have used Sobchack's typology in another essay on mockumentary and discuss there the ways in which these different modes of viewing represent different levels of 'knowing' the worlds we see depicted on the screen. See Paul Ward, 'The Future of Documentary? "Conditional tense" documentary and the historical record' in Gary Rhodes and John Springer (eds) *Docufictions* (Jefferson, NC: McFarland Press, 2005).

21. Joanna Bouldin, 'Cadaver of the Real: Animation, rotoscoping and the politics of the body', *Animation Journal*, volume 12 (2004): 7–31.

22. 'The creative interpretation of actuality' is the now-famous 'first definition' of documentary offered by John Grierson. The phrase originally appeared in his article 'The Documentary Producer', *Cinema Quarterly*, volume 2, no. 1 (1933): 8. It has since gone through various (synonymous) forms – 'the creative treatment of reality', 'the dramatic reconstruction of actuality' etc. – all of which, despite any other shortcomings, do manage to capture the central dilemma of *all* documentary productions: i.e. that they will have to negotiate the tension between the real world of actuality and the creative construction inherent in all representations of that world. In this respect, these animations are no different from any other documentary output.

23. Bouldin, 'Cadaver of the Real': 9.
24. Though it should be remembered here that some aspects of these 'interactions' are minimised or effaced entirely, so as to inflect the interview material in a different way, as is the case in *Going Equipped*.
25. These comments were made in a personal email to the author.
26. John Elli, *Visible Fictions* (London: Routledge, 1982): 58.
27. Nichols, *Blurred Boundaries*: 81.
28. Bill Nichols, *Introduction to Documentary* (Bloomington and Indianapolis: Indiana University Press, 2001): 131.
29. See Nichols, *Representing Reality*, 3–4. He states: 'Documentary film has a kinship with those other nonfictional systems that together make up what we may call the discourses of sobriety. [For example:], Science, economics, politics, foreign policy, education, religion, welfare ... Discourses of sobriety are sobering because they regard their relation to the real as direct, immediate, transparent'. Nichols goes on to point out that 'Documentary, despite its kinship, has never been accepted as a full equal' – something I would suggest is even more the case for animated documentaries, making their critical analysis even more important.
30. See Stephen Mulhall, *Heidegger and 'Being and Time'* (London: Routledge, 1996).

Dr **Paul Ward** is Lecturer in Film and Television Studies, School of Arts, Brunel University, UK. His main research interests are documentary and animation. Publications include '"Rotoshop" in context: Computer rotoscoping and animation aesthetics' in *Animation Journal* (2004), 'Distribution and trade press strategies for British animated propaganda cartoons of the First World War era' in the *Historical Journal of Film, Radio and Television* (2005) and essays in edited collections on various animation and documentary-related topics. He is also the author of *Documentary: The Margins of Reality*, an entry in Wallflower Press's 'Short Cuts' series of books. He is a Reviews Editor for *animation: an interdisciplinary journal*.

Chapter 9

New Media Worlds

Thomas Lamarre[1]

Although there had been experimentation with digital animation for some years, the ballroom scene in *Beauty and the Beast* (Gary Trousdale and Kirk Wise, USA, 1991) is frequently cited as a key moment in pushing cel animation to new heights and announcing the wonders of digital animation for films produced for mass audiences. Depth had never looked so endlessly, volumetrically deep, and viewing position had never appeared so mobile and lively. Digital animation promised to renew our sense of wonder, not only for animation but also for cinema, and digital media promised to produce amazing new worlds, things never before seen. As in the early days of cinema, anything produced in this new media appeared to dazzle and beguile audiences. While some producers fretted over how to combine digital animation and cel animation (which latter was now designated as traditional or 2D in contrast to the new 3D animation), others began to buzz about the possibility of a completely digital animated film. The only obstacles were budgets and computing power. New media worlds seemed almost within the grasp.

Not many years later, as digital animation trounces 'traditional animation' at America's global box office, a relatively stable digital look and feel has already emerged in those films. Digital animation in a film like *The Incredibles* (Brad Bird, USA, 2005) combines iconic characters (reminiscent of cel animation) with a 'hypercinematic' movement in volumetric depth.

Abstract: This paper explores the ways in which the use of digital media can create different sets of material orientations for viewers, thus generating diverse kinds of media worlds. In particular it looks at the construction of media worlds in two animated films, both targeted for mass audiences: the photoreal or hyperreal world of *Final Fantasy: The Spirits Within* (Sakaguchi Hironobu, 2001) and the multilayered world of *Metropolis* (Rintarô, 2001). While far less successful commercially than much of the recent digital fare at the American global box office, these films tell us far more about how new media orientate viewers, especially in relation to worlds of cinema and cel animation.

Derived from cinema, and especially from big budget action cinema, hypercinematic movement relies on the ability to produce volumetric spaces digitally in conjunction with an amazingly mobile 'camera' (that is, simulated camera-like viewing position).[2] Such digital animation tends to extend the ballistic effects prevalent in action films while steering away from photoreal or hyperreal environments and characters, in favour of a slightly cartoonish, iconic style of figuration. This shrewd, smoothly nego-tiated conjoining of cinematic paradigms and animated ones results one kind of media world, one set of orientations for verisimilar actions and stories. Yet this is but one possible world, one among many other possibili-ties opened by digital media. While it does produce its share of thrills, it has, in the manner of much successful mass cultural production, all too neatly resolved the tensions and antimonies implicit in digital animation. Here I would like to explore two other new media worlds, both targeted for mass audiences, far less commercially successful but more challenging in their use of digital media – the hyperreal world of *Final Fantasy: The Spirits Within* (Sakaguchi Hironobu, Japan/USA, 2001) and the multilectical world of *Metropolis* (Rintarô, Japan, 2001). Crucial are the ways in which these films orientate us, especially in relation to cinema, but in relation to 'traditional' cel animation as well.

The fascination of consummated worlds

Final Fantasy: The Spirits Within,[3] an animated film based on the (once and now again) extremely popular video game series, appears determined to become the 'ultimate digital cinema', exactly as Lev Manovich proclaimed it in his essay 'What is Digital Cinema?' (1999). 'In principle', Manovich writes, 'given enough time and money, one can create what will be the ultimate digital cinema: ninety minutes of 129,600 frames completely painted by hand from scratch, but indistinguishable from live photogra-phy'.[4] Similarly, the makers of *Final Fantasy* insist, 'No reference models were used or digitizing of real humans done to create these characters; they were all built from scratch within the computer'.[5] In other words, the ultimate digital cinema aims to produce the look and feel of 'live action cinema' (as it will now be called) but without 'live photography'.

In *Final Fantasy*, budgets and hype lavished attention on the creation of the character Aki Ross, a completely digital woman who was to be indistin-guishable from a real woman. Needless to say, the media hyped the possibility that men would now be able to create a dream woman who looked entirely real. There was even speculation about whether actresses and actors could be replaced.

If there is something odd about such an attempt, it lies in the idea of an animated film indistinguishable from live action cinema.[6] Which is to say, the very goal is to make the boundary between cinema and animation indistinguishable. This is the situation that Manovich announces, and appears to champion, in *The Language of New Media*: new media make possible the dissolution of the boundary between (live action) cinema and (digital) animation. Yet Manovich also declares, surely to provoke discussion, that, with the advent of new media, animation, once lesser and subordinate to cinema, now subsumes cinema. All is now animation, and cinema is but a subset of animation. Likewise, the *Final Fantasy* movie aims to subordinate cinema to animation, by replicating and thus subsuming cinema within digital animation. But why did so much attention settle on digital actors, and especially the digital actress, Aki Ross?

Everyone is fairly comfortable with the dissolution of the boundary between animation and cinema when it comes to producing backgrounds and special effects and even non-human characters (as with Jar-Jar Binks). But it is something of a commonplace in animation that the more one adds cinematically realistic detail to the figuration of human characters, the more audiences expect equally cinematic-real movements of those characters. Naturally, there are many types of realism or verisimilitude, and I am referring here to a certain sort of realism – the cinematic conventions for realism that are usually evoked as a point of reference for animation. Live action cinema has created certain expectations about how photoreal images of humans can and should move. Because live action cinema relies on filming real humans performing movements that obey physical laws such as gravity, we come to expect photographically realistic characters to act and move in accordance with the physical laws observed in our world. In animated worlds, however, effects of mass and gravity are not given but must be somehow produced, simulated, or fudged.[7] For these reasons, when digital animation strives to replicate and thus subsume live action cinema, it is human figures that become the test case. It is not only the photorealism of their appearance that comes under scrutiny, but also the verisimilitude of their movements in relation to physical laws. It is strange then that *Final Fantasy* and Lev Manovich's *The Language of New Media* seem far more concerned with photography than with movement. And their tendency to define new media in contrast to photography and the photoreal is not without consequences.

In Manovich, the emphasis on the digital generation of photographically real footage comes of an underlying opposition between analog and digital media. This has become a fairly common opposition, and Philip Rosen provides a nice summary of it: 'Whereas analog inscription is relatively continuous and depends on physical contact between different substances (artist's paint with canvas, for example), digital inscription is relatively discontinuous and depends on a seemingly arbitrary code of discrete, relational elements (numbers)'.[8] In other words, as Manovich makes clear, photography, as an analog medium, has an indexical relation to reality. Photography records reality, it captures the real. Digital cinema, on the other hand, is characterised as 'painted by hand' – by which Manovich means not only painting in the manner of gallery art or of cel animation (with ink pens, brushes, celluloid and other surfaces). He also means the use of computer software such as paint programs and other software. These all generate a reality 'by hand' rather than record or otherwise capture it indexically, via physical contact.

Naturally, with such an expanded definition of 'by hand', one might well ask whether photography too should not be considered as by hand – acknowledging the photographer's manipulation of lens and apertures. Or one might otherwise acknowledge that every media production entails the production of a variety of different kinds of signs, indexical and iconic and others. Yet the characterisation of photography and, by extension, live action cinema as inherently indexical is essential to Manovich.

The same is true of *Final Fantasy* movie as it strived to produce its cinematically realistic digital characters from scratch, that is, without cameras, with computers. But it quickly ran into trouble with its efforts to simulate an indexical reality. Initially, for instance, the hype surrounding the movie emphasised the photoreal quality of Aki Ross, and magazines featured photoreal images of her – images that were as realistic as photographs, and yet, uncannily, not photographs. Subsequently, however, in his interviews, director Sakaguchi shifted the characterisation of the digital actors from photoreal to hyperreal.[9] While there is no explanation for this shift of emphasis, I think that the answer lies in Aki Ross's hair. It turned out that, in order to produce hair that moves realistically, one has to generate thousands of individual strands with some degree of autonomous movement. Individual strands of hair must be individually animated – at great expense. In brief, the problem is one of movement, which Aki's strands of hair, waving in a breeze or billowing with movements of her head, came to exemplify. You can make a photoreal image of a face but when it moves, other criteria for realism come into play.

Similarly, literal-minded viewers of *Final Fantasy* were quick to detect something deceptive about the film's claims to have made its actors entirely from scratch within the computer. The problem lay in the film's use of motion capture. As the liner notes to the DVD remind us, motion capture took the form of 'a staff member, wearing a skin-tight black costume laced with 37 reflective markers, simulated true-to-life human motions for 16 specialized cameras that were connected to computer screens'. Programmers then used these captures to construct 3D stick figures that served as the basis for designing and animating the CGI actors. In other words, as many early viewers protested in on-line reviews, this was not the ultimate digital cinema – cameras had been used, to capture motion. Although the filmmakers did not capture real actors photographically, they captured the movements of a real person in order to construct actors who moved realistically, that is, in a manner consonant with the conventions of cinematic movement. Thus, for those who take 'from scratch' literally, *Final Fantasy* had cheated.

It is not such a surprise that *Final Fantasy* resorted to motion capture. After all, viewers will expect photoreal characters to move in accordance with the physical laws conventionally depicted in cinema, and it is not so easy to simulate the effects of mass and gravity 'by hand'. In fact, even with the realism available through motion capture, the characters in *Final Fantasy* appear quite weightless and hollow, as animated characters often do. But we tend to notice their weightlessness more in the context of a photoreal world.

For such reasons, it was surely safer to characterise *Final Fantasy* as hyperreal rather than photoreal. Nevertheless, audience expectations for the film, and much of its fascination, comes of what might be called its 'photoreal address', its apparent presentation of a live action world with photoreal actors that are not produced photographically. What remains interesting, even fascinating, about *Final Fantasy* is the way in which the film strives to give the sense of an indexical real by replicating or simulating a brand of cinematic realism. *Final Fantasy*, like Lev Manovich, thus stumbles into a situation in which live action cinema is treated as a stable, immutable world with a defined origin and end, which world new media must replicate or simulate in order to come alive. In effect, cinema must be pronounced dead for new media to come alive. In this sense it matters little whether one calls the *Final Fantasy* movie photoreal or hyperreal. The basic problem remains. How can the replication or simulation of something dead result in life? To become animated (or reanimated), cinema must be seen as dead or at least completely motionless.

In *The Language of New Media*, Manovich circles anxiously around cinema, as if caught by its fatal tides. On the one hand, he frets that new media might repeat the history of cinema. He worries that new media will lose their experimental edge, their openness, and will be only put in the service of producing stable, systematic, closed-off story worlds. On the other hand, he seems ready to announce that new media have already fallen, or will soon. There could indeed be a language of new media. In either case, cinema appears as a thoroughly formalised, stabilised form of representation or expression. In this respect, Manovich has internalised much of the wisdom about the history of cinema as the history of the rise of a hegemonic mode of representation. There are many variations on this history, so many that I cannot possibly write about them all; and each implies different strategies of resistance that follow from its view of film history. Let me simply mention some of these stories of the fall of cinema.

Noël Burch mentions the work of

> Marcelin Pleynet, Jean-Louis Baudry and others [who] decreed that the optical properties of the photographic lens (and hence the cinematic lens), a monocular technology arising directly from bourgeois ideology, were a kind of 'original' sin of the seventh art, a historical fatality adhering to its very being and that only disruptive practices could free it from.[10]

Burch argues, to the contrary, that there was nothing inevitable about the rise of a certain mode of representing space and volume; although that mode may today appear hegemonic, it did not follow inevitably from the properties of the apparatus. He speaks of an 'institutionalized mode of representation', to underscore that the hegemonic mode of cinematic representation is a product of institutional pressures, which are in turn linked to financial concerns (capitalism).[11] In other words, socio-economic concerns 'condition' the directions taken by cinematic representation. Nonetheless, one confronts a mode of representation that is now stabilised, homogenised, and institutionalised. The question then is, how does one re-open cinema?

David Bordwell, Janet Staiger and Kristin Thompson offer another, less polemical, less despairing, apparently neutral and empirical version of the tendency of cinema toward systematisation: the establishment of a 'classical film style'. Unlike Burch, they do not stress how socio-economic concerns condition filmic expression but rather gesture toward parallel historical developments. To borrow Miriam Hansen's description: they

> conceive of classical cinema as an integral, coherent system, a system that interrelates a specific mode of production (based on Fordist principles of industrial organization) and a set of interdependent stylistic norms that were elaborated by 1917 and remained more or less in place until about 1960.

The result is the classical Hollywood style, a style with

> thorough motivation and coherence of causality, space, and time; clarity and redundancy in guiding the viewer's mental operations; formal patterns of repetition and variation, rhyming, balance, and symmetry; and overall compositional unity and closure.[12]

Manovich sometimes presents a new variation on apparatus theory (cinema is indexical), but at other junctures he sees cinema in terms of the formation of a stable code, style, form or language. What is crucial for Manovich is that cinema appears somehow closed and completed. Even though Manovich is interested in more experimental fare such as *Man with a Movie Camera* (Dziga Vertov, Soviet Union, 1929), it is *The Birth of the Nation* (D.

W. Griffith, USA, 1915) that becomes representative of cinema for him. In sum, cinema appears a closed and completed world with a stable code or style or form of expression, which results in self-contained story worlds. Presumably, cinema tends toward closure and completion precisely because it is indexical – as if indexicality entailed a linear relation to the real that resulted in causal formations, which inevitably tend toward teleological closure.

Simply put, for Manovich, cinema has to be somehow stable and immutable if it is to become just another medium within the new media mix. Indexical media involve a stable relation to the real, based on contact with it, which allows for stable points of reference and thus for identity and for self-contained worlds. New media, however, do not touch the real or impress it into images. Rather, digital media generate images from numbers, at a remove, as if no longer beholden to the real. Moreover, because any of the old media can be digitised, new media loosen the grip that old media have on reality, by opening them to manipulations and transformations that cast doubt on their hold on reality. Digital media generate realities rather than record them. New media threaten to dispense with the logic of origins. At certain junctures, Manovich explores the possibility that new media entail a regime of simulation, in which all realities are generated, in which reference to an underlying reality is no longer important.

Yet, insofar Manovich defines new media in contrast to indexical media (photography and cinema), indexical media are not just another element. Manovich continues to evoke indexical media precisely because they provide proof that there is a real out there, which can be touched and captured – even if new media do not connect with it directly. Put another way, because Manovich has no theory of the subject and of its relation to the real, the real is, by default, something out there to be captured by cinema, which cinema in turn transmits faithfully to digital media. Thus the indexical continues to provide the foundation for new media – yet the so-called indexical media are deprived of any power to construct realities. Thus cinema is transformed into a brute materiality, a diegetic closure, dead world, into which new media are to breathe new life, to reanimate it.

This is what I think of as a 'consummated world'. It is a world that is consummated in the sense of completed. It is also consummated in the sense of consumed; it is already swallowed and digested, or always ready for consumption. Of course, if cinema can be seen as a consummated world, it is partly because it has for so long been a staple for consumers.

Manovich remains fascinated by cinema as consummated world. He sees in cinema entire worlds of possibilities, but these possibilities have been closed and contained, made for ready consumption. While he fears that new media too will become consummated, it is only because he himself has consummated cinema that he can make any claims for the life of new media.

Final Fantasy betrays a similar fascination with cinema as a consummated world. As with Manovich, the result is a paradoxical attempt to destroy the logic of origins while desperately pinning everything on the photoreal qualities of cinema. Simply put, cinema serves as the model and foundation for this digital animation, yet the replication or simulation of cinema via digital media is supposed to undermine cinema's status as an origin. At the level of its production and narration, *Final Fantasy* relentlessly circles around this problem.

The film presents a challenge to the logic of origins in several ways. In addition to bypassing the need for real places as shooting locations, the film destabilises relations to a place of production. It is a movie produced everywhere and nowhere, bits of information transmitted electronically between computers in various locations in Japan and the United States. Moreover, its story and actions seem to derive at once from video games, Hollywood films, and Japanese animation. Apparently, director Sakaguchi, who developed the video game narratives, worked with screenwriters Al Reinhart and Jeff Vintar to make the 'Japanese' story consonant with Hollywood conventions. Indeed, contrary to those who read the story as somehow Japanese (and therefore difficult for Westerners to understand), Sakaguchi protests that the film was penned in Hollywood. Needless to say, doubts arise about the extent to which Japanese conventions can be considered outside Hollywood and international cinematic conventions (and thus incomprehensible). But the point is that the production itself was billed as one produced from different locations – without a single real reference, place or source. In its very production, the film poses a challenge to the logic of origins by multiplying its places of production or origination. And isn't this precisely what digital media are supposed to do – generate multiple origins, or at the very least, multiple relations to an origin?

Yet, for all *Final Fantasy*'s bid for multiple origins at the level of place of production, at the level of its story and the production of digital actors, it is as anxious about origins and the indexical as Manovich is.

The film opens with Aki Ross recording one of her dreams of the violent extinction of an alien world, which I'll call for the sake of convenience, the Red Planet. Subsequently we learn through her dreams that the Red Planet has been destroyed in the course of a war, with weapons of mass destruction. Chunks of the destroyed planet, hurled into space when it exploded, found their way to earth, bringing with them the life forms of the alien world, but in spectral form – phantoms. On earth, which is coded as a blue-green world, the red-coloured alien phantoms proceed to suck the life out of all that lives on earth. When the reddish phantoms make contact with a human, for instance, they pull the human's life force out of its body – a sort of human-shaped radiantly bluish figure. The surviving humans have been reduced to living within cities protected with special energy shields to keep the phantoms out. In the meantime, the military is trying unsuccessfully to seek out and destroy the phantoms. A particularly militarist faction, led by a leering fascist type, is developing plans to use a weapon of mass destruction against the earth itself, targeting the red mass of phantoms that is burrowing its way deeper into the planet.

In contrast to the increasingly militarist army, Aki Ross and her mentor do not believe that the phantoms can be (or need be) destroyed by force. Because Aki harbors a phantom (she was infected by a phantom but managed to contain it with an energy field within her chest), she has made contact with the aliens in her dreams. She comes to understand that the phantoms are not alien invaders but life forms that were violently dislocated in the course of planetary destruction. These spectral aliens are feeding on the life forces of earth not in order to destroy it but in an attempt to heal themselves. Conveniently, it turns out that they are simply out of phase, and Aki is tracking down the remaining spirits of earth in order to unlock and restore the life-giving wave of the earth, Gaia. Thus she aims to heal both the phantoms and the earth. In other words, the story and moral message of *Final Fantasy* is straightforward: it is best not to resort to weapons to solve matters but rather to try to understand the sources of anger and violence, to heal rather than to combat. Oddly, however, both killing and healing seem to demand one to be willing to sacrifice one's life. In the end, it is the self-sacrifice of Aki's lover, a soldier named Grey, which allows her to make the final connection as it were, and reboot Gaia. (Grey is literally an inseparable mixture of angry militaristic red and compassionate blue-green love.) The suicidal gesture of their fascist opponent, who unwittingly aims to save the earth by destroying it, is on the order of a bad sacrifice. We understand his suicidal tendencies as bad largely because he sneers a lot, wears black leather and looks crazy. Which is to say, suicidal gestures are at once condemned and condoned on the basis of which kind of sacrifice truly makes for life. This is a not a comfortable distinction under any circumstances, but the film carefully codes the correct path with colours, so we know to follow the way of compassion and peace.

Still, as the necessity for self-sacrifice suggests, *Final Fantasy* is fraught with contradictory impulses. On the hand, it plays with multiple origins, as if digital media itself had overcome the problem of origins. Aki Ross, for instance, need not be designated as Japanese or American, and more importantly, she harbors an alien close to her heart, literally. She is a creature of multiple origins. And we might say the same for the digital actors in general: an actor's motions derive from the motion capture of one actor, the voice from another, and their physical appearance has indeterminate, multiple origins, insofar as the animators used various sources to fashion them. All this seems cause for celebration. On the other hand, the story betrays a certain obsession with origins. Clearly, to have one's world violently destroyed, to lose one's origins, is not a good thing. Moreover, the solution to such trauma is a holistic one, a search for origins that heals the traumatic dislocation. At this level, *Final Fantasy* treats the loss of origins as a traumatic situation that demands treatment, even to the point of demanding heroic self-sacrifice for one's home world. In brief, *Final Fantasy* pays tribute to the beauty and unity of the home world, a unitary origin, which is precisely what new media are supposed to render obsolete. Whence this holistic, mythic return to a unitary origin?

In effect, like Manovich, *Final Fantasy* remains under the spell of the indexical as a marker of the real. Even as they celebrate the ability of digital media to bypass or move beyond indexical media, to work from multiple sources and to generate multiplicity, they are thrall to the power of indexical signs. In the absence of indexical signs, digital media must simulate indexicality. That is the ultimate mission of the ultimate digital animation: indexicality in its absence. The result is a fascination with consummated worlds, an insistence on them in their absence. If *Final Fantasy* appears torn between possibilities at the level of its narrative about healing the relation between two worlds (can there really be two different origins in one world?), its fascination with consummated worlds is all too evident in its treatment of digital actors and the phantoms.

The reddish spectral images of phantoms seem calculated to serve as indexical markers of the life forms from the alien planet. Every effort was made to give them the feel of photography (a look of double exposure), as if the photographic feel of spectral images could establish retroactively the reality of the digitally generated models of alien life forms. The look and feel of indexicality is supposed to prove that there is, or was, a reality out there. Yet, as the digital humanoid actors make clear, there is a strange shift of emphasis involved in this fascination with indexicality. The blue human-shaped forms that the red phantoms suck out of bodies are reminiscent of the blue CGI shells built upon the 3D stick figures (generated with motion capture), on which animators 'painted' layer upon layer of musculature and skin textures. Ultimately, it is these blue shells that are the site of life, of animation, more than the actor's lifeless eyes, or weightless musculature, or undulating hair strands, or depthless skin textures. The film's visual conceit – the blue spirits are the life of humans – underscores this promise that life lies just under the skin as it were. Is life then just another layer, easily stripped away? In any event, the film is here calling attention away from the photoreal or hyperreal of images toward the process of animation

– especially to the humanoid blue screen animated through motion capture. But, as if fearful of undermining its indexical enjoyment, *Final Fantasy* can only give the site of animation (motion capture and the blue screen) a mythical status. This is how the replication or simulation of cinematic reality so easily turns into myth. Its fascination with consummated worlds results in a panicked quest for signs of life, a desperate hunt for the Gaia that will mythically reanimate the world of cinema that it has laboured technically to render inert.

The redemption of multilectical worlds

Although touted as a big-screen adaptation of Tezuka Osamu's 1949 manga entitled *Metropolis* and as a tribute to Tezuka, the animated film *Metropolis* is clearly a disappointment in those terms. Probably the film's commercial failure in Japan was due in part to audiences' expectations that they would see Tezuka's manga brought to the screen. Instead viewers encountered a story that departed significantly from its source, and a collage of the work of diverse talents with exceeding different visions of animation. In Europe and North America, rather than bill it simply as a Tezuka adaptation, advertisement stressed the collaboration of two well-known figures in the world of Japanese animation, Rintarô (director) and Ôtomo Katsuhiro (screenplay and storyboards), as well as the film's relation to the silent film *Metropolis* (Fritz Lang, Germany, 1927). The film met with greater success in North America, which led to a respectable commercial revival in Japan on DVD. Nonetheless, the film is not without difficulties, precisely because it brings together such different talents. The result is a film with distinct 'signature layers', which demand some individual attention.

First, the film obviously bears some relation to Tezuka's manga. As one of his earliest full-length manga stories, which is often grouped together with *Lost World* and *Next World* as Tezuka's SF trilogy, the manga *Metropolis* tells the story of an 'man-made human' (*jinzô ningen*) named Michi who, in addition to the ability to change genders, possesses various superhuman abilities. Michi the robot believes itself to be human and comes to think that Duke Red is his/her father. When Duke Red informs the robot that it has no father, that it is a man-made human or robot that was designed to further the agenda of the Red Party, Michi joins forces with other, far less human-looking robots, leading them in an attack on the metropolis. Michi's friend Ken'ichi tries to prevent Michi from destroying the city. As Ken'ichi and Michi battle, another group finds and destroys the source of Michi's power on a nearby island, and Michi slowly dissolves, finally melting away in a hospital bed as Ken'ichi and the other children watch and mourn its passing. In the end, there is nothing left of the robot but its heart, which then too melts.

The animated film *Metropolis* uses many of the elements of this story and adds to them, borrowing characters from other Tezuka manga in order to introduce new characters and situations. Insofar as Tezuka himself developed a 'star system' in which he would reuse famous characters from manga in different roles in other manga, the producers of the animated film are true to Tezuka in this gesture. Yet, because they transform Tezuka's story into one arc of a larger story, Tezuka is visible in the film largely in the form of his characters, which character designer Nakura Yasuhiro carefully updates in accordance to their original sources. In this respect, Tezuka's signature layer risks appearing as little more than a set of nostalgically familiar characters formatted to more contemporary tastes.

Second, there is the work of Ôtomo Katsuhiro, which tends to overwhelm the other signature layers. Renowned internationally as a manga artist and animation director, especially for the manga *Akira* (serialised 1982–90) and its film adaptation (1988), which is credited with launching the transnational manga and anime craze that gathered steam in the early 1990s, Ôtomo not only meticulously laid out the entire film in a series of detailed storyboards but also took the leap of combining Tezuka's *Metropolis* with Fritz Lang's film. Building on a fortuitous comment by Tezuka to the effect that the images of Lang's robot coming to life in the 1927 *Metropolis* had a great impact on him, Ôtomo deftly wove the plotlines of the two films together.[13] The result is a third signature layer that evokes Lang's film alongside Tezuka's manga.

As for Rintarô who began his career as an in-between animator on big-budget animated films in the late 1950s (under the name Hayashi Shigeyuki) and subsequently gained renown as a director of animated films as well as OAV series, it is difficult to say what he brings to *Metropolis*. While he has worked in the animation industry in various capacities, he has more recently found acclaim producing topnotch film versions of famous television series (as with *Galaxy Express 999* (1979) and *X* (1996)) as well as high-quality OAV series that revisit well-known series (such as the recent *Space Pirate Captain Herlock: The Endless Odyssey*, 2002). But no one thinks of Rintarô as contributing a signature style as a director. On the contrary, he seems to roll with the transformations of the industry, relying on long experience to make solid versions of beloved works. One can well imagine that the company that tightly controls the rights to Tezuka's works would be as delighted with Rintarô as it would be dismayed over Ôtomo. Rintarô brings competency, fidelity, and quality.

Now, with so many distinct talents adding at least four signatures layers – Tezuka, Lang, Ôtomo, Rintarô – one wonders what will hold them together. The film risks turning into a grab bag of different animators' styles, with each talent paying homage to Tezuka Osamu in its distinct way. The film risks becoming little more than series of citations of well-known talents – with no other apparent motivation than a profitable repackaging of hallowed styles.

One of the interesting aspects of the animated *Metropolis* is that media itself tends to become the mediator. In fact, media orientations provide the basic orientations for viewing the film. This is not to say that Ôtomo's story does not hold together. His story goes in a number of directions, however, and demands repeated viewing to appreciate; what is more, even though there is a comprehensible outcome, the story does not seem to drive the movie inevitably forward. Rather, Ôtomo's careful combination of Lang and Tezuka tends to call attention to media as a mediator. Let me explain.

A tension between digital animation and cel animation structures the film visually. First and foremost we see characters in the style of cel animation (flat, unmodelled, iconic) moving through three-dimensional architectures in a world of volumetric depth associated with recent developments in digital animation. Insofar as the characters in the style of cel animation are largely produced digitally, this is clearly a stylistic choice, partly dictated by the need to remain faithful to Tezuka's vision. In many scenes, the cityscapes and architectures directly evoke those of Lang's film, and it is as if manga characters had been set loose in the world of Lang's film. Yet character/architecture tension does not strictly follow a distinction between Tezuka and Lang. Rather, various polarities and differences tend to coalesce around what might be called a 2D/3D interface – with the caveat that so-called 2D characters always imply other dimensions, and so-called 3D environments appear on 2D screens. This is something of a relatively old or at least familiar problem in animation: how to combine cel and digital technologies with their very different (2D versus 3D) sensibilities?

The 2D/3D interface is localised and embodied in the figure of the robot Tima. Some of the most arresting images in the film are those of the angelic figure of the robot Tima in a halo of light. She appears pale and radiant, with a shock of blond hair and limpid blue eyes, against the rectilinear forms of the towering Metropolis. In particular, the ziggurat, designed to dominate the city, presents a stark contrast to Tima's soft, rounded radiance. Much of the promotional material for the film highlighted this contrast. The image of Tima against the ziggurat appears, for instance, on the dust jacket of the reprint edition of Tezuka's manga. The cover of the film book takes the contrast a bit further, with an image of Tima's head in profile, the face soft, angelic and radiant, while the cranium shows what lies within: gears, wheels and other mechanisms. This is an astute imaging of the central problematic of the film: Tima is a robot that looks supremely human yet also betrays an inhuman nature. She is, on the one hand, a beautiful and innocent child. On the other hand, she carries within her a darker, mechanical nature. Angelic in appearance, Tima is an angel whose intervention in human affairs cannot be predicted or trusted – an angel of destruction or redemption?

The final sequences of the film dwell on the dark destiny of Tima. Much of the film follows the development of robot Tima's friendship with the boy Ken'ichi, as together they flee her pursuers. Tima disappears immediately after her 'birth', and her 'father' Duke Red wants her back. It turns out that Duke Red had the robot (in the image of his deceased daughter) designed to ascend to a throne atop the ziggurat. The throne is actually an interface with computer weapons system that will allow Duke Red (via Tima) to rule over the city and the world. Eventually, Duke Red captures Tima, who knows nothing of her origins or destiny. She does not know that she is a robot designed for global domination. Nor does Ken'ichi.

In the final sequences, once Duke Red forces her to sit upon the throne, the contrast between the two Timas plays out violently, with the underlying mechanical Tima erupting through the radiant skin of the angelic Tima. Machinery invades her body, exposing her inner mechanisms, leaving only patches of her angelic appearance. Then, as Ken'ichi pulls her from the throne and tries to recall her to her angelic self, we see Tima's face half-angel, half-machine. In the ensuing scenes, as the ziggurat crumbles, the demonic, machinic Tima pursues Ken'ichi, intent on destroying him. Yet the robot still retains traces of the angelic side of her. And the good Tima makes a last appearance. Not loathe to twist the strings of viewers' hearts, the filmmakers allow Tima to return to her beautiful self and to recognise her beloved Ken'ichi before she plummets to her destruction.

In sum, right till the end, we see Tima as a being that is quite literally torn between two possibilities, between two identities, two natures, and two worlds. She is also the site where the different sources of the film – Tezuka and Lang – meet. The contrast between the two Timas allows writer Ôtomo to resurrect a conceit familiar from other projects – a self-organising all-consuming machine reminiscent of those in *Akira*, *Roujin Z* (1991), and *Spriggan* (1991). At the same time, the contrast is in keeping with Tezuka's manga, in which the robot Michi embodies a tension between the demonic and angelic, between evil and good, between adults and children, between domination and innocence. Yet, unlike the robot Michi in Tezuka's manga who readily changes gender from boy to girl and girl to boy, the robot Tima is decidedly a girl. In this respect, Tima also follows from the robot Futura in Fritz Lang's *Metropolis*. In effect, the contrast between the two Timas allows three different kinds of robot stories to coexist, distinct yet apparently not contradictory.

Recall that, in Lang's film, the evil father (Johhan Fredersen) constructs Futura in the image of the saintly Maria, in order to crush the spirit of the workers to whom she gives hope and inspiration for a better future. The animated *Metropolis* clearly builds on Lang's (and novelist Thea von Harbou's) story of unjust exploitation, in which the conflict between head and hands (thinkers and workers) is resolved by the heart, which becomes manifest in the romance between Maria and the son (Freder Fredersen). The animated *Metropolis* combines Lang's revolt of the workers against exploitation with Tezuka's revolt of the robots against human discrimination, as well as with Ôtomo's scenerio of machinic forces coming to life and going out of control. Ultimately, in the animated film, the heart or innocence promises to heal the range of problems evoked in these different stories – a 1920s story of technological exploitation (Lang), a 1950s story of human discrimination against those deemed 'non-human' (Tezuka) and Ôtomo's critique of the developmental State that emerged at a time when postwar Japanese economic growth seemed unstoppable (in the late 1980s).

Although the film makes a general appeal for humans to learn to understand, appreciate and even love robots, it has presented so many different relations to robots and technology that the viewer is left with a sense of uncertainty about what it would mean to nurture the robot. In effect, as the intersection of different stories on the figure of Tima makes clear, the animated *Metropolis* overdetermines the robot.[14]

Significantly, however, the animated *Metropolis* wears its overdetermination right on the surface. It thus stresses the impossibility of ever fully determining the robot. In this respect, the robot appears full of potentiality yet remains decidedly underdetermined.[15] In Lang's film, for instance, it is always possible to distinguish between the real woman Maria and the robot Futura. In the animated *Metropolis*, however, although the two natures of Tima are distinct, they are not separable. Nor does the film have a psychologically motivated transition from the innocent robot in search of love to the robot that would destroy the city. The two natures of the robot coexist in one being, which allows Tima to catalyse different actions without fully becoming a part of them. Needless to say, in film without any female roles (with the exception of a maid who is later impersonated by a young man), it is significant that the only character coded as female is a robot, and the girl robot's action are largely on the order of catalyst.[16] It is no small wonder then that Tima's signature line is 'who am I?' (*watakushi wa dare*). Insofar as she is a mediator of a range of tensions and polarised actions, the film must assure that she cannot know who she is, or understand her position. For Tima must potentially play many roles simultaneously, providing the orientation for different narrative lines.

Of course, we know who Tima is. We know her origin in the sense of who created her, when, how and why. But she is divergent at her origins: in appearance she is a replica of Duke Red's daughter, her inner structure is that of a robot, and her subsequent development in the company of Ken'ichi adds another layer or dimension to her makeup. In this respect, we might think of Tima as an overdetermined figure. Yet, at the level of media, this overdetermination actually functions as a sort of underdermination. This is evident in Tima's neither active nor passive catalytic function in the film. Something underdetermined is something that does not determine actively or thoroughly; nor is it entirely passive. In effect, this is how media operates in *Metropolis*. Media does not determine the audio-visual field in the sense of providing an origin and end or telos. Yet it does provide a basic set of orientations, which coalesce in the 2D/3D interface.

Put another way, the 2D/3D interface makes us aware of differences between different media, which become most obvious in the difference between flattish characters and voluminous architectures. Yet the film does not mediate the relation between sheets and volumes. It does not provide for mediation of the different media, in the sense of a synthesis that would raise up and resolve or cancel contradictions and tensions. Rather we have a mediator (Tima) that embodies the contradiction. This means that, at the level of narrative and its events, Tima is overdetermined. Yet, at the level of media, Tima functions as a mediator, as a force of underdetermination that allows for multiple relations to a (divergent) origin.

In this respect, Tima presents one solution to a general problem of new media. Many commentators speak of the way in which new media use the power of digitalisation to combine many different media. The goal of much new media art is not to level the differences between media (or to transcend it with effects of speed as in so much of the action-orientated digital animation) but to leave those differences visible and palpable, on the surface. The trouble is, the consequent vision of new media tends toward that of an omnivorous machine that incorporates all manner of media without digesting them. Again, the work of Ôtomo seems prescient here, with its self-organising all-consuming entities that absorb bits and pieces of everything at hand without really assimilating them; rather we continue to see the pieces as what they formerly were – a chair, a electric pillar, a car – and as part of an eclectic and gigantesque new life form. This is literally multi-materiality or multimedia.

The problematic of Tima is exactly that of new media – it is a problematic of multiple origins without mediation. This is far from the consummated world of *Final Fantasy*, in which one media formation (cinema) served as a traumatic origin for digital animation. Here we see the possibility of a 'multilectical' media world, a world in which one is orientated vis-à-vis different media and toward a whole (rather than a totality). The animated *Metropolis* repeats this multimedia gesture in its signature layers; there, too, it is a problem of the co-presence and cooperation of multiple layers.

146

Nonetheless, as I mentioned previously with respect to signature layers, there is a tendency for multiplicity to take the form of an asymmetry – the 2D/3D interface. This asymmetry, however productive, runs the risk of turning into a simple binary opposition, say, 2D versus 3D, or cel animation versus digital animation, or the human (and humanoid) emotion versus exploitation and domination. In the absence of mediation will all lapse into simple binary oppositions, contradiction or dualism? Will the multilectical world collapse into a binary code?

One of the ways in which the animated *Metropolis* strives to sustain its multilectical world is through the use of colour.

Compositing cel and digital animation is a common technical problem in animation (analogous in many ways to compositing live action 'analog' cinema with digital animation or CGI). Naturally, the *Metropolis* team had recourse to a range of techniques to composite these different layers, to de-emphasise the difference between the different kinds of dimensionality evoked by cel and digital styles. Yet, and this might be said to be Rintarô's most important contribution, the film often highlights the contrast. The difference between the two media remains visible and palpable, by design – as if the tension embodied in Tima had diffused throughout the filmic world. Or has she appeared as a crystallisation of this tension? This is an experience of multiple media, condensed in the form of a productive asymmetry between cel and digital animation – much as the two Timas condense the different sources of the narrative.

Rather than smoothly composite the 'flat' cel and 'deep' digital layers by masking or smoothing out the evocations of different dimensionalities (sheets and volumes), however, the filmmakers opted for colour to hold the layers together.[17] On the one hand, they used colour to lessen the sense of disjunction between cel and digital layers, by hand painting the digital architectures and by digitally colouring characters. On the other hand, with digital software, they let colour run in two seemingly incompatible directions. For instance, they painted entire scenes in complementary colours – reds and greens, or purples and yellows. The result is a stark, rather unsettling contrast. Moreover, the colour scheme sometimes jumps suddenly from red/green to purple/yellow, as in the sequences in which Duke Red's son Rock discovers Ken'ichi and Tima in the lower levels and pursues them. At the same time, in conjunction with the high contrast of complementary colours, the filmmakers deploy such a vast palette of red and green hues that the high contrast spreads across the scene in a play of subtle variations: scarlet, olive green, crimson, forest green, and an infinite number of other reds and greens. As a consequence, although colour seems to offer mediation (in the form of compositing), it replicates the asymmetry in the experience of multiple media in the form of high contrast and infinite variation.

At times, we watch the film only in terms of colour, and colours create continuities and introduce divides without settling into contradiction or affording mediation. Colour conjures up a dimensionless depth in which the two or three or four layers might coexist. Colour hints at another kind of time or depth that promises to redeem the perplexing coexistence of multiple media – of multiple origins, identities, worlds and histories. Colour provides a sense of an all or a whole (that is not a totality), such that this world, continually on the edge of destruction, hangs together. We sense that the ziggurat will fall, for its volumetric depths feel hollow, yet the colours that bring its surfaces into the world of characters promise redemption in advance.

The multilectical world of *Metropolis* verges on an experience like that which Walter Benjamin discussed in terms of the 'dialectical image'.[18] The dialectical image derived from the coexistence of incommensurable times and spaces within the same world. These different times and spaces defied dialectical resolution or mediation, simply holding together. Unfortunately, by refusing to produce contradictions and mediate them, the dialectical image threatened to stop historical movement altogether; revolutionaries would not arise and enter into conflict, for the dialectical image would not make basic contradictions palpable enough to politicise humans, to make them demand a new life. Yet Benjamin also saw in the dialectical image the promise of redemption, the advent of Messianic time.

Is this not precisely what happens in the animated *Metropolis*? The revolutionaries who would overthrow the State fail, as do the intrigues of the various other factions, and even Duke Red's plans for global domination. Agency always fails on the eve of mass destruction. In the end we see a flattening of the city's verticality, and the emancipation of the robots. The robots, however, are not revolutionaries, agents of historical transformation. Inspired by Tima, robots are angels of destruction (flattening) – and of redemption (colour).

While the multilectical world does not offer resolutions to conflicts or mediation of difference, neither does it treat difference as closed. Neither cinema nor cel animation are consummated worlds. Each follows its bliss. But how are they to act or work together? Just as humans can learn to work with robots by opening themselves emotionally to them, so *Metropolis* asks us to open our hearts to the digital – not its volumes but its colours. Still, colour alone will not suffice to redeem the 2D/3D interface or the human/robot divide. Redemption will demand a new humanoid figure – the girl/robot in the role of angel – who will announce the coming of a new world beyond the conflicts of history, making us see that the colours of the heart were always hovering over the divide, showing us the beyond by blinding us now.

Notes

1. I first presented this material at the 'Animated Worlds' conference in 2003 and wish to thank Suzanne Buchan not only for hosting the event but also for her subsequent encouragement and assistance with this paper.

2. For a fuller discussion of the problem of speed and hypercinematism (versus animatism, see Lamarre, Thomas, 'The Multiplanar Image', *Mechademia: A Journal of Manga, Anime and the Fan Arts* 1:1 (forthcoming).

3. A second digitally animated film related to the *Final Fantasy* games, *Final Fantasy VII: Advent Children*, was released in September of 2005, after significant delays in production. Judging from the trailer and the parts of the uncompleted film that have been screened at media festivals over the past year or so, I think it safe to say that this production considerably mutes the photoreal or hyperreal human figures of the first *Final Fantasy* film but has not altogether abandoned the idea. Andy Jones's digital entry in the *Animatrix* collection, *The Final Flight of the Osiris*, also affords a point of comparison with respect to muting the photoreal.

4. Lev Manovich, 'What is Digital Cinema?' in *The Digital Dialectic: New Essays on New Media* (MIT Press, 1999): 173–192. Chapter 6 of Lev Manovich, *The Language of New Media* (Cambridge: MIT Press, 2001), also entitled 'What is Cinema?' repeats much of the argument, with even greater emphasis on cinema as 'the art of the index'.

5. This was deemed important enough to stress in the otherwise brief liner notes to the DVD.

6. Such a project also demands a kind of double vision in which we would see cinema and not see cinema – whence analyses of the film in terms of the uncanny (Livia Monnet) or rotoscoping (Mark Langer). Livia Monnet, in 'Invasion of the Movie Snatchers', suggests that *Final Fantasy*'s effort to construct a cinematic real results in a repetition that is uncanny; cinema haunts digital animation. See *Science Fiction Studies* 31:1 (March 2004). Mark Langer discusses *Final Fantasy* in terms of the end of animation history, by which he means the end of a boundary between animation and live-action cinema; and he calls attention generally to the hyperreal computer-generated effects that have blurred that boundary – see asifa.net/SAS/articles/. More recently, at the SAS Animated Worlds conference in Farnham (2003), he calls attention to another kind of 'impossible' or uncanny doubleness in animation – that of rotoscoping. In effect, we might see *Final Fantasy* as a special instance of double vision in which the digital tries to overcome the indexical – which generates uncanny effects in its very failure.

7. For a fuller discussion of weightlessness in animation, see Thomas Lamarre, 'From animation to anime: Drawing movements and moving drawings', *Between Cinema and Anime*, special issue of *Japan Forum* 14:2 (2002): 329–367.

8. Philip Rosen, *Change Mummified: Cinema, Historicity, Theory* (Minneapolis: University of Minnesota Press, 2001): 302.

9. Barbara Robinson, 'Reality Check', *Computer Graphics World* (August 2001).

10. Noel Burch, *Life to Those Shadows* (Berkeley: University of California Press, 1990): 162.

11. Ibid.

12. Miriam Bratu Hansen, 'The Mass Production of the Senses: Classical Cinema as Vernacular Modernism', in *Reinventing Film Studies*, Christine Gledhill and Linda Williams (eds) (London: Arnold, 2000): 336.

13. This evocation of Lang's robot finds its justification in an afterword written for one edition of the manga, in which Tezuka commented that, although he had not seen Lang's *Metropolis*, he had seen a still from the movie, apparently from the scene in which the robot Futura comes to life.

14. See Louis Althusser's discussion of overdetermination and contradiction in *For Marx* (London: Gresham Press, 1997).

15. I adopt the term 'underdetermination' from Paul Dumouchel's discussion of Gilbert Simondon, in 'Simondon's Plea for a Philosophy of Technology', in *Technology and the Politics of Knowledge* (Bloomington: Indiana University Press, 1995): 225–271.

16. Gender is also a central problematic with respect Tima, as with Aki Ross. It is crucial to note that the association of femininity with materiality makes female or feminine characters the site of imagining the materiality of media. Whether this reverses or continues the abjection of the female body is an issue that merits fuller discussion in the context of new media. Clearly, however, this association of femininity with a sort of powerful (mediatic materiality) is a central problem in *shôjo anime*.

17. Music is also exceedingly important in the animated *Metropolis*. Brassy 'colourful' jazz often accompanies scenes with rainbow palettes or high-contrast complementary colour schemes, and the use of Ray Charles in the final sequences of destruction sounds a note of loss and nostalgia (echoed in the figure of the radio). In many respects, the use of music repeats the layering of old and new media in order to generate a sense of a non-relation – a pure heart, pure colour, or pure affect – that redeems rather than mediates historical relations. Yet it is colour that operates most effectively in the media interstices of the film, producing what might be thought of as so many tiny redemptions, which follow in the wake of the tiny robot-angel.

18. See Susan Buck-Morss, *The Dialectics of Seeing: Walter Benjamin and the Arcades Project* (Cambridge: MIT Press, 1989): 114; 120–121.

Thomas Lamarre is an Associate Professor of East Asian Studies at McGill University. He is the author of *Uncovering Heian Japan: An Archaeology of Sensation and Inscription* (2000) and *Shadows on the Screen: Tanizaki Jun'ichirô on Cinema and Oriental Aesthetics* (2005). He is also the co-editor, with Kang Nae-Hui, of *Impacts of Modernity* (2003).

Chapter 10

Style, Consistency and Plausibility in the Fable Gameworld

David Surman

Introduction

In 2004 British videogame developer Lionhead Studios, in association with its subsidiary company Big Blue Box, released *Fable* on Microsoft's XBOX console, a role-playing videogame in which you play an orphaned boy who matures into a hero and whose moral alignment relates to how you play the game. While the videogame enjoyed substantial commercial success in the UK and North America and was appraised in established videogame magazines such as EDGE, it received a lukewarm reception among hardcore role-play gamers and fans of Peter Molyneux's prior achievements. Their tastes had been sharpened by the trail of 'teasers' released by the developers,[1] as well as Lionhead Director and lead designer Molyneux's frequent mention of the revolution in gameworld design that *Fable* would offer. Extraordinarily, these frustrations motivated Molyneux to confront his audience in the gaming press, in an online documentary, and on his own Lionhead online forum. In answer to the frustrations of his gaming public, Molyneux writes:

> There is something I have to say. And I have to say it because I love making games. When a game is in development, myself and the development teams I work with constantly encourage each other to think of the best features and the most ground-breaking design possible.

Abstract: Gameworlds are the expression of a complex cultural and textual interaction, in which the foundational structures of the videogame solicit investment and belief from the player. Style arbitrates this solicitation, causing all aspects of the gameworld to conform to a common aesthetic line. This process is rarely so efficient however, and contemporary videogames such as *Fable* demonstrate the messiness of this ideological contract between the ambiguous roles of producers and consumers of videogames.

> However, what happens is that we strive to include absolutely everything we've ever dreamt of and, in my enthusiasm, I talk about it to anyone who'll listen, mainly in press interviews. When I tell people about what we're planning, I'm telling the truth, and people, of course, expect to see all the features I've mentioned. And when some of the most ambitious ideas get altered, redesigned or even dropped, people rightly want to know what happened to them.[2]

In an unprecedented dialogue with consumers, Molyneux apologised for the underwhelming release of *Fable*, which was to be the videogame to simulate an unprecedented experience of exploratory player freedom. Trees would grow, the environment could be directly affected, and there would be new levels of player/environment interaction: in short, the gameworld would provide a heightened experience of realism and immersion. When these flights of fancy failed to materialise in the final retail product, the intentionality of the videogame designers was held to task, through the new system of direct accountability inadvertently created by Lionhead Studios' own online forum.

Molyneux and his production team made available their imaginary projections of what the *Fable* gameworld *could* be – and the company's unspoken policy of transparency had backfired. Audiences had gauged the quality of this particular videogame against the imaginative projections of the lead developers alongside their own consumer expectation, and the online forum designed to extend the gameworld through discussion, mythmaking and speculation had instead served as a channel through which the *Fable* producers were directly accountable to the *Fable* consumers. As lead programmer Dene Carter and lead designer Simon Carter reflect, such criticism is representative of both the importance of imaginary preconceptions of the gameworld, and the close scrutiny brought to the videogame by those gamers who pay close attention to the creative possibilities of development.[3] In his online post Molyneux goes on to write:

> If I have mentioned any feature in the past which, for whatever reason, didn't make it as I described into Fable, I apologise. Every feature I have ever talked about WAS in development, but not all made it. Often the reason is that the feature did not make sense. For example, three years ago I talked about trees growing as time past. The team did code this but it took so much processor time (15 per cent) that the feature was not worth leaving in. That 15 per cent was much better spent on effects and combat. So nothing I said was groundless hype, but people expecting specific features which couldn't be included were of course disappointed. If that's you, I apologise. All I can say is that Fable is the best game we could possibly make, and that people really seem to love it.[4]

As this essay will investigate, the control of ideologies of freedom that permeate the construction/consumption of gameworlds is a central concern for both developer and gamer alike. Here I specifically examine the role of style in this ideological equation. Two issues are immediately apparent: the utopian expectations of a significant proportion of gamers, and the way in which information that emerges during development creates an imaginary game against which the final production is measured. No matter how much Molyneux and the Carter twins justified the need to remove certain elements in order to improve the holistic experience of the game, certain gamers felt betrayed that their anticipated gameworld, an assemblage of imaginary negotiations and scant information sources, is not vindicated in the commercially available *Fable* gameworld. This consumer anxiety is motivated in part by Molyneux's rhetoric, and he admits that 'I have come to realise that I should not talk about features too early [and] so I am considering not talking about games as early as I do'.[5] This complex response to the *Fable* gameworld involving both developers and gamers provokes a series of associated questions: what is (and what is not) an acceptable gameworld? What strategies do games employ to create a sense of completeness while never truly being so?

Of particular interest to me are the textual strategies through which games developers rationalise both the material and imaginary limits of the worlds they create. While a videogame may suggest a spatial and temporal infinity in its worldview, nonetheless those edges are eventually encountered. While we can see the distant hilltop horizon or gaze out to sea in *Fable*, the restricted exploratory potential means that we can never reach that place. The imaginary investments of gamers overcome this boundary, extending both positively and negatively beyond the limits of play, either to praise or criticise the potential gameworld.

My study of gameworlds relates primarily to role-playing games and action-adventure videogame 'genres', in which exploratory play and interaction with non-player characters (NPCs) is of paramount importance. From a game studies perspective, the study of gameworlds presents us with a discursive point in which theories of representation and theories of play are consolidated. The overriding governance of interrelated conceptual principles of style, consistency and plausibility affect both representational and play aspects, be it as recognisable player/character (e.g. Eidos' *Tomb Raider*, 1996) or controlling deity (e.g. Lionhead's *Black and White*, 2001).

In the first section I examine the way in which the gameworld – a term which is regularly used, and yet rarely qualified, in both industrial and academic circles – relates to the older broadly accepted idea of the diegetic fictional world. By association, existing theories on the fictional world help us to understand the under-theorised notion of the gameworld. Through recourse to certain literary and film discourses, I suggest that the psychology and function of style in gameworlds differs radically to conventional diegetic worlds of live-action film and television, and has more in keeping with animated film, comic books and the science fiction and fantasy genres across various media. I suggest that style, as a unifying determinant, creates the basis upon which the ideological effects of consistency and plausibility are constructed in videogames.

In a second move, I look at the specific way in which the participatory act of play differentiates the gameworld from other associated forms of fictional world, with the noted exception of tabletop role-playing and war games such as White Dwarf's *Warhammer* franchise. In the transition from a non-interactive to interactive experience of fictional worlds, what is gained and what is lost? And on reflection, as James Newman has noted, are videogames interactive at all?[6] As such I must further explain developments in the play theory of game studies. Through an examination of *Fable*, I reflect on the ways in which modes of representation and play coincide to create a believable diegetic space.

Fictional worlds

Before we examine gameworlds, further enquiry must be made into certain recurrent terms and their uses. The theoretical use of 'world' in various media discourses is yoked to the creation of a foundational 'reality'. To be in the 'world' of a novel, film or performance suggests an experience with strong continuities with aspects of our real-world experience; an experience that is immersive and all-encompassing, without the kinds of reflexive punctuation that would destroy its holistic effect. A fictional world, then, is on one level a realist discourse since it deals with the construction of a naturalised space to be disavowed, and which is ancillary to the noteworthy things that happen, and the events take place in that world. However, simultaneously one is able to look to the corners of that world and note that things are happening outside of the terms of a restricted narration, as part of a holistic 'sphere of activity'.[7]

Moreover, the fictional world is simultaneously an episteme, a legitimating source to which discrete activity such as flora and fauna, cultures and societies connect; and yet the fictional world is itself a product of the overriding creative motivations and stylistic choices of the production team – it is both created and serves the role of creator. Fictional worlds are constructed, and are found primarily in the tradition of serialised or open fictions that rely on a core matrix of spaces, cultures, characters and places to unify them. The generalist, open access Wikipedia defines them thus: '[a] fictional universe is usually differentiated from the setting of, and the cosmology established by, ancient or modern legends, myths and religions, although there are countless fictional universes that draw upon such sources for inspiration'.[8] Videogames are the most recent addition to this fictional mode. Role-playing games such as *Fable* rely heavily on the transposition of religious and mythological narratives in real-world cultures.

In addition, role-playing videogames that are recognised for their immersive and expansive gameworlds (like the Square-Enix *Final Fantasy* and Nintendo *Zelda* franchises) rely heavily on serialisation, and on a complex intertextual knowledge base expanded as each new title is developed, played and contextualised by discerning fans. Though I limit my discussion to gameworlds, this distinction necessitates a further excursion into literary theory and film studies, alongside videogame and animation studies. And though I use literary criticism and traditional film theory, in a cross-disciplinary enterprise I shall be mapping their methods onto the videogame text. The various worldviews offered by new media have rarely been studied as such, and as a consequence, in an effort to enrich our conceptual understanding of videogames, I knowingly make lateral and sometimes tenuous leaps from established debates in studies of literature and live-action film.

The place of style in gameworlds

The stylistic basis of the gameworld and its accompanying 'second-order realism'[9] have evolved from the ongoing remediation of worldviews from preceding and contemporaneous media that share narrative themes, stylistic tropes, points of distribution and, at times, even audiences. Gameworlds incorporate the codes and conventions of animated, science-fiction, comic-book, televised and cinematic worlds. In its wholesale consolidation and expression of the media it encounters, the gameworld is exemplary of the contemporary notion of new media convergence. For example, in his essay 'Videogames as Remediated Animation' Paul Ward outlines the complex way in which videogames can be understood through the lens of animation discourses, and he examines the migration of the stylistic conventions of animated movement from animated film to videogame.[10] His analysis foregrounds Jay Bolter and Richard Grusin's theory of 'remediation' to describe the migration of the representational modality of movement from one media (animated film) to another (videogames) in a new media culture. He writes that '[r]ather than 'new' media simply replacing 'old' media they will, at any historical point, necessarily *remediate* previous media forms. By remediation they [Bolter and Grusin] mean the ways one medium appropriates the representational strategies of another ...' – in this case the remediation of animated movement from animated film to videogame – '... to further its transparency/immediacy but with the apparently contradictory consequence of foregrounding the process of mediation itself'.[11] While Ward presents a qualitative analysis of remediated movement in which he notes the loss of nuance and expression in videogame animation,

Fig. 1: The Fable game screen.
[©Microsoft Corporation.]

I simply want to note that stylised animated movement contributes to the gameworld by remediating the illusionism and immersive strategies of the animated film. In the remediation from drawn animation to two-dimensional videogames such as *Sonic the Hedgehog* (SEGA, 1991), parallax-scrolling was carried over to give the illusion of depth-of-field. In computer animation, the remediation of three-dimensional modelling and texture mapping into contemporary videogames creates the same illusionist effect.

As a remediation of a variety of diegetic strategies from a range of media, the gameworld seeks to produce as immersive an experience as possible, reflecting our real-world experience of reality as an interconnected continuity of spaces, times, and experiences; a seemingly borderless space that invites participation. Bolter and Grusin categorise this imperative as 'immediacy', the desire to erase the traces of mediation in the construction of a singularly immersive experience.[12] However, the diegetic worlds in 'new' videogames can only be appreciated for their immediacy when juxtaposed against prior 'old' gameworlds. Ward notes a similar predicament in the assessment of a text's realism: 'We can only understand and conceptualise how "realistic" these forms are by reference to our actual lived reality – including, however, our experience of other media representations such as "realistic" live-action films'.[13] Similarly the 'worldliness' of the gameworld is qualified through comparison with other media texts for whom the explicit criteria of 'world' is paramount, such as cult media. As such, videogames invite comparison with other so-called cult media, for instance the science fiction franchise Star Trek. Importantly, the activism of audiences seen in studies of cult media fandom – specifically in the way they hold producers to task for taking the 'world' in a direction felt inappropriate – echoes the relation between the developers and gamers of *Fable* discussed here.

Bolter and Grusin categorise this opposing intertextual tendency as 'hypermediacy', in which an emphasis on the new (in the case of gameworlds) necessitates recourse to a multiplicity of other texts against which the 'newness' of 'new' is qualified. This is not to be confused with the aesthetic hypermediacy of the game screen (such as that of *Fable*) with its multiple information sources relating health, wealth and location). I feel this contributes to the immediacy of the gameworld, since all information sources are pseudo-indexical representations of the players' causal status within the gameworld. The information presented does not refer to an experience outside of the diegetic space of the videogame, and instead adds depth and complexity to the player avatar in caricature of our lived experience of geography, health and wealth. These abstractions are indexes to the reality of the gameworld and thus substantiate its plausibility as a possible world. To compare, the hypermediacy of the contemporary newsscreen refers to multiple non-continuous realities (sports, celebrity, news coverage, tv listings, stocks and shares) within one screen space, whereas the gamescreen information is connected to the singular reality of the played gameworld.

Ward identifies that in both animated film and videogames representation does not depend on any indexical link with reality, save for certain uses of motion-capture technology in the animation of moving characters.[14] Whereas live-action film captures reality and augments and transforms it (through production techniques) to create its fictional world, animated film and videogames create diegetic worlds from scratch. I concur with Ward that this distinction has limited currency given our accelerating media convergence and the blurring between animation/film/videogames. However, both the conceptual and conspicuous place of style differs in the historical development of different media. Therefore the place of style in a stylistic history of comic books is not comparable to the place of style in a stylistic history of celluloid-based film.

Cinematic and literary concepts of style

In live-action film production, style is most commonly connected to the treatment of the pro-filmic reality through production design, casting etc., and through subsequent post-production processes including editing, sound design and now digital manipulation. David Bordwell writes in his stylistic history of film of the formal nature of style:

> In the narrowest sense, I take style to be the film's systematic and significant uses of techniques of the medium. Those techniques fall into broad domains: *mise-en-scène* (staging lighting, performance and setting); framing, focus, control and colour values, and other aspects of cinematography; editing; and sound. Style is, minimally, the texture of the films images and sounds, the result of the choices made by the filmmaker(s) in particular historical circumstances.[15]

Filmmakers cannot, in principle, effect pro-filmic reality beyond a certain point, though I recognise that the digitisation of live-action film practices has undermined this. For the sake of distinction, in live-action filmmaking style does not extend to the *total* aesthetic reconfiguration of an actor's physical body, the colour of the sky on the day of filming, and so on. Reality is manipulated, but not created: style is a principle guiding the aesthetic transformation of the pro-filmic 'real world'. Erwin Panofsky summarises that

> [e]xcepting the very special case of the animated cartoon [and, I propose, the videogame], the movies organise material things and persons, not a neutral medium, into a composition that receives its style, and may even become fantastic or pretervoluntarily symbolic, not so much by interpretation in an artist's mind as by the actual manipulation of physical objects and recording machinery.[16]

In the wholly artificial worlds of videogames and animated film along with extending and legitimating cross-media franchises, style serves a different function (since no pro-filmic reality exists and every attribute of the text is artificially created) similar to the governing role style plays in certain literary forms and genres, in particular science fiction. Particular styles often precede the release of the referent text in the form of toys, artwork, advertisements and so on. They also follow the text in fan art, dress styles and fan cultures such as *cosplay*, and of course imitation in other videogames. In his introductory essay 'Reflections on Style in Science Fiction'[17] George Slusser writes that

> [a] form like science fiction causes us to ask whether style can be the world as well, and SF[18] worlds creations of style. This conjunction of style and world creation raises some interesting questions. Indeed, how can the "creation" of a fictional world be an act of style when style is traditionally seen as belonging to the realm of the individual rather than collective utterance?[19]

Slusser argues that traditional prose – much like live-action film – relegates the place of style to the order of additional effects secondary to the predominant realism of syntactic rhetoric, comparable to the indexical 'material' realism of film photography. Literary style, in that traditional rhetorical sense, is the preserve of an individual author's *parole*, or word choice, rather than the *langue*, or governing language of the world. While in live-action film, style extends, in equally traditional accounts,[20] from the choice of *what* to put in front of the camera and *how* to do it, it is also disavowed as the foundation from which the spectrum of effects conceived as 'realism', 'diegesis' and 'fictional world' emerge. This is not the case for the 'new' world of SF. Slusser notes that '… the primary function of SF and what gives it its generic identity: the creation not just of narrative worlds but of *new* narrative worlds. And these new worlds, conversely, reveal a new role for style.'[21] The fantastical nature of the literary SF genre provokes a shift in both the place and function of style within the contexts of other literary modes: '[t]he stylistic utterance, then, defined in relation to this idea of world, can be little more than idiomatic, an exception to the rule. Despite these traditional expectations, however, style plays a significant role in SF world creation.'[22] The wholly fictional world of most SF elicits the same remediation paradox as the diegetic worlds of animated film and videogames – to be uniquely immersive while at the same time understood and appreciated in the context of other comparable works.

Consistency

In the creation of fictional worlds what role does style serve common to SF literature, animated film, and videogames? This question brings us to the consequence of totalising stylisation shared by SF, animated worlds and gameworlds – the effect of dynamic *consistency*. Slusser cites the work of Richard Ohmann on the role and function of style in prose fiction. Importantly, Ohmann emphasises the way in which style should be considered experientially rather than rhetorically. Slusser writes that

> [h]e offers, in contrast to the old manuals of rhetoric, an expanded role for style. In statements such as "style is the hidden thoughts which accompany overt propositions" Ohmann defines style as the point at which acts of thought separate from the hegemony of propositional or formal acts of language. To Ohmann, language is, ultimately, a system that permits the individual speaker to explore his or her natural world, making this latter a realm of experiential referents rather than simply one of signs and codes.[23]

Style then becomes a means of constructing a world in which heuristic experiential navigations are emphasised over systems of signification, a point that clearly resonates with the topsy-turvy logic of the animated world and the interactive realm of the videogame, in which the experiential is at times the only means of sense-making.[24] On a side note, this pheno- menological approach has been emphasised elsewhere in film and anima- tion studies.[25] Slusser adds that

> [t]he ancillary role to which rhetoric has traditionally relegated style has in a sense hidden its true potential, which is in reality a means for individual

speakers of a given language to explore and understand realities that lie on the fringes of, or just beyond, its syntactical limits.[26]

In relation to film theory, similarly confining rhetoric can be found in the over-determination of photographic indexicality and its technological truth claim associated with writers such as Stanley Cavell and André Bazin. In Bazin's thesis, the convergence of cinema technology is motivated by an idealised imaginary construct driven by pure immersion and complete realism, a 'myth of total cinema', in which the 'facts' of cinema's representation of a singular reality override the apparent 'fiction' of non-indexical reproduction.[27]

As part of my call for an expanded theory of style in videogames (and to some degree animated film, SF, and comic books) I propose that style provides a means of governing a fictional space that operates at the limits or beyond our 'real world' conception. The emergent logic of the stylised fictional world provides a consistency reflective of the foundations that underpin the logic of our everyday experiences since '[t]he very idea of *world* implies a complex set of laws and relationships …'.[28] Ward writes that: 'A game … offers us a simple coherent world … not complicated by references to anything but the most general sense of reality and the world of the game seems largely *self-contained*'.[29] At points in which new elements are integrated into the gameworld they are conditioned by the predominant style of the host. This conditioning extends to games which permit players to submit modified material, as in the player portrait submissions of Black Isle/Bioware's *Baldur's Gate* series, in which players create portraits clearly following both in-game conventions and those of fantasy illustrators such as Frank Frazetta.

In these sandpit realities where real-world complexities are pared down, style arbitrates the (albeit artificial) rules and regulations correspondent to our real-world experience. For instance: Newtonian physics (through game engines), evolutionary diversity in the natural world (through complex 'bestiaries' of creatures and monsters), and even consciousness (in artificial intelligence programming). In a gameworld which is fantastical and surreal (such as *Fable*) the gameplay, physics engine and aesthetic treatment of characters (Fig. 2) and environment all follow this implicit logic to create a consistent experience that (while radically different to our lived experience) has a cosmology which acts as the 'temporary episteme' Ohmann identifies in SF stylistics.

In accordance with Ohmann's account, I suggest that style, then, is a regulatory system of aesthetic and physical values spanning all textual elements of the fictional world. Style provokes immediacy, since it ensures a naturalistic consistency across all representational and non-representational elements within the text. At the beginning of many role-playing

Fig. 2: Character concept artwork for Fable, *featuring clearly styled costume design.* *[©Microsoft Corporation.]*

games (an excellent example, aside from *Fable*, being *The Legend of Zelda: The Wind Waker* [Nintendo, 2002]), when the player/character is in his 'hometown', his costume, his tone of skin, his dialect, his *accoutrements*, all pertain to a governing stylistic principle that ceaselessly promotes the solidarity of all constituent aspects. As the game progresses and the player/character moves further and further from his homestead, the stylistic juxtaposition of player with a consistent-yet-different environment (for instance rural character in urban environment) serves to emphasise the geographic worldliness through a caricature of the ubiquitous real-world experience of cultural solidarity and cultural difference.

At this point you might be thinking 'why is he describing as *style* what I know to be generally referred to as *design*?' This is understandable since a videogame *designer's* role involves conceiving of a consistent diegetic space. In a theoretical context however I feel the term design to be insufficient in describing the continuities between animated film, live-action, literature and videogames. I use style then as a synonym for design as it is used in videogame development, and in recognition of its remediation between various media.

To recall, in SF Ohmann suggests that style is an episteme, and not simply a rhetorical strategy. Style becomes an invisible unifying logic that creates an effect of immediacy; everything looking and functioning in a perceived rightful place, cultural history evidenced in the artefacts, architectures and design practices of this (albeit constructed) world. As an episteme, style assumes the function of a myth of origin, a primordial point to which everything is linked in the fictional world. For the fact that the buildings share aesthetic principles with the dress codes, the treatment of physics, and non-player characters – that there is a degree of homogeneity when rightfully there should be heterogeneity – style as 'surface level expression' is representative of an assumed cultural depth and a utopia of cultural solidarity common to the majority of fictional worlds across a variety of media.[30] In the gameworld successful consistency relates to the extent that a guiding principle of style has penetrated and unified all corners of games aesthetic (both representational and non-representational) aspects.

From this assertion it is clear that style therefore serves both a formal aesthetic and ideological function. By creating a fictional world with its own internal logic videogame developers can construct experiential expressions to be associated with particular gaming *brands*. This was most pronounced in the console wars of the mid-1980s to early 1990s between SEGA and Nintendo, whose in-house videogame franchises created stylised worlds with distinct ideologies rehearsing, with each play experience, a projected company image. The cyberpunk chic of SEGA's *Sonic the Hedgehog*, *Streets of Rage* and *Turrican* series presented a clearly different set of aesthetic and cultural values to the 'cutesy' chaos of Nintendo's *Super Mario World*, *Kirby's Dreamland* and *Pop n' Twinbee* series.

When looking at *Fable* we can note the ways in which the various stylised attributes contribute to the production of an ideological effect. While these are many and varied, and would warrant further study, I want to consider the ideology of player freedom that is the mainstay of developer rhetoric and consumer expectation, and that seems to be so central to both the praise and criticism levelled at *Fable*.

Plausibility, and playing gameworlds

In the previous section I examined gameworlds as primarily representational phenomena through an analysis of the role of style. In this section I shall foreground the role of play in the experience of gameworlds. In a cinematic, televised or literary experience the construction of a diegetic sense of world extends from a predominantly non-interactive narrative text. As discerning readers, we consume the action as it unfolds before us, negotiating the layers of information that constitute a believable diegesis. Our experience is individuated through what Martin Barker has called prefiguration, the preformed judgements and experiential negotiations that precede the media experience, which are brought to the text in the act of interpretation.[31] Mark J. P. Wolf identifies the changes brought about by interactivity to the diegetic fictional world:

> By the time the video game appeared, the concept of the diegetic world was already familiar to most audiences through film and television. The video game used much of the visual grammar from these media in the construction of its worlds, and was able to build upon established conventions (such as conservation of screen direction when cutting from one space to another) through added participatory elements. Some of these elements, such as navigation and

interaction, place certain limits on to the diegetic world that are unlike those found in film or television. And as with film, the development of the diegetic world did not occur in a smooth, straightforward fashion.[32]

The non-interactive apparatus remains unaffected, at the discrete level, by our experience of it. Conventionally speaking, written prose is not alterable, though we can chose not to read. Likewise we can choose to leave the cinema, pause the DVD or video, change the channel – the content will remain the same. Newman writes, 'In the *Tomb Raider* movie, I can go to sleep or walk out and Lara will still save the day. But the game needs me ... The game is nothing without the player.'[33] However I recognise one can argue that, through the circuitous system of cultural production and consumption, the fashions, twists and turns of collective audience taste direct the development of popular media.[34]

Regarding interactivity, videogames present a substantial change in the history of mechanical and electronic media experience.[35] In videogames, play is the central activity through which meaning is produced. Play dominates the hierarchy of the different modalities found in videogame experiences: it individuates videogames from other media and as such is their defining characteristic. While games contain systems of representation and narrative comparable to prior media forms, emulating cinematic and literary modalities,[36] the simulation-oriented activity of play is the primary agent through which these other processes are expressed. That is not to say that such modes of communication do not exist, but rather that they are expressed through the moderating and modifying activity of play. I want to make clear that while discussing play, I do not want to overstress its place to the detriment of other ways of studying videogames. As I have said, a study of gameworlds incorporates both theories of representation and theories of play.

Given the centrality of play, the construction of gameworlds requires an increased level of stylised 'attention to detail' to counter and negotiate the inevitability that players reach a point where they encounter the limits of the gameworld; a limited repertoire of moves, a finite exploration space, glitches and cheats. As such, videogames invite considerable testing and scrutiny by consumers as a consequence of the interactive nature of play. In a similar way, interactive arts such as installation often suffer from participants focussing on play to the detriment of the production of meaning intended by the work. The pleasures of the interface override the disclosure of the artist's intent.

Cinematic composition and editing direct the attention of the viewer to focal points and centres of action, as do syntagmatic structures in literature. In videogames, players direct their attention through play, and while the game is furthered through a set series of 'core' interactions, nonetheless the player is (predominantly) in command of the ways in which that is approached. For instance, standing in a corner is a viable option, as is running in a circle, or devoting hours to clearing an area of enemy characters. Newman writes, '... without a player, "Lara" just stands there'.[37] While these activities are often unproductive in terms of narrative flow or game completion, they are certainly available to the player and highlight the way in which play constitutes a predominant norm defined by the average gamer; and a peripheral 'other', associated with the extremes of play proficiency, is often referred to as the 'casual' or 'hardcore' gamer.[38]

In his review of game and play theory dating back to the 1950s, Newman writes that '[t]he game is a voluntary activity, engagement with which represents an end in itself rather than operating as a means to an end; game play is its own reward and is clearly distinguished from ordinary life'.[39] Play therefore generates the same effect of self-containment and immediacy found in the way style creates coherence across the representational (and certain non-representational) aspects of the gameworld. The played gameworld remediates both our real world experience of childhood exploration and simultaneously our experience of games played in relation to certain sets of rules. Though 'distinguished from ordinary life' such worlds are dependent on the plausible correspondence to real-world laws as a system of stylising parameters through which players and audiences can negotiate the fantasy. Ward writes that gameworlds

> ... offer more compelling gameplay if certain rules (such as those of gravity and the solidity of objects) are obeyed up to a point even when characters are performing actions that seem unbelievable by real-world standards. A certain degree of plausibility at one level helps to emphasise the pleasure of engaging in vicarious activities that go beyond the bounds of normal physical capability.[40]

Even in a heavily abstracted game series like *Super Bomberman* which nonetheless features characters and environments, the remediation of the real-world rules of board games like 'chess' and 'connect four' into the gameworld provide a tacit system through which players can rationalise and negotiate the gaming experience. The experience of another prior form of game authenticates through subtle continuities of form and structure of play. Frauenfelder (quoted in Ward) writes that '[a]lthough game developers like to boast about the realism of the experiences they create, they're actually talking about making sure that the world within a game, which may be entirely unlike the one we live in, is consistent and accessible'.[41]

Newman writes that the play theorist Roger Caillois 'distinguishes between *paidea* and *ludus* referring to games with simple and complex rules respectively.[42] As such skipping a rope (*paidea*) can be distinguished from more complex games such as bridge or football (*ludus*).'[43] Therefore, the vast majority of play activity within a gameworld can be placed on a continuum between simplicity (*paidea*) and complexity (*ludus*). It is important to stress that a durable use of these categories necessitates placing them on such a continuum, noting all the shades of grey between the poles. Gonzalo Frasca has added that we can further distinguish between *paidea* and *ludus* through the recognition of the role of outcome in the two categories.[44] As Newman notes, *ludus* is characterised by an effort to achieve an objective, while *paidea* is not. Frasca, quoted in Newman, writes that *paidea* is 'physical or mental activity which has no immediate useful objective, nor defined objective, and whose only reason to be is based in the pleasure experienced by the player ... . *Ludus*, therefore, requires reference to an external suite of rules where *paidea* is understood and delimited by the player'.[45]

Caillois' notion of *ludus* has clear associations with the idea of style as I have outlined it, since style acts like a 'suite of rules' governing all aspects of the gameworld. Play is then by association subject to the overarching rule of style, since stylisation touches all aspects of the constructed gameworld. The range of abilities, speed and strength of the player/character in a given point in the game is contemporaneous with the stylised world in which s/he resides. An expanding world, opened up through exploration and narrative exposition, is echoed by an expanded repertoire of play abilities. As a consequence, the return of an 'expanded' character (with the abilities and *accoutrements* of later areas of the gameworld) to an early area of the gameworld has an implicit experiential meaningfulness; a dramatic quality extending from the juxtaposition of stylistic complexity and simplicity.

Given the predominance of the rule of style in all aspects of the gameworld, I concur with Frasca's suspicion that we can never be truly free from rules, per se, in videogame worlds; there is no state of utopian pure *paidea*.

Elsewhere, Newman has made key observations which are integral to the way play distinguishes the gameworlds from its animated, cinematic and literary predecessors. To summarise, in those non-interactive diegetic worlds the protagonist character is identified as separate to the audience participant. No matter the degree of identification, the majority of audiences recognised the status of the filmed subject as 'other'. In videogames, a radically different system of subject association is constructed, in which players partially collapse on-screen characters with the first-person referent 'I', and (in an admittedly simplistic account) games characters become a surrogate second self. As Newman notes, this has a substantial consequence on the way in which we negotiate the gameworld as a diegetic space.[46] Further, in his argument Newman suggests that those players actually playing the game, which he terms 'on-line' players (not including the audience of secondary players who do not control but instead spectate) do not distinguish between character and world, and instead understand 'character' to be '… a complex of all the action contained within the gameworld … The situation and action within the gameworld are inexorably bound into the players conception of the experience of being within that gameworld'.[47] I suggest style is integral to the creation of this holistic character complex.

Conclusion: 'imagining what freedom means'

At the core of the gameworld is a dichotomy. For a belief in player freedom to be solicited, then the restrictions of the rule of style must come into play to create necessary senses of consistency and plausibility. Freedom then becomes what one can do within overarching constraints. The imagination of the videogame developer recognises these conditions, while the imagination of the gamer largely does not. For the gamer the concept of freedom, like Bazin's myth of total cinema, constantly exceeds that of the developer since it is not constrained by the hum-drum of pragmatic technological development. It is a driving imperative in the popular consumption of videogames, and is (like any sales pitch) exaggerated by the developers, publishers and advertisers of videogames. *Fable*'s Dene and Simon Carter note that what developers and gamers imagine freedom to mean is central to either the success or failure of a videogame. If a videogame exceeds the imagined preconception of freedom held by gamers then it is sure to be a success, if it falls short, then it is sure to fail.[48] *Paidea* – Caillois' experiential play without restriction – might be considered analogous to Bazin's imagined total cinema. Certainly, the freedom to explore gameworlds without restriction is the mainstay of tradeshow demonstrations of the latest role-playing videogame.

One telling example from *Fable* relates to the inclusion of homosexuality among the repertoire of choices available to the player (Fig. 3). NPCs exhibit growing affection to the player/character as the videogame progresses and the player/character is able to seduce whom he chooses, man or woman. This feature represents a significant move in videogames culture, away from the simulation-based dolls-house sexuality of *The Sims* to a main protagonist in whom gamers can realise more complex structures of desire. However, here we encounter a rupture in the consistency of the gameworld, since the videogame erroneously refers to your same-sex male spouse as 'wife'. Moreover, to fully explore the gameworld at one point the player must marry Lady Grey, the head of the largest town Bowerstone. This act revises the sexuality of the player/character to bisexual; the fullest exploration of the apparent freedom of the gameworld leads to a narrative restriction contrary to the defining choices the gamer had made. This particular contradiction is representative of the broad criticisms of gameworlds gamers recurrently make. It is a hole in the consistency.

Fig. 3: Gay seduction in Fable.
[©Microsoft Corporation.]

Revealingly, gamers criticise holes in the ideology of the gameworld and the associated lack of consistency. Illusionism is not something to be deconstructed as in the radical cinema and associated film theory of the 1960s and 1970s, but instead something to be cultivated and extended. This tells us something of the socio-cultural role games are playing in the domestic sphere, perhaps as an escapist fantasy, or space for legitimate experimentation with subjectivity not permitted in real-world social structures. In this essay I hope to have sketched some preliminary ideas regarding the role of style and discourses of consistency and plausibility in the gameworld. The immediacy of *paidea* and the ideological discourse of freedom are central to the role-playing gameworld. A dialectical appreciation of such freedom however necessitates a foundational rule set. What is *paidea* without *ludus*, immediacy without hypermediacy, and freedom without constraint? This dichotomous realisation is overshadowed by the rule of stylisation, a temporary episteme within which we can experientially negotiate our artificial realities.

Acknowledgements: I would like to thank Seth Giddings, Tanya Krzywinska, Bob Rehak and Paul Ward for their invaluable suggestions during the writing of this essay.

Notes

1. For tradeshow previews and TV trailers see: http://www.gametrailers.com
2. Available online at: http://www.lionhead.com/boards/nonflash.html
3. *Fable: The Big Feature: In-depth with Lionhead and Big Blue Box*, production documentary, available online at: http://www.kikizo.com
4. Available online at: http://www.lionhead.com/boards/nonflash.html
5. Ibid.
6. James Newman, 'The Myth of the Ergodic Videogame: Some thoughts on player-character relationships in videogames', *Game Studies* vol. 2, no. 1 (2002), available online at: http://www.gamestudies.org/0102/newman/
7. Oxford English Dictionary.
8. 'Fictional universe', *Wikipedia, the free encyclopaedia*, available online at http://en.wikipedia.org/wiki/Fictional_universe
9. Andy Darley, 'Second-order realism and post-modernist aesthetics in computer animation', Jayne Pilling (ed.), *A Reader in Animation Studies* (London: John Libbey, 1997): 16–24.
10. Paul Ward, 'Videogames as Remediated Animation', Geoff King and Tanya Krzywinska (eds), *Screenplay: Cinema/Videogames/Interfaces* (London: Wallflower Press, 2002): 122–135.
11. Ibid., 128.
12. Jay David Bolter and Richard Grusin, *Remediation: Understanding New Media* (London: MIT Press, 1999): 21–31.
13. Paul Ward, 'Videogames as Remediated Animation': 132.
14. cf. Stephen Prince, 'True Lies: Perceptual Realism, Digital Images, and Film Theory', *Film Quarterly*, vol. 49, no. 3 (1996): 27–37; Warren Buckland, 'Between science fact and science fiction: Spielberg's dinosaurs, possible worlds, and the new aesthetic realism', *Screen* vol. 40, no. 2 (1999): 177–192.
15. David Bordwell, *On the History of Film Style* (London: Harvard University Press, 1997): 4.
16. Erwin Panofsky, 'Style and Medium in the Motion Pictures', Angela Dalle Vacche (ed), *The Visual Turn: Classical Film Theory and Art History* (London: Rutgers University Press, 2003): 69–84.
17. George Slusser, 'Reflections on Style in Science Fiction', George Slusser and Eric S. Rabkin (eds), *Styles of Creation: Aesthetic Technique and the Creation of Fictional Worlds* (London: University of Georgia Press, 1992): 2–23.
18. 'SF' is an acronym for Science Fiction.
19. George Slusser, 'Reflections on Style in Science Fiction': 3.
20. cf. Ralph Stevenson and Guy Phelps, *The Cinema as Art* (London: Penguin, 1989, revised 2nd edn); Victor F. Perkins, *Film as Film* (New York: Da Capo Press, 1993); Stanley Cavell, *The World Viewed: Reflections on the Ontology of Film* (Cambridge: Harvard University Press, 1979, enlarged edition).
21. George Slusser, 'Reflections on Style in Science Fiction': 3.
22. Ibid.: 3. One can even speculate that in the late-nineteenth century animation remediated both the style and worldview of the science fiction literature of the time, evidenced in the multimedia works of Windsor McCay and Emile Cohl, as both textual forms enjoyed a degree of popularity in the Victorian culture of curiosities.
23. Ibid.: 6.
24. This is particularly true of the burgeoning imported games market. While many Japanese games are illegible to their western audience, the audiences' tacit knowledge of videogames in general allows for an experiential navigation of the gameworld.
25. For a summary discussion see Suzanne Buchan's essay in this book.

26. George Slusser, 'Reflections on Style in Science Fiction': 6.

27. André Bazin, 'The Myth of Total Cinema', *What is Cinema? Volume 1* (London: University of California Press, 1967): 17–22.

28. George Slusser, 'Reflections on Style in Science Fiction': 3.

29. Ward, 'Videogames as Remediated Animation': 123, my emphasis.

30. Siegfried Kracauer, 'The Mass Ornament', *The Mass Ornament: Weimar Essays* (London: Harvard University Press, 1995): 74–86.

31. Martin Barker, 'The *Lord of the Rings* Project', paper presented at the Association for Research into Popular Fictions annual conference, Liverpool John Moores University, 20–21 November, 2004.

32. Mark J.P. Wolf, 'Narrative in the Video Game', Mark J. P. Wolf (ed), *The Medium of the Video Game* (Austin: University of Texas Press, 2001): 94, for a brief history of diegetic and non-diegetic aspects in videogames see pages 93–111.

33. Newman, 'The Myth of the Ergodic Videogame' *Game Studies* vol. 2, no. 1 (2002), available online at: http://www.gamestudies.org/0102/newman/

34. cf. John Fiske, 'Commodities and Culture', *Understanding Popular Culture* (London, Routledge: 1989): 23–48; Joanne Hollows, 'Mass Culture Theory and Political Economy', Joanne Hollows and Mark Jancovitch (eds), *Approaches to Popular Film* (Manchester: Manchester University Press, 1995): 15–36.

35. The reason I delineate mechanical and electronic media relates to the interactive and participatory modes of certain classical forms such as baroque sculpture, in which viewers are provoked to circle the work in order to ascertain its implicit narrativity. For further examples, see: Angela Ndalianis, *Neo-Baroque Aesthetics and Contemporary Entertainment* (London: MIT Press, 2004).

36. For an analysis of the relation between cinema and videogames see: Geoff King and Tanya Krzywinska (eds), *Screenplay: Cinema/Videogames/Interfaces* (London: Wallflower, 2002). For literature and videogames see: Barry Atkins, *More Than a Game: The Computer Game as Fictional Form* (Manchester: Manchester University Press, 2003); Janet Murray, *Hamlet on the Holodeck: The Future of Narrative in Cyberspace* (London: MIT Press, 1997); Marie-Laure Ryan, *Narrative as Virtual Reality: Immersion and Interactivity in Literature and Electronic Media* (London, John Hopkins University Press: 2001).

37. Newman, 'The Myth of the Ergodic Videogame', available online at: http://www.gamestudies.org/0102/newman/

38. David Surman, 'Downtime and Online Debate in Hardcore Gamer Culture', paper presented at the *Association for Research into Popular Fictions* annual conference, Liverpool John Moores University, 20–21 November 2004.

39. James Newman, *Videogames* (London: Routledge, 2004): 18.

40. Ward, 'Videogames as Remediated Animation': 126.

41. Ibid.: 127.

42. Roger Caillois, *Man, Play and Games* (Urbana: University of Illinois Press, 2001).

43. Newman, *Videogames*: 19, my italics.

44. Gonzalo Frasca, 'Introduction to Ludology', Mark J. P. Wolf and Bernard Perron (eds), The Video Game Theory Reader (London: Routledge, 2003): 221–236.

45. Ibid.: 19–20, my italics.

46. Newman, 'The Myth of the Ergodic Videogame', available online at: http://www.gamestudies.org/0102/newman/

47. Ibid.

48. *Fable: The Big Feature: In-depth with Lionhead and Big Blue Box*, production documentary, available online at: http://www.kikizo.com

David Surman is Senior Lecturer in Computer Games Design at the University of Wales, Newport. He is author of *The Videogames Handbook* (in press), a Reviews Editor for *animation: an interdisciplinary journal* and an editorial board member for *Games and Culture*. His work on animation and videogames has featured in *EDGE*, *The Age*, *Gamasutra.com*, *Entertext*, *Videogame*, *Player*, *Text*, and *The Boston Globe*. His research focuses on design theory and practice, style and fictionality in screen media.

Chapter 11

Final Fantasies: Computer Graphic Animation and the [Dis]Illusion of Life

Vivian Sobchack

y title takes its point of departure from Alan Cholodenko's introduction to his edited anthology on animation, *The Illusion of Life*. There he tells us, 'Animation always has something of the inanimate about it ... a certain inanimateness that both allows and disallows animation ... And this would suggest that in a sense the "uncanny" is never not with us, for it would mark the always already returned of the ghost, the zombie, and the dead in us – lifedeath'.[1] It is this 'lifedeath' of animation I want to engage here, particularly, however, as it is foregrounded – but reversed – into the 'deathlife' of animation (the 'dis-illusion of life') in a film that is literally (or, should I say, computergraphically) an overt exploration of 'lifedeath' and 'deathlife' and filled with ghosts, the dead, and zombies (the latter taking the form of 'synthetic human actors'). I am referring, of course, to *Final Fantasy: The Spirits Within* (Columbia Pictures and Square USA, 2001), conceived and directed by Hironobu Sakaguchi who was also the originator, in 1987, of the 'Final Fantasy' interactive video game franchise.

Touted as 'the first major release to feature an entire cast of computer-generated human characters',[2] *Final Fantasy* was also a major flop at the box

Abstract: What is the underlying urge in the history of animation, particularly computergraphic animation toward photorealism? Why does the desire persist to turn Pinocchio into a 'real' boy? Touted as the first major animated release to feature an entire cast of computer-generated human characters, *Final Fantasy: The Spirits Within* (2001) was a major box office flop. Using this film as a paradigmatic text, this essay asks not only what we want from animation but also what animation wants from us, and explores both the rhetorical lure and semiotic disappointment at the irresolvable paradox of this impossible desire for complete computergraphic simulation of human beings.

office, its failure attributed primarily to its apparently confusing and emotionally unengaging narrative. While its CGI attempts at 'photorealism' were acknowledged as 'ground-breaking', the general sense was that – for a variety of reasons, not all having to do with the convoluted story – the majority of reviewers and the audience found *Final Fantasy* an unsatisfying experiment that just 'didn't work'. Why is this? One possible reason comes from a thoughtful viewer posting on the Web's International Movie Data Base. 'Well', she writes, 'it's quite simple in my opinion. Animation films are entertaining when we know that they are animation films. They are something different from reality, and all the imperfections we find in them don't count. All the holes we … find are filled with our imagination … But, when the level of perfection of an animation film crosses the line between animation and reality, then we change our scale of values, and we judge the film by comparing it with non-animation film. [This] is when we notice … that there is still an abyss between a real and a virtual actor.'

In what follows, then, I want to focus on 'our scale of values' as it slides and shifts in our phenomenological relation to animated film in general and, as I go, to explore as well the computergraphic conundrum – or 'lifedeath' – of animation presented to us as 'deathlife' by *Final Fantasy* in particular. Thus, although I will begin with rather 'grand' theoretical questions about 'the "problem" of animation', most of my subsequent remarks will be of smaller scale and more 'piecemeal' in approach – this called for not merely by the conference brief but also (and markedly) by the way in which *Final Fantasy* itself calls intense spectatorial attention to the smaller scale of the 'detail' and, in a 'piecemeal' fashion, constitutes our epistemological engagement with the ontology of its CGI characters and world as a 'patchwork' of heterogeneous, shifting, and incompatible values impossible to reconcile and resolve in either narrative or representational satisfaction.

The 'grand' questions, then, are 'What do we want from animation?' and 'What does animation want from us?' In terms of the first question, as spectators, there are some of us – although we are in the minority – who do prefer from animation its reflexive acknowledgment of its own (and our) 'metaphysical effort': that is, the visible struggle or play of 'becoming' we see in the work of the Brothers Quay, on the one hand, and on the other – and 'lightning' – hand, the Brothers Fleischer. What we privilege is animation always visibly marked by the threat of inertia and 'lifedeath', animation filled with the 'uncanny' gaps, starts, stops, and stutters that, as Cholodenko suggests, 'simultaneous[ly] bring … death to life and life to death'.[3] Nonetheless, what the majority of spectators seem to want and value from animation is not a gloss on 'metaphysical effort' but rather, as film theorist Noël Carroll has said of 'trick films', 'metaphysical release'[4] – that is, the vicarious playing out of the 'plasmatic' possibilities for subverting and/or substituting the laws of physics (and here I might add, the laws of mathematical calculation) with the laws of imagination.[5] Furthermore, if one reads through reviews and IMDB viewer comments about *Final Fantasy*, it also seems that what we want from animation is not 'sterility' or 'coldness' but, rather, the 'emotional substance', 'flowing rhythm', and sense of 'improvisation' of line, action, and world primarily associated with 'auratic' hand-drawn pen-and-ink animation, if also apparently achieved by the 'playful' CGI animations of the *Toy Story* films (Pixar 1995/1998); *A Bug's Life* (Pixar, 1998); *Antz* (Dreamworks, 1998); *Shrek* (Dreamworks, 2001); *Monsters, Inc* (Pixar, 2001); *Ice Age* (Blue Sky, 2002); and, most recently, *Finding Nemo* (Pixar, 2003) – all films that have assiduously shied away, both in narrative and representation, from character 'realism' of any kind but emotional.

The second question, 'What does animation want from us?', seems, at least on the surface, of another order – one not only about aesthetics but also about the technology of the medium and its utopian dream of 'overcoming' the inertia and stasis that would stall its freedom of expression. In this regard, film critic Anthony Lane's ironic comment about CGI and the recent *Finding Nemo* might well be said of the earlier *Final Fantasy*: 'the ideal vehicle for the demonstration of an improving medium. To authenticity and beyond!'[6] And here, for its analogical – and, dare I say, analog – value, I would invoke André Bazin's famous essay, 'The Myth of Total Cinema', which argues that cinema was 'an idealistic phenomenon', and, very early on, was imagined by its various inventors as 'a total and complete representation of reality ... [a] reconstruction of a perfect illusion of the outside world in sound, colour, and relief'.[7] Thus, Bazin tells us, 'The guiding myth, then, inspiring the invention of cinema, is the accomplishment of ... an *integral realism*, a recreation of the world in its own image'.[8] What, we might ask, is the comparably idealistic 'myth of total animation'? Is it identical to cinema's? Or, in its perceived place (rightful or not) as a 'subset' of cinema, is animation guided by a similarly-directed but, nonetheless, 'second-order' idealism – that is, by a desire for the 'perfect illusion' not of the 'outside world' but of the perceptual correspondences that inform 'photorealism', and, in particular, '*cinematic* photorealism', with 'authenticity'?[9] But then, again, perhaps insistent on its own discrete metaphysics, animation might desire not 'integral realism', but 'integral *irrealism*' – and thus be guided by an alternative ideal founded on the 'total' creation (not re-creation) of the world in its own image (the referent of 'its' here *not* that of the 'outside world' but, rather, of 'animation' itself).

The answer, then, to 'What does animation want?' is certainly ambiguous – if not as downright ambivalent as it turns out to be in *Final Fantasy*. Here CGI animation wars with itself – attempting, on the one hand, to *re-create*, through the simulation of cinematic photorealism, 'perfect computer generated human beings' (this the initial hype and later changed to 'hyper-real' human beings) and, on the other, to *create* and animate an imaginative and irreal (if perceptually realistic) world in – and through – its own CGI imagination. Again, both analogically and in terms of the analog image, it is worth looking backward to make the 'problem' of animation, particularly the CGI animation in *Final Fantasy*, even more problematic. Thus, I will evoke *Pinocchio* (1940) and ask, again, 'What does animation want?' Is it the fulfilment of Pinocchio's dream of 'authenticity' – that is, to become a 'real boy'? And, if so, 'authentic' and 'real' according to what criteria? – for Pinocchio the wooden puppet and the 'real boy' he is finally rendered (the word here no accident) both draw upon and are drawn through the *same* representational logic that would assert their ontological *difference*, each from the other. The irony of this theoretical 'il-logic' is that, in practice, it produces its own kind of 'integral realism' from the coherence of the patently irreal, and thus a very emotionally satisfying phenomeno-logic – one not found, significantly, in what would seem to be the similar representational circumstances of *Final Fantasy*. Unlike in *Pinocchio*, as one reviewer notes, here the CGI 'real boys' (and girl) give 'emotionless "performances"' in a film with 'a distinctly stiff, *wooden* flavour'.[10]

The conundrum, then, is that while we never really question either Pinocchio's 'wooden-ness' or his later 'fleshiness', in relation to CGI heroine, Dr. Aki Ross, and the 'real boys' of *Final Fantasy*, we hear again and again – and down to the most minute details – litanies of disappointment at their rendering. If we're willing to accept animation's 'irreality' in its *representation* of human beings (a tradition that continues in the CGI of *Toy Story* and *Monsters Inc*), why, then, is there such a problem with accepting *Final Fantasy*'s 'hyper-real' *simulation* of human beings? Clearly, in this particular instance, the problem has something to do with a significant 'incompatibility' that emerges between the different scale of values and expectations attached to representation and simulation when a particular kind of utopian 'myth of total animation' – as the IMDB viewer wrote – 'crosses the line between animation and reality'. And, indeed, in *Final Fantasy*, this 'incompatibility' can be found everywhere: not only in the differing epistemological demands made on the spectator by the semiotic status of the animation but also in the irreconcilable rhetoric that surrounds the film and in the incompatible premises of the narrative that serves as their perverse allegory.

Let me touch first on the narrative which focuses on 'humanity's' need to defeat a highly successful 'alien invasion' of a futuristic and decimated Earth by creatures (later found to be the 'phantoms' of beings from a devastated planet) who, for their energy, 'suck the life' out of (CGI) human beings. (In this regard, one reviewer notes both a basic ontological and epistemological incompatibility between the narrative and its CGI realisation when he asks: 'Is this some kind of sick joke, or at least an in-joke? A virtual human plays one of the few real humans left',[11] while another highlights the irony underlying – or is it over-laying? – the fact that these CGI 'human facsimiles have devoted every pixel of their beings to preserving life as we know it'.[12]) One faction of the remaining and 'mechanistically'-inclined 'humans' wants to blast the red-orange and multi-formed aliens with a 'Zeus cannon' which may also end up destroying the Earth. The other more 'animist' faction, led by scientists Dr. Aki Ross and Dr. Sid, believes the invasion can be stopped if a certain small number of remaining and representative Earth 'spirits' (eight to be exact) can be amassed to form a 'wave' of positive and life-giving energy that will overtake and transform the alien phantoms and their angry planetary spirit – or 'Gaia' – into a more 'pacific' (and literally blue) form.

In short, the narrative serves up a simplified version of James Lovelock's 'Gaia theory'; that is, both the Earth and, here, the destroyed alien planet and its ghostly remnants as well, are regarded as a purposeful, animate, and organic totality. As noted, however, the use of CGI animation confuses and ironises this opposition between 'mechanists' and 'animists', between the technological and the organic, between what it means to 'suck the life' out of human beings and to 'inspire' or 'animate' them with an *élan vital*. Here, quite literally and computergraphically, *in toto* and in the end, the 'organic' phantom spirits of both alien and Earth 'Gaia' co-constitute what, for Sergei Eisenstein, constituted animation itself: 'plasmaticness', or 'the potentiality of the primal plasma, from which everything can arise'.[13] Nonetheless, the graphical 'plasmaticness' of this Earth- and life-affirming 'modulation, transitivity and the continuous coming into being of images' is, paradoxically, accomplished by – and allegorises – the same CGI that would and does, in *Final Fantasy*, appear to 'suck the life force' from organic human representations (and from the representation of organic humans)![14] Here, while CGI gives us the 'infinite changeability, modulation, and transitivity' of the 'plasmatic' in its passionate orange-red and pacific cool-blue visualisations of Gaia and its phantom spirits, in its human form, the 'plasmatic' is bent on 'being' a 'fixed entity' and the rigidity of its CGI algorithms and geometric forms forestall any sense of improvisational, or organic, 'becoming'. As Keith Broadfoot and Rex Butler put it (long before *Final Fantasy* was ever released), 'Animation corresponds, as Eisenstein implies, to a condition of organic production. Animation is not the result of the lifelessness of a mechanical reproduction but is itself life-giving. What, however is the form of life it creates? Is it a life that we know?'[15] And the answer is that it is not – or, at least, not 'quite' – for, as one reviewer notes of his experience: 'You miss the unchoreographed wayward tilt of a head or an improvised double take; the unpredictable physical chemistry of actors that computer science hasn't mastered'.[16] What emerges is not organicity but, quite visibly, 'the lifelessness of mechanical reproduction'.

We can see, then, that the foundational 'visual premises' of *Final Fantasy* – that is, the computational computergraphic grounding of the film's 'humans' – are semiotically incompatible with the film's narrative or 'visual argument': that what animates, inspires, and gives life is organic, not technological, production.[17] Faced by this deeply structural incompatibility – one that affects both the process of our 'reading' and our emotional engagement with the film – we watch *Final Fantasy* in a state of what, in another context, Scott Bukatman has called 'epistemological hesitation'.[18] What might this mean? – particularly since *all* cinematic imagery is technologically achieved? Again, why do we have problems with *Final Fantasy* and not *Pinocchio*? Peter Wollen, in *Signs and Meaning in the Cinema* is helpful here. He tells us in relation to all cinema and its iconicity: 'The iconic sign is the most labile; it observes neither the norms of convention [the symbol] nor the physical laws which govern the index'. Thus, given its iconicity, '[cinematic] depiction is pulled toward the antimonic poles of photography and emblematics. Both these undercurrents are co-present in the iconic sign; neither can be conclusively repressed.'[19] If this antimonic tension is an undercurrent in *all* cinematic iconicity, nonetheless, *one* of its poles – the indexical photograph or the symbolic emblem – usually tends to dominate, regulating our phenomenological perception not only of genre but also of the representational 'ontology' of what we see on screen. Here we might safely generalise that iconic indexicality is dominant in live-action, photorealistic film whereas the emblematic is dominant in animation – both, in their own semiotic modality, able to create an 'integral realism' or 'irrealism' that immerses the viewer in a coherent textual world. Thus, in *Pinocchio*, where both the wooden puppet and the 'real boy' are hand-drawn and posited in the integrity of an irreal world, there is little antimonic tension between indexicality and emblematics at the level of resemblance. In *Final Fantasy*, however, this antimonic tension is not only heightened but also ambivalently 'double-valued'. The film attempts to achieve indexical, photorealistic 'human characters' in a world that is emblematic, symbolic, irreal – and thus it visibly *equivocates* within what, narratively and semiotically, is supposed to be an integrating 'perceptual realism'. That is, without textual *purpose* (as is the case in a film such as *Who Framed Roger Rabbit?* (Robert Zemekis, 1988)), *Final Fantasy* solicits from the viewer two different and incompatible modes of epistemological apprehension and aesthetic judgement. Finally, then, what we pay most attention to (or what most distracts us) is the antimonic struggle between indexicality and emblematics, and this phenomenological attention (or distraction) reveals, even if only latently, the 'illogical' or contradictory foundations of the narrative.

The deep structural incompatibility that exists between *Final Fantasy*'s narrative rhetoric and the semiotic mode of its visual representation also finds expression in the deep structure of the rhetorical discourse that has surrounded not only the film's promotion and reception but also the perceived 'success' – or not – of its then 'state-of the-art' CGI renderings of human characters. In this regard, rhetorical theory (not often used in film studies) is particularly illuminating about what constitutes the 'double bind' of animation that sits on the fence between representation and simulation. Chaim Perelman and L. Olbrechts-Tyteca's seminal *The New Rhetoric: A Treatise on Argumentation*, in a chapter aptly titled 'Arguments Based on the Structure of Reality', provides us with a rhetorical – and structural – companion to 'the myth of total cinema' and 'total animation' called the 'argument of unlimited development'.[20] Such an argument, we are told, 'insist[s] on the possibility of always going further in a certain direction without being able to foresee a limit to this direction, and this progress is accomplished by a continuous increase in value'.[21] This said, however, it bears emphasis that the argument of unlimited development can progress in either direction – that is, either toward 'diminution' or 'enlargement' (on the one hand, *Dumb and Dumber* and now *Dumb and Dumberer* and, on the other, *Fast and Furious* and now *2 Fast 2 Furious*).[22]

Unlimited development is, of course, the argument that accompanies the industrial (if not aesthetic) promise of CGI, particularly as it pursues what has been regarded (per one IMDB viewer) as 'the Holy Grail of CGI creators' – 'a realistic, living, breathing and acting human being'. Hence statements from Sakaguchi and Square, made in 1999, about the CGI planned for *Final Fantasy*: 'It is beyond anything that has ever been done before', and 'We are creating "perfect computer generated human be-ings"'.[23] (By 2001, it was 'We can do anything we want now. In this type of filmmaking, there are no limitations', although the 'perfect computer-gen-erated human beings' were now described as 'hyper' real, not 'photo' real.[24])

Of particular relevance to *Final Fantasy* is the fact that the argument of unlimited development can be used not only to project 'limitless' extension but also 'to *depreciate* a state or situation which *could* have given satisfaction but to which a more favourable condition is supposed to be able to follow'.[25] Hence, the following viewer comments on IMDB: 'A level of CG detail that really has never been seen before, but it isn't completely perfect'; the terse dictum, 'Don't ever make a movie about real people if you can't portray real people'; and '[There was a lack of] chemistry and warmth between the characters ... [but] to dismiss computer animation as inferior to live action is to not give the spirit of technological advancement its due. I have no doubt in my mind that someday we will not be able to the tell the difference between computer-generated people and real people without serious evaluation.'

Confronted with an argument of unlimited development (whether in the interests of an increase or decrease of value), Perelman and Olbrechts-Tyteca also tell us that listeners (in this case, viewers) 'are often more interested in the value which such argumentation confers on *certain terms which fall short of the ultimate term*, but are really the *center* of the debate, than they are in the ultimate, always receding term in a given direction'.[26] Thus, throughout the discourse surrounding *Final Fantasy*, while the 'ultimate, always receding term' may be an ideal 'realism' indistinguishable from 'cinematic photorealism', the term that 'falls short' but is central to the debate is *'hyper-realism'* – a realism that is, at one and the same time, *'not real enough'* and *'too real'*. Thus, on the one hand, IMDB viewers present extraordinarily detailed litanies of CGI 'errors' of movement, wooden facial expressions, poor lip-synching and the like. On the other, they make comments such as 'Something about the animation ... makes the whole thing a bit too perfect'. Particularly ironic in this context, then, is Lev Manovich's point in *The Language of New Media* that 'although we normally think that synthetic photographs ... are inferior to real photographs, in fact, they are *too perfect*. But beyond that we can also say that paradoxically, they are also *too real* ... From the point of view of human vision, [what we see] is hyperreal. And yet, it is completely realistic.'[27]

Final Fantasy can't win for losing – and, given the semiotic and ontological incompatibilities and contradictions of its visual and narrative premises as well as the discursive field the film's CGI animation generates, this is no mere accident. What is perhaps most fascinating about the argument of unlimited development in the context of *Final Fantasy* is that, as Perelman and Olbrechts-Tyteca explain it, the argument *contains the premises for its own rebuttal*. That is, the argument's 'refutation ... lies in the statement that it is impossible to go indefinitely in the direction indicated, either because one encounters an *absolute* or because one ends up with an *incompatibility*'. Furthermore, the argument is always also in 'danger of appearing *ridiculous* as a result of incompatibility with values one is loath to give up'.[28] This awareness of the absolute and ridiculous extension of *Final Fantasy*'s visual argument and its two 'incompatible' ontologies (or 'myths of total animation') are rendered strikingly clear in two reviewer 'rebuttals' of the film. One writes, 'The photo-realism of the humans doesn't always work, and frankly that is a relief. ... If the illusion always worked, how would we know they weren't really human actors, and some joker just told us they were computer generated?',[29] while the other notes: 'If computer animation could ever get to the point of creating an entirely believable human representation (and that is a dubious possibility), then, as animation, it will have entirely missed the point. If you can create a computer being ... unmistakable from a real human being, why not just use a real human being? Is it animation any longer, except in the most technical sense?'[30] In sum, the argument of unlimited development always asserts the premises for its own rebuttal and, in the case of *Final Fantasy*, CGI animators, the film itself, and the film's viewers are all caught up in a version of it – a misguided (and doomed) dream of a 'totally' photorealist animation that constitutes, through even its tiniest failures, the grounds for its own refutation and rebuttal.

Which, in conclusion, brings me to Dr. Aki Ross's hair. Writing about the 'too real' nature of CGI animation, Manovich points to (among other things) its capacity for 'unlimited resolution and an unlimited level of detail'.[31] In a sense, then, the 'hyper-reality' of CGI resolution and detail (as well as some of CGI's other features) constitutes a 'hyperbolic' effect in relation to what we perceive (conventionally or otherwise) as 'the structure of reality'. Thus, the 'hyper-reality' of the human characters in *Final Fantasy* stands as a visual articulation of the major rhetorical trope that Perelman and Olbrechts-Tyteca identify as central to the argument of unlimited development: *hyperbole*.[32] The hyperbolic nature of *Final Fantasy*'s CGI detail in particular relation to its 'hyper-real' humans demands, from the viewer, a heightened and hyperbolic form of judgmental attention. That is, where, in our normal mode of attention, we might have only looked at either cinematic photorealism or irreal CGI animation 'in general' (as we do with the non-human representations of the film), the CGI detail of *Final Fantasy*'s human characters solicits a directed and intensified *scrutiny*. As one admiring IMDB viewer put it: 'The detail to the faces and hair can't be denied. You could see every spot of stubble, ... every mole and freckle, wrinkles, eyelashes, even moisture in the eyes if you look closely enough ... If you pay attention, there's another world of detail to appreciate here, you just have to be watching for it'. In either a live-action photorealist film or in an animated fantasy metaphysically 'released' from 'the structure of reality', our scrutiny and judgment would not be activated at the small-scale level it is in *Final Fantasy*. The film's own semiotic and rhetorical construction as well as our distancing 'epistemological hesitation' at the film's dual ontology ask us to scrutinise – to either admire or judge wanting – *smaller and smaller semantic units of the image*: to wit, every one of the 60,000 hairs on Aki's head. Thus, as another admiring IMDB viewer unselfconsciously writes: 'Subtleties such as hair movement that are generally lost were not so with this film'. It is not for nothing that, speaking of the CGI 'ideal of photorealism' and the difficulty of 'creating fully synthetic human actors', Manovich notes a 1992 SIGGRAPH paper titled 'A Simple Method for Extracting the Natural Beauty of Hair'.[33]

But not everyone was pleased at having their attention directed to the micro-level of the putatively 'natural' beauty of CGI hair. 'When I read that animating Aki Ross's 60,000 strands of hair gobbled up one fifth of the entire budget for *Final Fantasy* I was just amazed', says one viewer. 'How can they spend so much money on what is really nothing more than an *irrelevant detail*, and in comparison give so little thought to things like dialogue and storyline?' Yet another finds Aki's hair 'really, really annoying, like someone must have followed her round and cyberbrushed it every five minutes. It actually detracted from the movie because it was *so irritatingly noticeable*.' And another notes that, in rendering time, Aki had 'something like $35 million of hair care', and that 'not even Jennifer Aniston has worried that much about her hair'. Furthermore, given the level of scrutiny demanded by the film's rhetorical and semiotic structure, even the hair is doomed to photorealist failure: 'There was overemphasis on the main character's hair, but at the same time', says one viewer, 'not one strand goes out of place. How could someone with straight limp hair, when faced down, still have it fall toward the shoulder instead of covering the face?'

The great irony here, of course, is that the detail is in the observer. Aki Ross's hair is *not* constantly foregrounded in the film, but that is what we look at. We look at the characters' skin, their liver spots, their freckles and wrinkles, and – given the epistemic call – watch the physics of clothing, movement, and (oh, yes) the way hair falls. In reverse – but in concert with the CGI animators – we, as viewers, also get caught up in the film's 'argument of unlimited (photorealist) development'. And thus we spend a large portion of our own time (dare I pun?) 'rendering' judgement and 'splitting' ontological hairs. Unfortunately, then, our attention – and that of the filmmakers – is greatly misdirected from a focus on 'the illusion of life' to the 'dis-illusion of life'. Watching the film, we are most certainly more in the realm of animation's 'deathlife' than 'lifedeath' – and at the limits of a 'final fantasy' of animation that is not so much uncanny as it is unmoving.

Notes

1. Alan Cholodenko, *The Illusion of Life: Essays on Animation* (Sydney: Power, 1999): 28–29.

2. *Variety*, 9 July 2001: 20.

3. Cholodenko: 29.

4. Noël Carroll, 'Notes on the Sight Gag', in *Comedy/Cinema/Theory*, Andrew Horton (ed.) (Berkeley: University of California Press, 1991): 25.

5. It is worth noting here that narrative animated films provide us 'metaphysical relief' by doing both – that is, *subverting* physical laws within a world perceived by the viewer as physically akin to our own (hence the delight when a character walks off a recognisable representation of a cliff and doesn't fall); and *substituting* physical laws with created ones (the film creates a consistent physics of its own).

6. Anthony Lane, Review of *Finding Nemo*, *The New Yorker*, 9 June 2003: 109.

7. André Bazin, 'The Myth of Total Cinema', in *What is Cinema?*, trans. Hugh Gray (Berkeley: University of California Press, 1967): 20.

8. Bazin: 21.

9. On 'perceptual realism' and 'correspondence', particularly in relation to photorealism and CGI, see Stephen Prince's seminal essay (originally published in 1996), 'True Lies: Perceptual Realism, Digital Images, and Film Theory', in *Film Quarterly: Forty Years – A Selection*, Brian Henderson and Ann Martin with Lee Amazonas (eds) (Berkeley: University of California Press, 1999): 392–411.

10. Sean Axmaker, Review of *Final Fantasy: The Spirits Within*, *Seattle Post-Intelligencer*, 11 July 2001.

11. Bob Graham, Review of *Final Fantasy: The Spirits Within*, *The San Francisco Chronicle*, 11 July 2001.

12. Stephanie Zacharek, Review of *Final Fantasy: The Spirits Within*, Salon.com

13. Sergei M. Eisenstein, *Eisenstein on Disney*, Jay Leyda (ed.) and trans. Alan Upchurch (London: Methuen, 1988): 45.

14. There has been another allegorical reading of the film which sees the opposition set up between Earth's Gaia and the Phantom Gaia 'as an allegory for the rivalry between analog cinema/analog media and digital cinema/new media ... , as well as for the digital's obligatory detour through the analog' (Livia Monnet, 'Invasion of the Movie Snatchers: Mimesis and the New Uncanny in *Final Fantasy: The Spirits Within*', unpublished manuscript).

15. Keith Broadfoot and Rex Butler, 'The Illusion of Illusion', in *The Illusion of Life*: 273.

16. Elvis Mitchell, *The New York Times*, 11 July 2001.

17. Of interest here is the relation between semiotics and rhetoric, particularly in relation to the iconic sign. Umberto Eco views a variety of codes as operative in the iconic sign, including 'perceptual codes (the domain of the psychology of perception)' and 'iconic codes proper, subdividable into (a) figures, (b) visual premises, and (c) visual arguments' (Robert Stam, Robert Burgoyne, and Sandy Flitterman-Lewis, *New Vocabularies in Film Semiotics: Structuralism, Post-Structuralism and Beyond* (New York: Routledge, 1992): 31.

18. Scott Bukatman, 'Online Comics & the Reframing of the Moving Image', (unpublished manuscript, forthcoming in *Matters of Gravity* (Durham, NC: Duke University Press, 2003).

19. Peter Wollen, *Signs and Meaning in the Cinema, New and Enlarged* (Bloomington: Indiana University Press, 1972): 152.

20. Ch. Perelman and L. Olbrechts-Tyteca, *The New Rhetoric: A Treatise on Argumentation*, trans. John Wilkinson and Purcell Weaver (Notre Dame: University of Notre Dame, 1971): 287–292.

21. Perelman and Olbrechts-Tyteca: 187.

22. References are to *Dumb and Dumber* (Farrelly Bros., 1994) and *Dumb and Dumberer* (Troy Miller, 2003), and to *The Fast and the Furious* (Rob Cohen, 2001) and *2 Fast 2 Furious* (John Singleton, 2003).

23. Tim Ryan, 'It's reel Fantasy', *Honolulu Star Bulletin*, 15 January 1999.

24. Barbara Robertson, 'Reality Check', *Computer Graphics World* (August 2001): 24.

25. Perelman and Olbrechts-Tyteca: 288.

26. Perelman and Olbrechts-Tyteca: 290.

27. Lev Manovich, *The Language of New Media* (Cambridge: MIT Press, 2000): 202.

28. Perelman and Olbrechts-Tyteca: 289.

29. Bob Graham, Review of *Final Fantasy: The Spirits Within*, *San Francisco Chronicle*, 22 July 2001.

30. David Luty, Review of *Final Fantasy: The Spirits Within*, *Film Journal International* (August 2001): 74.

31. Manovich: 202.

32. Perelman and Olbrechts-Tyteca: 291.

33. Manovich, 194. Reference is to K. Najyo, Y. Usami, and T. Kurihara, 'A Simple Method for Extracting the Natural Beauty of Hair', *Computer Graphics* 26.2 (1992): 111–120.

Vivian Sobchack is Professor in the Department of Film, Television, and Digital Media at UCLA School of Theater, Film and Television. The first woman elected president of the Society for Cinema and Media Studies, her essays and reviews have appeared in many books and journals, including *Quarterly Review of Film and Video*, *Artforum International*, *camera obscura*, *Film Quarterly* and *Representations*. She is author of *Screening Space: The American Science Fiction Film*; *The Address of the Eye: A Phenomenology of Film Experience*; and *Carnal Thoughts: Embodiment and Moving Image Culture*, and has also edited two anthologies: *Meta-Morphing: Visual Transformation and the Culture of Quick Change* and *The Persistence of History: Cinema, Television and the Modern Event*.

Chapter 12

An Unrecognised Treasure Chest: The Internet as an Animation Archive

Karin Wehn

New media – old mistakes

In recent media history we have seen an exponential and accelerating growth both in mediated communication and in the number of media. Methodologies of contemporary media history increase the pressure on media historians to collect, structure and preserve the content of new media, starting with their emergence in order to avoid the same mistakes that have been lamented by historians across all mass media. No matter what area one looks into, the historiography of all mass media (be it film, radio and television) is based on as little as 10 or 20 per cent of generated material, and the rest has fallen into oblivion as it is no longer available.[1] The new media histories of the Internet, CD-ROM and DVD have surprised us all, mainly because of the speed with which new media infiltrated almost all areas of society and, at least in the First World, it has become a matter of course in our lives. These recent changes have been called revolutionary, and justifiably so, when compared to the evolution of earlier

Abstract: This paper investigates as to what extent the Internet is an archive for animation. Starting off with some general observations on the challenges for digital archives, it is argued that Internet has the potential to be an archive for animation in a double sense. On the one hand, it is a repository for traditional animation. On the other hand, the Internet as a new medium has brought about its own art forms that need to be preserved. The new forms of web animation (Flash, brickfilms, machinima, demos) are introduced briefly. The article closes with some reflections on what human and computerised equivalents of gatekeepers, curators, archivists exist and what further action should be taken from there.

media, where only one stage of cultural communication was impacted upon: this time all stages of media and all types of media are affected.[2]

The advent of new media has had a considerable effect on the field of animation. Until recently, animation aficionados and researchers who wanted to keep up-to-date with the less mainstream fields of animation had to visit film festivals and look out for special programmes in art house cinemas. Contemporary and emergent new media formats have created several new outlets for animation that offer hope that animation will become more accessible for both research and fan interests in the future, and many historical, experimental and rare collections of animated film-making have been be re-released on DVDs.[3] On the other hand, techno-logical innovation, the consolidation of software standards and increasing bandwidth caused a renaissance of animation on the Internet which – despite its short history – has seen some dramatic ups and downs. Unfor-tunately, most of them go largely unnoticed by animation studies which remains focussed on the traditional media of film and television.[4] How animation has conquered the Internet and how it has been changed both as a technique, an art form and as a social practice is a subject that animation studies have yet to discover. The discipline has both failed to recognise the new distribution outlets that emerged on the Internet and the new anima-tion techniques that emerged with them. Thus, by neglecting the new forms of production and distribution for animated films, animation re-search is not only missing out on a challenging stage in animation history. It is also in acute danger of repeating the aforementioned mistakes once again.

It is the task of archives to preserve documents that are important for our culture. According to the Collins Dictionary, an archive is 'a collection of records of or about an institution, family ... a place where such records are kept'.[5] Both libraries and museums can be seen as a sort of archive, 'but the word "archive" is often used when stressing its role of preservation, rather than that of dissemination'.[6] Etymologically, the word 'archive' is derived from the Greek *arkhé* meaning government, indicating its importance in the continued life of a community.[7] This essay investigates the extent to which the Internet is an archive for animation. To answer this, I ask whether the notion of the Internet as an archive makes sense or whether it needs to be revised. In addition I query what legal and illegal attempts already exist to preserve films, what we can find, what the access conditions are like, which human and computerised equivalents of gatekeepers, curators, and archi-vists exist, what should be conserved with regard to the Internet and how it should be conserved. Before delving deeper into these matters, an explo-ration of precisely how animated films are prepared for and distributed over the Internet, and how that affects the quality of the viewing experience, is warranted.

Distribution over the Internet

Venues and types of distribution

Different methods have evolved to distribute films over the Internet. Currently, the two main ways are as website content and through file-sharing systems. Films are exhibited at websites for quite different purposes. Online cinemas and entertainment portals showcase hundreds of films and experiment with new venues for films and new opportunities to create revenues on the web (e.g. by advertising, subscription). Artists and animation companies exhibit lavish digital portfolios in order to flaunt their talents and to gain recognition and publicity. Many amateur filmmakers release films just for fun. Within the case of online cinemas and entertainment portals that primarily pursue a commercial interest, viewing a film tends to be more hypermediated than watching a film on the big screen or on television. Regardless of whether the films are embedded in a website or open up in a new window, they tend to be accompanied and surrounded by additional information (e.g. biography and other works of the director), fun-facts, interactive games and brightly coloured advertising, often more eye-catching than the film itself. File sharing systems – also referred to as peer-to-peer or P2P – such as Gnutella, EDonkey, FastTrack (Kazaa) or BitTorrent enable users that have downloaded the peer-to-peer client software to share audio and video files with their unknown 'friends' by allowing a direct and temporary exchange between systems. While they are logged on, users can search the public directories of all other users that are online at that time and download files directly from these. If the download is interrupted it is indexed by the software , and, once the connection has been re-established, the download is restarted automatically at the point where it previously stopped.

After a boom in film piracy on the Internet illegally anticipating the official release in theatres, the film industry, represented by the Motion Pictures Association (MPA), alerted that they may have to face similar losses as the music industry started rather aggressive campaigns and legal actions against illegal file-sharing. However, so far, all these strategic moves to stop illegal swapping of copyrighted content appear to be ineffective. Quite the contrary – they turned out to be the best promotion to introduce a larger public to peer-to-peer clients. Also, new generations of file-sharing clients sprouted up with improved and more user-friendly features. Not only do they operate from geographically remote insular states in the Pacific, where copyright is hard to be implemented but they also have a completely decentralised structure which makes it even more difficult to take legal action.

Storage-eating film files vs. web-friendly compression

Both digitised analog animations, for example film files of claymation or cel-animated shorts, and 'born-digital' animations, for example brickfilms and machinimas (see below), are created and stored in a variety of formats. The crucial problem regarding their transmission over the Internet is the discrepancy between the huge size of film files and the small bandwidth with which the majority of users are currently connected to the Internet. For instance, one second of uncompressed video animation at 30 fps (frames-per-second) operates at 27 Mb/s (megabytes-per-second).[8] At present, a modem can transmit at best 56 Kb/s (kilobytes-per-second), but depending on network overhead and heavy traffic the effective bandwidth might be as low as 1 Kb/s. Therefore, films have to be squeezed into smaller streaming formats, which can be achieved in two ways.

A first option to diminish the amount of data is to reduce the resolution of the image, the frame rate and/or the quality of the sound track which may result in qualitative aggravations.

Typical compromises for re-encoding a film for the web:

	Cinema/TV	Web
Image size and resolution	PAL: 768 x 576 pixels	320 x 240 pixels 160 x 120 pixels
Frames per second (fps)	Cinema: 24 fps TV: PAL: 25 fps TV: NTSC: 29 fps	10–15 fps
Sound	Stereo	Mono Lower sampling rate

The second possibility to overcome bandwidth constraints is to apply revertible mathematical transformations to the data stream, a procedure referred to as compression. For compression, mathematical algorithms, so-called codecs (portmanteau word for compression/decompression) reduce media files into smaller streaming formats which are then decoded by the end-user's player.

This way of reducing file size has its downside too, as in most cases lossy compression procedures have to be applied which are best understood as a 'trade-off between the amount of compression achieved and the amount of image quality sacrificed'.[9] In a single still image, runs of pixels that share the same colour are identified and recorded in the run. Also, fine details in the image are sacrificed which predictably leads to unwanted side-effects like pixilation and blurring of fine detail. Furthermore, consecutive images are compared with each other and only the areas of the image that have changed over time are recorded (temporal compression). How well spatial and temporal compression methods work depends on the film material.[10]

Compressing the video also requires making decisions about how the audio-visual data are delivered. Progressive streaming (or download) refers to the transmission of audio or video files which a user can watch, once the file or a sufficient part of it has been downloaded in the cache (buffering). It is suitable for films that are intended to be shown in superior quality, because the part of the film that is to be seen will only play after it has been downloaded without loss. The disadvantage is that especially with slower connections it might take a long time before the film plays. Progressive streaming is also used for pirate copies of movies which are often compressed to roughly the size of 650 Mb so that they just fit on one CD-ROM, or for films if the filmmaker (or other parties) either does not mind or is actually interested in encouraging the movie's visibility.

Realtime streaming refers to technologies that adapt the media signal bandwidth to the user's connection so that films are *always* watched in realtime. To achieve this, realtime streaming ignores information (packets) that have not been delivered in time, for example, if the network is clogged up and skips images, which may cause the mediocre image quality at modem speed. Nevertheless, the majority of online cinemas and entertainment portals prefer realtime streaming because a complete file is not transferred to the user's hard disk. After viewing there are no data left in the cache, so streamed films are much better protected against theft and copyright violations than downloaded ones.[11]

So how do compressed and digitised animations for the web relate to their originals? Most scholarly research on animation emphasises that the fascination of animation has to do with the fact that still images are transformed into moving images.[12] Keeping in mind the dramatic miniaturisation of the image (sometimes the size of a postage stamp) and the lossy compression procedures discussed above, currently in many cases smooth movements have to be sacrificed for choppy motion to meet the web's requirements. Thus, a number of independent and theatrical animated films shown on the web are at best compromises that bear a vague resemblance to the originals but lack the qualities that distinguished the original. The quality is often average and contains artefacts like paiting effects and break-ups of the picture. For instance, especially when viewed with a 56 k connection, the streamed version of Aardman's famous clay animation *Creature Comforts* (Nick Park, 1989), showcased at the online cinema Atomfilms.com,[13] looks more like a slide show, and many of the delicate movements of the original are lost. At present, many compressed versions of films provide rather a thumbnail-like information about the film but do not come close to the original. Fortunately, as bandwidth is constantly increasing, these qualitative losses are quite likely to disappear with time.

Challenges for digital archives

Whereas traditional archives rely on some sort of material basis (mostly the printed word), in digital archives all media documents (images, sounds, films) are broken down in digital zeros and ones and transferred to digital storage media. Once digitised they can be stored independently from their original and authentic carrier material (e.g. a filmreel or a video-tape). What is attractive about this is that digital archives could be collection points for the products of all other media as they promise to liberate knowledge from being tied to space and matter and to make it available ubiquitously.[14] In other words, digital archives are suitable both for analog and digitised data as well as for digitally sourced data. However, this separation between information and storage media also raises questions about their material qualities and whether conservation should take place independently of its original material quality – a question that is by no means new but that first came up with the advent of other media than print, e.g. photography, film and television. If storage media and viewing apparatus are considered to be part of the artwork, with regard to computers this implies that original hardware, input-devices and software need to be saved in order to guarantee an authentic viewing experience.

Several organisations have taken on the responsibility of preserving digital data. With 'Memory of the World' UNESCO has released a 'Charter on the Preservation of the Digital Heritage'.[15] UNESCO sees its role both in preserving digital materials (texts, databases, moving images and so on) and as a reference point and forum. It intends to foster cooperation, awareness-raising and capacity-building, the proposal of ethical, legal and technical guidelines and the setting of standards for the promotion and preservation of digital heritage. In 2002, the National Science Foundation and the Library of Congress hosted a workshop where they brought together experts from different fields and sciences.[16] Finally, there is the San Francisco based Internet Archive whose aim is to prevent the Internet, as a new medium with major historical significance and other 'born-digital' materials, from disappearing into the past. Since 1996 it permits people to access and use archived versions websites stored at different points in time. Since 1999 the Internet Archive also contains several other collections (see below).[17]

All these organisations agree that the main issues of preservation of digital data concern guarding against the consequences of accidents and natural disasters, data degradation and maintaining the accessibility of data as formats become obsolete. Digital preservation strategies include:

- Normalisation: converting a document into an archival data format;
- Migration: periodically transforming digital data from obsolete to current formats; and
- Emulation: running obsolete application software from a current platform by simulating the original platform as perfect as possible.

The experts argue that protecting digital content is much more difficult than preserving the content of traditional media. On the one hand, digital collections are growing so rapidly that they outpace current ability to manage and preserve them.[18] On the other, the long-term perspective raises distinctive challenges. While it is one of the foremost aims of many digital archives to preserve data for decades, centuries or even longer, the half-life period of digital storage media is getting increasingly shorter because 'the storage media input and output devices, programming languages, software applications, and standards that are necessary to retrieve and interpret digital information are revised and replaced every few years'.[19]

Digital archives may profit from a 'continuous improvement in computer memory and storage performance and their simultaneous drop in cost'[20] and saving digital data has become relatively easy. The downside is that neither the technologies, strategies, methodologies nor the resources needed to manage digital information for the long run have kept pace with innovations in the creation and capture of digital information.[21] Some experts express the anxiety that digital archives are maybe not secure storage spaces after all and invoke the gloomy metaphor that digital archives may be an 'Alexandrine smouldering-fire', a gigantic mechanism for oblivion that does not need an arsonist to be destroyed but that slowly anneals anyway.[22]

Fuzzy, Flowing and infinite shelf-space: The Internet as a special form of digital archive

If we assume that the Internet, or rather part of it, is a special form of archive for animation it has several characteristic features that distinguish it from other archives. Like other digital archives on the Internet analog material is detached from its material basis, in other words, wine can be sold without the bottle.[23] The internet can be a repository for both digitised analog animations as well as for born-digital animations. However, as will be shown below, the internet is not only a repository for theatrical and TV animation, as a new medium it has also caused the emergence and consolidation of new forms of animation which need to be archived. The Internet lacks many of the stable characteristics associated with traditional archives

– it is rather 'fuzzy'. Its content changes daily, everything is in constant flow. Well-known websites disappear entirely over night, new ones appear, others change both their content and their design constantly – in fact, they have to, as websites which are not regularly updated are easily dismissed as 'dead'. Non-linear hyperlinked document structures make it difficult to decide where sites begin and end as sites link to the content of other sites, and with large sites the content is spread out on several servers or sites are divided in subsections hosted by different partners. As indicated in the definition cited above, traditional archives are envisioned as buildings or repositories that – expanding on this metaphor – contain rooms with shelves that are filled with dusty folders. Traditional archives have walls and borders, in other words, criteria for inclusion, allowing certain things in and others not. When an archive is full, items have to be thrown out in order to make room for new ones. While this may seem to be a limiting and restrictive factor, Boris Groys has pointed out that borders are actually necessary for the healthiness of an archive.[24]

If everything is included in an archive, there is no selection based on qualitative criteria. This necessary delineation between system and environment is hard to draw, because unlike traditional archives with limited room, the Internet has no walls, no borders and potentially infinite shelf space. Part of this problem is the fact that on the Internet, not only can everyone be a producer but also a publisher. Compared to traditional filming the costs of digital filming are very low. By now people can produce a complete film on their PC without having to buy expensive film stock or hiring a team and equipment. They can then release the film themselves on the Internet. Also, the gap in function and price between professional and amateur software is diminishing.[25] Finally, filmmakers are able to bypass traditional gatekeepers and produce and distribute what they like. For these reasons, an abundance of animation has been originally produced primarily on the computer with the distribution for the net in mind.

Consequently, the spectrum of film creators who release films on the web reads like a continuum, with film celebrities such as Tim Burton and David Lynch and comic legend Stan Lee at one end, followed by many professional filmmakers in the middle range and lots of enthusiastic amateurs and no-names at the other. Both highly skilled animators and would-be artists release their films on the web for a variety of reasons, for instance, to promote their talent, to test new concepts, or just for fun. Therefore, selective access to animation is also challenged by the sheer amount of material available: on the web it is very difficult to separate the wheat from the chaff. Thus, the need for archivists to make a breach and to establish borders becomes even stronger and is much more complicated. In a culture of consumption which dictates ever-shortening cycles of renewal and throwing away, the accumulation of discarded inventory becomes an eco-logical problem, something Jaques Derrida draws attention to with his notion of 'biodegradability'.[26] Known for her studies on cultural memory, Aleida Assmann has pointed out that former threats to archives such as decomposing and decay are now viewed in a different and more positive light.[27]

Traditional archives have various one-dimensional indices (alphabetical, subject etc.) and catalogues to simplify access to their documents. The World Wide Web has no coherent filing system that suggests a hierarchical order. Instead, all documents and websites are intertwined by links in a rhizome-like structure that is as fuzzy and flowing as its contents. With the Internet and its abundance of films available, the main problem is how to find them in the first place. Search engines such as Google are valuable and efficient tools, but in the case of animation they are little help, as they list many thousands of entries, but do not yet provide a selection based on qualitative criteria. Thus, the first pages often tend to be filled up with advertising. However, once an anchor site, in other words a well maintained topical site, has been found, most valuable websites on the same topic are within reach of a few mouse-clicks.

Scholars or interested people who want to peruse the contents of an archive usually have to physically access their repositories during their opening hours. While researching in the archive itself is usually not a problem, taking documents home or copying them is either impossible or, especially with film material, a rather pricey affair, partly because the films have to be converted to different formats. On that score, the Internet is much more convenient: with a few mouse-clicks its content is instantly accessible in the living-room or the office or anywhere there is an online computer. With regard to films, access barriers are not opening hours but bandwidth: Users connected to the Internet with a modem or ISDN-connection are more or less excluded from participating in film experiences on the web, as com-fortable viewing and downloading of even highly compressed films requires high speed Internet access.

Traditional animation on the Internet

Traditional animation in this context refers to all forms of animation that were not originally produced for the Internet, but rather for the theatrical screen or the TV. Different types of websites showcase a great variety of animated films online that would be either hard or impossible to find in the offline world. Online cinemas or sites by individual artists re-publish animated short films that were produced primarily with traditional meth-ods (e.g. cel animation, puppet animation, stop-motion etc.) and materials (e.g. on 35 mm film or video) for the traditional media film and television. For instance, with *Origins of American Animation 1900 – 1921* the Library of Congress in Washington, D.C. provides a rare collection of 21 animated films and two fragments that includes early treasures such as *Humorous Phases of Funny Faces* (James Stuart Blackton, 1906) or excerpts from *Gertie on Tour* (Winsor McCay, 1921) from the first twenty years of the 20th century.[28] The Library of Congress encourages the download of the films for research purposes.

Since 1999 the Internet Archive also collects films and provides easy access to them in a separate film section. The information section of the film archive explains their aim is 'to encourage widespread use of moving images in new contexts by people who might not have used them before'.[29] The film archive contains more than 15 different film collections: The Prelinger Archives is a famous American collection of advertising, educational, industrial and amateur films, whose goal is it to collect, preserve, and facilitate access to poorly preserved films of historic significance. The Prelinger Archives include films produced by many hundreds of important US corporations, non-profit organisations, trade associations, community and interest groups, and educational institutions. Currently, 2000 films from the collection are available at the Internet Archive, for copyright reasons all of which were released prior to 1964. The most frequently downloaded film of the Prelinger Collection is *Duck and Cover* (Archer Productions, 1951) an educational film from the Cold War period which provides advice on how to act in the case of a nuclear war.[30] Using a mixture of live-action and animated sequences with a tortoise to get the Cold War nuclear warning message across, 'duck and cover' is visually and acoustically hammered into peoples heads. As hilarious and naive as the film seems today, it is a valuable source for a socio-political climate at a certain time.

Other collections in the Internet Archive include 300 feature films, among them *Gullivers Travels* (Max Fleischer, 1939), a collection of feature film trailers, amateur collections such as open source films, brickfilms (see below), game-based films such as machinimas and speedruns (see also below), collections related to both significant and or tragic political events such as elections and 9/11 and computer-related TV series such as the Computer Chronicles and Net Café. All audio-visual material is provided in more than half a dozen different formats and file sizes so that varying bandwidths and quality demands of different audiences are best-possibly considered.

Commercially oriented online cinemas with less of an archival interest showcase many recent award winning films. An example is Atomfilms.com that re-releases many festival winners which are not available anywhere else: all the Aardman shorts, the puppet film *The Periwig Maker* (Steffen

Schaffler, 1999), the claymation trilogy *Uncle* (1996), *Cousin* (1998) and *Brother* (1999) by Australian Oscar-winner Adam Eliot, experimental films by German animator Bärbel Neubauer that were painted, drawn and scratched directly on film or the irreverent Bill Plympton shorts that were originally aired at MTV. Even banned films are made available. Ifilm showcases a *Popeye*-episode with anti-Japanese propaganda from the early 1940s.[31]

Institutions such as the National Film Board of Canada,[32] online journals like the Animation World Network[3] or individual artists do not provide complete films at their websites, but do offer clips or at least stills and additional information about the films. Both Cartoon Network[34] and Warner Bros.[35] occasionally showcase Chuck Jones and Tex Avery cartoons from the Golden Age and clips from more recent shows at their websites in order to promote their brands.

Not only commercial sites, but also private sites aspire to archiving films: For instance, a fansite[36] provides the anarchic short *The Spirit of Christmas* (Trey Parker/Matt Stone, 1995) for download: The trashy short about Jesus and Santa Claus having a fight in front of a shopping mall while being watched by four foul-mouthed three-graders is interesting for everybody who wants to know more about the history of *South Park* (Trey Parker/Matt Stone, 1997). Originally a video Christmas card commissioned by a Fox executive that mushroomed both by word-of-mouth and the Internet, it became the point of departure for *South Park*.

Among the animated films that are shared in file-sharing clients are classic feature films, e.g. *Snow-White* (Disney, 1937), *Pinocchio* (Disney, 1940), recent feature films, e.g. *Toy Story* (Pixar, 1995), *Shrek* (Dreamworks, 2001), television shows, e.g. almost all episodes of *The Simpsons, South Park* and *Ren & Stimpy*. There are also classic cartoons, e.g. *Donald Duck, Mickey Mouse, Looney Tunes*, erotica and animated porn (often made by amateurs), video clips, e.g. *Sledge Hammer* (Peter Gabriel, 1986), *One More Time* (Kazuhisa Takenôchi, 2001) and also banned cartoons such as Disney's and Warner Bros.' anti-Nazi propaganda films from the era of World War II. Nevertheless, a precise diagnosis of what file-sharing communities have in store is difficult. At best one finds all the titles one has searched for. Also, the availability of films changes continuously, depending on how many file-sharing users are online and on what kind of films they consider interesting to share with others. It seems that all current blockbusters are easily available, but that experimental animations are less common. In 2004, entering the names of Norman McLaren, Paul Driessen, Alison Snowdon or Caroline Leaf yielded no results. Reasons for the absence of experimental animation in this semi-illegal realm might be that experimental animation is not so much sought after, or that there is a lack of an initial digital copy in order to distribute them with file-sharing-clients.

Web animation

The World Wide Web is not only a home for the products of other media. Despite its short life, it has already brought about its own born-digital art forms. While the aesthetic styles of web animation are not the focus of this article, the most influential techniques will be briefly outlined, as they are not well known and in great danger of being irrecoverably lost. Some of these animation techniques adapt to the Internet's demands in an ideal way. Others existed independently before the breakthrough of the World Wide Web but spread and mushroomed with it.

What is most important is that these different techniques of web animation are particularly vulnerable to oblivion as technology is still in constant flux: the power of the hardware is steadily increasing, which may cause animations designed for older and slower processors to play too fast on contemporary computers. Several formats compete for market penetration – some succeeded, other did not. For instance, VRML (virtual reality modelling language), a text file-based approach to 3D, did not make the breakthrough with a larger audience because it lacked standard support within browsers.[37] Without VRML, *Floops* (Brad de Graaf, 1996) often credited to be the first episodic web series, can no longer be viewed.

Flash

The vector-based animation software Flash by Macromedia has been referred to as a 'killer application' as both its small file sizes and the close to 100 per cent market penetration of the Flash plug-in make it an ideal tool for producing and distributing web animation and webtoons. Flash has also been called a 'happy accident': when the software first came out in 1996 it was never intended for the production of cartoons but for sprucing up websites, yet it was soon exploited for cartoon production. Depending on the final medium (television, cinema, web), Flash films can take on a variety of styles and are very hard to nail down to a certain aesthetic style. However, when Flash films are produced for the web, the assumed bandwidth of the viewer dictates what is possible and what is not. When a low bandwidth user is targeted, either a cut-out-animation style or a cartoony style best suits the software's current specifications and the specific requirements of web distribution.

Early Flash films were seldom longer than one to two minutes and featured an extremely limited animation style. With increasing broadband audiences

Figs. 1–3. (above and on the following page)
Manege Frei, Ljubisa Djukic, 2005. [Images courtesy Ljubisa Djukic.]

more recent Flash films have grown in length, file size and richness of detail (Figs. 1–3). Due to easy implementation of interactive elements many Flash animations share elements with the narrative structures of greeting cards and computer games. Due to the small file sizes of Flash movies compared to compressed video films, and the relatively easy-to-learn software, there are millions of Flash movies on the web. Hotwired's Animation Express[38] holds a carefully selected collection of about 250 experimental Flash cartoons (many of them in the range of less than a 100 Kb to 1 Mb) that provides a valuable overview on the artistic development of Flash cartoons between October 1998 and December 2002. The look of Flash cartoons that cater for high-speed internet access is best illustrated by the results of Macromedia's yearly prestigious competition FlashForward.[39]

Brickfilms

Brickfilms are stop-motion animated films with Lego 'minifigs' in settings primarily or entirely built of Lego bricks. More than 1000 films by more than 400 filmmakers can be downloaded from the scene's hub, Brick-films.com,[40] smaller collections are stored at the Internet Archive,[41] New-grounds.com[42] and Ifilm.com.[43] The origins of brickfilms date back to the mid-1980s, however, streaming video, webcams and easy availability of editing software as well as the communicative and distributive opportuni-ties of the Internet gave the genre a great boost. As late as 2000, the Lego company recognised the trend and released a MovieMaker Set for US$ 200 that contains a webcam (actually in a Lego shell), a simple editing software and a four hundred piece set. Several other subsets that followed were

closely tied to theatrical blockbusters (*Jurassic Park*, *Indiana Jones*, *Star Wars*) and explain to some extent why so many brickfilms imitate recent popular films. However, many adherents of the brickfilms scene argue that the pricey commercial version offers nothing that had not been done before. They also complained about the 'grainy footage' produced by the camera that looks as if 'someone was shooting with a permanent mask' and the many specifications dictated by the set.[44] Vice versa, the Lego company tends to deemphasise any connection to the amateur scene as the violent content of quite a few brickfilms (cf. *The Lego Chainsaw Massacre*) does not match the company's philosophy of being an active supporter of creative learning and child development. Brickfilms are a great animation technique to get started with as the figures are readily available, and both the sets and

figures are much easier to control than those of other stop-motion techniques. Despite the restrictions of the material, some brickfilmers have produced great artwork with witty and original story-telling, great timing and highly creative sets.

Machinima

Machinima films (neologism consisting of machine and cinema) exploit game engines of mainly first person shooters such as *Quake 2, Unreal Tournament* or *Half-Live* to generate their visuals. A game engine is the software which regulates the physics of the virtual world as well as the possible actions and movements of the players. By tracking both the position of the user in the virtual world and the direction they are looking in, the game engine renders a seamless image in realtime that the user can see from his currently and spontaneously chosen perspective. Machinima filmmakers take advantage of this realtime rendering, usually network several computers together and steer altered game-characters like puppets through modified game settings. The result is then recorded in real time. The degree of variation of the game characters and the settings depends on the filmmaker's skills and ambitions. The captivating thing about machinima is that filmmakers with a very small budget can create 3D movies in realtime on their home computers – an area that was previously not open to amateurs since 3D animation software packages are both a pricey investment and difficult to master for beginners. In addition, because of the virtual nature of machinima films, filmmakers do not have to follow the usual chronology of 3D animation but can start anywhere they like, e.g. directing, animating characters or building sets and objects from the scratch.

The first machinima films were released in 1997 and required considerable programming skills from/on the creator's part. With early machinima films, not only producers but also viewers needed both a copy of the game the films was made in as well as some technological understanding in order to play the film. Since probably only avid gameplayers have copies of the aforementioned and of other games, most machinima filmmakers currently also release their films in conventional media formats such as Real or Windows Media in order to broaden the viewers' scope. Lately, the game industry has taken up this trend by releasing tools together with the games that simplify the production of machinima films. Machinima has garnered significant attention from art institutions and media coverage as a creative and anarchic mode of subverting the cultural practice of gaming. Some machinima makers like to promote their art as 'the latest evolution of Computer Generated Imagery (CGI), the technology used in hit films from Jurassic Park to Toy Story'.[45] However, so far only few machinima films withstand artistic criteria as they lack great storytelling and a meaningful realisation of dramaturgical conflicts and remain too close to the games they use. Large collections of machinima films are available at Machinima.com,[46] the Internet Archive as well as at various game-portals and private websites. One rather exceptional machinima group whose work has shown considerable progress over the years is the ILL Clan.[47]

Theoretically web animation, whether Flash, brickfilms or machinima, can be of any genre. However parodies, one-to-one re-enacted scenes of recent blockbusters or cult films such as *Star Wars, The Matrix* and *Harry Potter,* and other forms of playful references to popular culture tend to be among the most popular role models for amateur films. Other than that, similar topics and strategies repeat themselves across all techniques: sex, splatter and cutting-edge humour. To some extent, this probably reflects on the producers' age and interests, predominantly male teenagers and students.

Demos

Demos are a somewhat different story. A demo is defined as 'a software program that renders a several minutes long collage of 3D animation, sound, music and text on a personal computer'.[48] Demos first appeared in Northern Europe, particularly in Finland, in the early 1980s, for early home microcomputers like the Commodore 64 and Apple, but they really took off after Commodore's Amiga was released in 1985. It was the first low-cost home computer with high resolution graphics, a 4,096-color palette, powerful video handling and four-channel digitised sound. Around 1990 the demo scene started producing demos for PCs. Demos started off as modified title screens ('cracked by ...') of illegally cracked computer games and introduced the name of the person who had been first to crack the game. These 'programmed signatures' were soon superseded by more sophisticated versions showing the programmer's skills. Soon demos became a means or currency for claiming status and respect and emerged as an independent art form no longer associated with game piracy. Demo coders made it their main task to strive towards discovery and exploitation of features available within the technological environment which were not publicly documented. They squeezed the maximum performance out of their machines in order to achieve extraordinary previously unseen visual effects. The results were and remain stunning for the technological state of the art at that time: textures, journeys through 3D worlds, tunnels with a psychedelic touch coupled with synthetic sound.

Demos were initially distributed via floppy disks, thereafter through bulletin broadcast systems and ftp sites. Since the files had to fit onto a floppy disk or were mailed via slow and expensive modem connections, file size had to be kept low which led to the emergence of subgenres such as the 4 Kb or the 64 Kb demo. Demos eventually became too complex and time-consuming to be written by an individual alone and this led to the formation of (frequently international) coding groups typically featuring a minimum of a programmer, a graphics designer, and a musician.

The demo scene is still active today. However, as with today's multimedia PCs with lots of RAM, powerful hard disks and graphic cards, graphic limitations are no longer an issue, the demo scene has shifted their aims somewhat. While new school demos pay respect to their roots by retaining the fascination for hardcore programming, the heavy use of highly stylised and animated texts with greetings to friends and other demo makers, and audio-visual quotes of the style and the content of some old-school classics in a retro fashion, new-school demos address themselves to narrative and visually spectacular forms such as video-clips in which the perfect matching of images and sound is the main goal.[49] Starting points to delve into the history of this fascinating, highly varied subculture and how it sees itself are Scene.org, Ojuice.org and Pouet.Net.[50] Since demos are by far the oldest form of web animation, its creators are familiar with the problem of how to preserve obsolete data formats, as a lot of demos were programmed for old machines such as the C64 or the Amiga. Demo coders help themselves by programming emulators to simulate old systems on more recent ones.

Accidents and the disappearance of web animation

As mentioned above, the prevention of 'accidents' is one of the major issues of digital preservation. The most dramatic accident with respect to web animation so far was the severe crisis of the Internet economy in 2000/2001. When the dot-com bubble burst, many filmsites and their entire content vanished over night. Numerous high-budgeted companies declared bankruptcy (e.g. Anteye.com, Eruptor.com; Stanlee.net) or applied for insolvency. Others had to slim their company structures dramatically in order to survive on a much smaller scale. For instance, the former giants Atomfilms.com and Shockwave.com, which used to operate two separate movie portals, merged in December 2000 to Atomshockwave and are currently running a joint website. In June 2001, the company announced pink-slipping 150 of its 200 employees and the shutting down of New York and Los Angeles offices.[51]

Even more dramatically, Icebox.com[52] was once a flourishing and thriving portal uniting the force of more than 100 artists from TV and cinema, including script-writers from TV series such as *X-Files, Simpsons, South Park, King of the Hill* and *Seinfeld*. Despite a great reputation among animation enthusiasts for its highly creative team and content, they had to close down. In March 2001 Icebox.com relaunched, staffed with just two employees. Only a fraction of the former content is still available for free. Whoever wants to see more than the pilot episode has to pay a fee for each episode. The site seems to not have been updated since November 2001. Proudly announced projects such as Pop.com, financed by Dream Works and Steven Spielberg's Imagine Entertainment, did not even launch, but piled up a deficit of US$10 million US. Digital Entertainment Network, supported by Microsoft, pulled the plugs in May 2000 after having spent US$67 million on episodic video and animation programming that failed to attract much of an audience.[53]

Various fans have tried to keep content of the 'dead' sites alive by distributing the movies and series on private websites or by emailing entire series on requests but were stopped by the licensing proprietors' lawyers with cease-and-desist-letters for of copyright violations. Nevertheless, all these examples are ample proof that collection and preservation has to start now in order not to lose any more early forms of web animation, many of which did not fail for lack of artistic creativity but for being exploited within the frameworks of poorly conceived business models.

Institutions, curators and archivists: Top-down and bottom-up efforts

The mere availability of films at websites or through file-sharing clients is an important first step but does not amount to an archive. What distinguishes an archive from a mere accumulation is that archival contents go through various carefully planned curatorial processes including selection, organisation, description, quality control and regular care. Archives are administered and guarded by institutions employing specifically educated and trained archivists and curators who not only collect and throw out material according to criteria that change over time but who also reflect upon how to preserve significant documents for the future. Envisioning the Internet as an animation archive[54] in the double sense discussed above – as an archive for traditional animation but also for its own animation forms – only makes sense if there are human or computerised institutions, gatekeepers and trustees that might take over the archivist's tasks. As mentioned before, the Internet is basically endless, ever-changing and always expanding which increases the demands for curators to separate the wheat from the chaff. This is further complicated by technology's constant developments. If part of the Internet is conceived of as an archive for animation, it has to be more than a one-to-one copy. If nothing is selected, the archive loses almost all of its rationale.

As will be further recapitulated in this section, there are numerous efforts from established institutions in the arts sector (top down) as well as from the web animation communities themselves to preserve these new art forms by imitating the selection processes of traditional archives (bottom up). Apart from the above mentioned organisations such as the UNESCO and institutions like the Library of Congress that have recognised the urgency to archive the contents of new media, and which have formulated sophisticated theoretical long-term strategies and aims, it is often private collectors, in many cases the artists themselves, who are accumulating valuable digital resources that need to be incorporated into the archiving process to a higher degree.

What is different about the preservation of new techniques is that the canonisation process becomes much shorter as the time that elapses between production and canonisation decreases. In fact, whereas in the past creators and archivists had clearly separate roles in the canonisation process, with new media, in many cases creators and archivists are the same people, since artistic communities are the only ones collecting their works, because they have not yet been recognised as art forms. While private collections are by no means a novelty, with the Internet it is much easier for fans with the same interests to combine different efforts across geographical borders and to make material available ubiquitously. Therefore, the co-presence of professionals and amateurs on the Internet who have equal chances to release films is mirrored by a similar co-presence of professional and amateur collectors. Because of the brevity of the canonisation process, one could also argue that the distinction between promotion and preservation disappears.

Interestingly, canonisation follows very similar routines in all these communities: Whether Flash movies, brickfilms, machinima or demos, almost all sites provide large collections of movies for download. For the visitor confronted with hundreds of films, access is simplified by automatically ordering the movies in various categories such as popularity, e.g. 'top-five most viewed', ratings within the community, e.g. 'top-five rated', or their creative value. On all these sites there are also extensive community-related activities including fora, tutorials on all aspects of movie-making and the announcement of awards to encourage continuous and enhanced movie production. Movies that have already gained some recognition in the scene are often accompanied by interviews with the director, making ofs or FAQs which explain the challenges of making them. The information provided may then serve as an instruction for other moviemakers. In all communities, user-friendly production tools eventually emerge that reduce technology-related barriers to movie-making.[55]

All new films entered are reviewed by members of the review committee who are usually active members that have gained respect and more responsibility over time. They also regularly review the current state of the art in more general articles. In order to move the art form beyond its current state, members regularly create new incentives, for instance by suggesting themes for competitions and contests that have not been exhausted yet. Contests and competitions are fundamental forces of productivity. They encourage continuous production, quality increase and turn many 'lurkers' (passive observers) into active participants. Contest organisers often impose additional hurdles and restrictions on the entry conditions: a highly limited production time, a restriction on movie length, maximum file size (as low as 5 Kb (!) at The5k.org[56]) or the specification of certain themes such as the concept of time with Flash (Flash.Beat, arranged by Swatch and Atom-films.com).[57] The next step for communities to foster and preserve their art will be writing a retrospective summary of the community's evolution, its most important personas and works. This needs to be followed by the emergence of online or offline journals, books and manuals about the techniques as well as CDs and DVDs with the most acclaimed works. It is important to mention that the community's life is not exclusively focused on production and distribution of films but also includes social activities such as celebrating awards and holidays with virtual meetings and chatlogs. In order to exchange ideas all film communities mentioned here organise different types of online and real-life gatherings; the latter are usually combined with a contest. For instance, the demo scene organises so-called demo parties ranging from simple copy parties with three or four attendees in a private home to large international events such as the Assembly in Finland which is attended by several thousands of people from all over the world. All these activities are organised by the web animation groups themselves, but there are also external activities from parties outside the web animation communities who contribute to the canonisation process.

Apart from media coverage of animation in the press, radio and television, festivals are a crucial part of the process of legitimising of what is considered art and what is not. Festivals help professionals in the film industry to spot new talents and foster communication between artists and journalists, film critics and art schools. All major traditional film festivals (e.g. Sundance online,[58] Annecy[59] and AnimaMundi[60]) have established web spin-offs and additional competitions for 'computer animation', 'digital film', 'webmovies', 'flash movies' etc. They frequently transfer part of the competition to the web: submitted films usually can be viewed online several weeks before the actual festival starts. Often there are two juries: a professional one made up by artists or film critics, and one made up by the users who, similar to audience awards, can vote for their favourite film online. And Flashforward is a prestigious business event consisting of a conference and a competition organised by software producer Macromedia. Awards are for Flash movies in categories such as originality, design, experimental, interactive, animation, sound, interface, e-commerce, entertainment and show. The conference for professionals guarantees that the winners are seen by the 'big' people.

Apart from traditional festivals with online components there are genuine Internet festivals: Portals organise festivals for amateur films, often in conjunction with the film industry or other parties, e.g. the Star Wars Fan Film Network sponsored by Atomfilms.com and Lucas Films. Apart from being named in the same breath with his or her (possible) role model George Lucas, the winner is awarded funding for his or her next project. For unknown filmmakers, festivals are a chance to get a wider exposure. For a company like Lucas Films which has an interest that its brands are not diluted by fan activities, such a contest is an easy way to control fan activities without making the fans aware of it.[61] However, one has to be aware that on the Internet, the term 'festival', due to its high-quality connotations, is often used as a marketing term.

Whereas traditional festivals take place at a fixed date and location (e.g. once a year or every two years) online festivals may extend to the whole year. The German portal Shorts Welcome shows ten shorts for the duration of three months. The winners are awarded prizes of €1,500, and their films are shown at the site for another three months.[62] To date they have collected more than 1,000 movies. Slamdance Anarchy follows a similar model showing three films a month. Each month's winners challenge each other once a year.[63] Online festivals experiment with new festival locations and with net-based forms of communication, for example by taking the notion of festivals from exclusive festival lounges to casual every-day-life places. The Going Underground contest[64] takes place during the Berlin Film Festival. Selected subway lines in Berlin show silent movies (max. length 90 sec) on television screens and a website features the same movies. Both passengers and web-surfing users can vote for their favourites via SMS or email. Only the award ceremony takes place in a traditional venue.

Conclusion

A significant number of institutions, communities and individuals have started to collect and evaluate various forms of web animation for different purposes. Now it is important to bring these puzzle pieces together. A first step to foster and unite communication between different parties and different levels of expertise could be a website that lists, categorises and describes the different efforts.[65] Other steps could be to collect hardware and software of well-known and less well-known players and plug-ins as they so quickly become obsolete.

Watching a film on the World Wide Web is a considerably different experience from watching a film in cinema or on television. Whereas films shown in cinema or television usually fill the entire screen, on the World Wide Web films are accompanied by additional, often hypertexual information. This ranges from site logos, navigation elements, static or animated advertising, a biography of the creator, a synopsis of the movie and information on the production process (software used, inspiration) to links to e-commerce shops selling videos or DVDs and community related activities such as opportunities to rate a film, add a small commentary or email it to friends.

Therefore, in order to retain the original viewing experience for web animation, it is important to not only save the animations themselves, but also the synchronic and diachronic context in which they are presented. To achieve this, archiving websites requires different and additional strategies such as saving not only single but networked pages, as well as regularly saving periodical updates, at best on irreversible storage media.

What is striking is that the most advanced efforts to preserve animation so far seem to come from Western, particularly US-American institutions. Accordingly, there is a stronger focus on the preservation of US-American movies than of movies from other countries. Therefore, efforts to preserve movies of other cultures should be encouraged. This implies also working on copyright solutions that protect the rights of the artists.

Notes

1. Paolo Cherchi Usai, 'Origins and Survival' in Geoffrey Nowell-Smith (ed.), *The Oxford History of World Cinema* (London: OUP, 1996): 12.

2. Lev Manovich, *The Language of New Media* (Cambridge, Massachusetts: MIT, 2001): 19: 'This new revolution is arguably more profound than the previous ones, and we are just beginning to register its initial effects. Indeed, the introduction of the printing press affected only one stage of cultural communication – the distribution of media. Similarly, the introduction of photography affected only one type of cultural communication – still images. In contrast, the computer media revolution affects all stages of communication, including acquisition, manipulation, storage, and distribution; it also affects all types of media – texts, still images, moving images, sound, and spatial constructions'.

3. Andy Mangels, *Animation on DVD: The Ultimate Guide* (Berkeley, California: Stone Bridge, 2003) for a collection of available DVDs on animation.

4. There is a considerable focus of research on theatrical animation, whereas the discourse on TV animation is significantly smaller. Worse, little research has dealt with animation displayed on computer screens, despite the fact that e.g. computer games are more than 40 years old, extremely varied and that the computer games industry is very vivid and vibrant with revenues that are by now topping the box-office results of the movie industry. Cf. Economist, 'Gaming Goes to Hollywood', *Economist*, 25 March 2004. http://www.economist.com/business/displayStory.cfm?story_id=2541401

5. *Collins Dictionary of the English Language*. (London, Glasgow: Collins, 1986): 76.

6. Wikipedia.org. http://www.wikipedia.org

7. Ibid.

8. Cf. Kit Laybourne, *The Animation Book: A Complete Guide to Animated Filmmaking – From Flip Books to Sound Cartoons to 3D Animation* (New York, Three Rivers, 1998): 266.

9. Cf. Manton, Rob, 'Understanding the technical constraints of creating for different digital media', Marcia Kuperberg (ed.), *A Guide to Computer Animation for TV, Games, Multimedia and Web* (Oxford: Focal Press 2002): 27–56, 38.

10. For instance, detailed (moving) structures, such as trees swaying in the wind or a finely striped shirt, are difficult to compress. Camera pans look wishy washy. Shots of many small distant objects (e.g. faces in a crowd) will be unrecognisable and distracting whereas a talking head that does not move very much lends well to compression.

11. Even movies that are streamed in realtime are not completely protected against copyright violations. Several types of software record a stream while it plays on the hard-disk of the user.

12. Paul Wells, *Understanding Animation* (London: Routledge 1998): 1.

13. *Creature Comforts* at Atomfilms; http://www.atomfilms.com

14. Cf. Aleida Assmann, 'Das Archiv und die neuen Medien des kulturellen Gedächtnisses', Stanitzek, Georg & Wilhelm Voßkamp (eds), *Schnittstelle Medien und kulturelle Kommunikation* (Cologne: DuMont, 2001): 268–281, 278.

15. Cf. UNESCO, Charter on the Preservation of the Digital Heritage. http://portal.unesco.org/en/ev.php-URL_ID=17721&URL _DO=DO_TOPIC&URL_SECTION=201.html

16. Cf. National Science Foundation, *'It's About Time. Final Report of the Workshop on Research Challenges in Digital Archiving and Long-Term Preservation'*, August 2003. http://www.digitalpreservation.gov/repor/ NSF_LC_Final_Report.pdf

17. While the Internet Archive http://www.archive.org is a valuable source for getting an impression of what certain websites looked like at a given point in time and how web-design changed over time, unfortunately, both images files (GIF, JPG) and movie files often do not load at all, and even HTML-pages take a long time to come up.

18. National Science Foundation Report, 3.

19. Ibid.: 6. This is to some certain extent caused by market forces that 'work against long-term preservation by locking customers into proprietary formats and systems, adding new features to encourage or to force upgrades, and phasing out useful but unprofitable hardware, software, and services. Ibid.: xii.

20. Ibid.: vii

21. Ibid.: vii.

22. Cf. Schüller 1993/94, 4f. quoted in Assmann, 2001: 276.

23. Cf. Johnny Perry Barlow, 'The Economy of Ideas', *Wired*, 2.03, (1993). http://www.wired.com/wired/archive/2.03/economy.ideas_pr.html

24. Boris Groys, *Unter Verdacht* (Munich, Vienna: Hanser 2000).

25. Cf. Manovich, 2001: 119.

26. Jacques Derrida, 'Biodegradables. Seven Diary Fragments', *Critical Inquiry* 15 (1988): 812–881.

27. Cf. Assmann, 2001: 272.

28. Library of Congress. 'Origins of American Animation 1900–1921'. http://memory.loc.gov/ammem/oahtml/oahome.html

29. Cf. Moving Images Collections at the Internet Archive; http://www.archive.org/movies/movies.php

30. *Duck and Cover*. http://www.archive.org/movies/movies-details-db.php?collection= prelinger&collectionid=19069&from=mostViewed

31. Ifilm; http://www.ifilm.com/ifilmdetail/2416886?htv=12

32. National Film Board of Canada; http://www.nfb.ca

33. Animation World Network; http://www.awn.com

34. Cartoon Network; http://www.cartoonnetwork.com

35. Warner Bros., http://www.wb.com

36. *The Spirit of Christmas*. http://www.killfile.org/soxmas/

37. Cf. Manton, 2002: 56.

38. Hotwired Animation Express. http://www.wired.com/animation/ (no longer online).

39. FlashForward; http://www.flashforward2004.com/default.asp

40. Cf. Brickfilms; http://www.brickfilms.com

41. Cf. Internet Archive; http://www.archive.org

42. Cf. Newgrounds; http://www.newgrounds.com

43. Cf. Ifilms; http://www.ifilms.com

44. Cf. Jared B. Gilbert, Cynicism of the Studios Sets, undated. http://www.brickfilms.com/index.php (under 'resources').

45. Strange Company, *What is Machinima*; http://www.strangecompany.org/about/machinima.htm

46. Machinima; http://www.machinima.com

47. The New York based ILL Clan is one of the few machinima groups whose works show considerable artistic progress: In their first short *Apartment Huntin'*, a slapstick-comedy about two lumberjacks looking for an apartment, based on the *Quake* engine, they changed only the skins of the characters but otherwise used default *Quake 1* models. Its *Quake 2* based sequel *Hardly Workin'* featured the same characters, but the two woodsmen looked totally different, because this time the group created almost all game assets themselves. With its more recent productions the ILL Clan founded an interesting subgenre of machinima: Live-machinimas using a mixture of improvisation and scripted comedy produced and performed live in front of an audience.

48. Cf. Shirley Shor; Aviv Eyal, 'DEMOing: A new emerging art form or just another digital craft?' http://www.shirley.friskit.com/text/demoing.htm

49. As most demos are abstract animations aiming at the perfect connection of sound and images, they could probably be fruitfully compared to the tradition of German Avantgarde films from the 1920s or visual music (although quite likely most demo producers are probably not familiar with this tradition).

50. Cf. Scene; http://www.scene.org; Ojuice http://www.ojuice.org; Pouet http://www.pouet.net

51. Cf. Noah Shachtman, 'Online Film Firms Look Offline'. 7 June 2001. http://www.wired.com/news/digiwood/ 0,1412,44319,00.html

52. Cf. Icebox; http://www.icebox.com

53. Cf. G. Beato, 'A Game Theory', 12 February 2001. http://www.business2.com/b2/web/articles/0,17863,528691,00.html

54. This also raises the question whether file-sharing systems are archives. Obviously, they are fragile and fleeting as their content and structure changes all the time. Of course there are no explicitly denominated archivists, at best one can think of as an entire file-sharing community as a collective archivist. Significance and popularity of a certain movie can be deduced both from the number of copies available and from their absence. The more often a file is listed, the better is its recognition and popularity with the file-sharing community. However, the co-presence of porn, mainstream blockbusters and TV series indicates that this quantitative approach does not reveal much about the quality. If at all, file-sharing clients are archives at a very low level.

55. Cf. the demo maker tool Werkzeug http://www.theprodukkt.com/werkkzeug1.html or the machinima tool Machinimation, which comes with Marino's manual on Machinima. Paul Marino, *3D Game-Based Filmmaking: The Art of Machinima*. Book and CD-ROM. (Scottsdale: Paraglyph, 2004).

56. Cf. The5k; http://www.the5k.org

57. Cf. Flash.Beat; http://www.swatch.com/specials/atomfilms/index_flash.html

58. Cf. Sundance Online Film Festival. http://www.sundanceonlinefilmfestival.org/

59. Cf. Annecy; http://www.annecy.org/

60. Animamundi; http://www.animamundiweb.com/
61. Cf. Star Wars Fan Film Network;
    http://atomfilms.shockwave.com/af/spotlight/collections/starwars/
62. Cf. Shorts Welcome; http://www.shorts-welcome.de
63. Cf. Slamdance; http://www.slamdance.com
64. Cf. Going Underground; http://www.going-underground.org/
65. The website 'Animation on the Internet' http://www.animationproject.org tries to be an anchor and reference point for all animation sites on the web.

Karin Wehn is a research associate of media and communication studies at the University of Leipzig, Germany and has been a guest professor at the University of Fine Arts Berlin, Germany and the Martin-Luther-University Halle-Wittenberg, Germany. Her research fields include animation, especially animation in new media, media theory, the relationship between old and new media, fictional formats on television and dubbing as a form of cultural mediation.